Messages of the Ascended Masters

Words of Wisdom

Volume 2

Dictations received by the Messenger
Tatyana N. Mickushina
December 12, 2005 to July 10, 2007

UDC 141.339=111=03.161.1
BBC 87.7+86.4
 M 59

M 59 Mickushina, T.N.
   Words of Wisdom. Messages of the Masters.
   In 5 volumes / T.N. Mickushina. — Volume 2: 2017.

About the Five-Volume Words of Wisdom Series of Books

This is the second book in a five-volume series that contains Messages given by the Ascended Masters through their Messenger Tatyana N. Mickushina from 2005 through 2016.

During this time the people of Earth have been given the Teaching of the True purpose of evolution — the aspiration of every soul to the Creator, to union with God, and adherence to the Highest Moral Law that exists in the Universe. This harmonious Unified Teaching also contains Teachings about the distinction between Good and Evil, the Path of Initiation, the change of consciousness, about Love, Karma, Freedom, happiness, nonviolence, about the Community, and many other Teachings.

Copyright © T.N. Mickushina, 2017
All rights reserved.

ISBN -10: 1540678954
ISBN -13: 978-1540678959

Contents

Book 2
Cycle 2: Messages of the Ascended Masters
from December 12, 2005 to January 7, 2006

We would like to incline you to fulfill new tasks
Sanat Kumara, December 12, 2005 17

New Divine Mercy
Beloved Surya, December 13, 2005 22

I come in order to ask you for the help that your ill planet needs
Beloved Alpha, December 14, 2005 26

A Teaching on responsibility for the received Divine energy
Lord Shiva, December 15, 2005 29

A Talk about the Path of Initiations
Lord Maitreya, December 16, 2005 33

You must prove your level of Christ consciousness every day
Beloved Lanello, December 17, 2005 38

Leave your holiday fuss. Start doing the real work on balancing the planet
Beloved Maha Chohan, December 18, 2005 43

A Teaching on Karma descending at the end of the year
Beloved Kuthumi, December 19, 2005 47

Create selflessly, strive for the Divine world without looking back, and you will receive what you deserve
Beloved Jesus, December 20, 2005 52

Faith is the remedy that you need
Beloved El Morya, December, 21, 2005 56

On letters to the Karmic Board
Gautama Buddha, December 22, 2005 60

I have come to warn you that this Dictation may be the last
Beloved Serapis Bey, December 23, 2005 64

We are joyful that our appeals have found response in your hearts
Great Divine Director, December 30, 2005 66

Let your holiday resemble the visit of the Higher, etheric octaves
Beloved Melchizedek, December 31, 2005 70

You have come to this world to learn a lesson of distinction
Lord Shiva, January 1, 2006 74

You should learn to evaluate your deeds and thoughts on your own and get rid of all those vain and human things that impede your advancement on the Path
Beloved Zarathustra, January 2, 2006 80

A Teaching on humility
Beloved Surya, January 3, 2006 85

We are waiting for you to grow up
Beloved Vairochana, January 4, 2006 89

We are looking for those who, in their consciousness, are able to go beyond the limits of the surrounding illusion
Lord Shiva, January 5, 2006 93

I am giving an opportunity, and I am opening a perspective
Beloved Alpha, January 6, 2006 97

I have brought you two pieces of news — one is sad and the other one is joyful
Beloved El Morya, January 7, 2006 100

Messages from the Ascended Masters between the second
and third cycles of Dictations

> When a chalice that we can fill with Light appears
> in the physical world, we always do that
> *Beloved Shiva, January 23, 2006* 105
>
> Use the help that Heavens give you, and do
> not disregard this help
> *Lord Shiva, March 13, 2006* 109
>
> We invite you to establish a new type of relations
> between the Guru and a chela
> *Lord Shiva, March 15, 2006* 113
>
> A Teaching on Divine Gratitude
> *Lord Maitreya, April 10, 2006* 117
>
> You have to be ready for constant changes
> in your consciousness
> *Lord Maitreya, April 11, 2006* 121

Book 3
Cycle 3: Messages of the Ascended Masters
from April 15 to April 30, 2006

> Give your Light, your Love, and your support to the people
> around you
> *Sanat Kumara, April 15, 2006* 127
>
> The process of returning to Reality, the process
> of folding up the illusion, will be accelerated
> to its maximum
> *Beloved Alpha, April 16, 2006* 132
>
> A Teaching on Divine Miracles
> *Beloved Surya, April 17, 2006* 135
>
> Your consciousness is the key to your future
> and to the future of the whole planet
> *Gautama Buddha, April 18, 2006* 139

A Talk about the Path of Initiations
Lord Maitreya, April 19, 2006 143

Instructions about your attitude to everything around you in your dense world and in the finer worlds
El Morya, April 20, 2006 147

A Teaching on extraterrestrial civilizations
Beloved Zarathustra, April 21, 2006 152

A Teaching on the Path of Apprenticeship
Lord Shiva, April 22, 2006 157

I am giving you a guaranteed way Home
Lord Maitreya, April 23, 2006 161

The natural evolution for your souls is following the Path we are teaching mankind of Earth
Lord Surya, April 24, 2006 165

We cannot make anybody go, but we call you to take the Path
Sanat Kumara, April 25, 2006 169

Expose yourself to the winds of change and do not be afraid to catch a cold or fall ill
Gautama Buddha, April 26, 2006 173

We ask you to act in your lives according to the knowledge and teachings received by you
The Great Divine Director, April 27, 2006 177

Only when you receive the Law from within your heart, do you become the executor of the Law
Beloved Kuthumi, April 28, 2006 181

Comments on the Path of apprenticeship
Lord Maitreya, April 29, 2006 185

We are calling you to follow our Path
Beloved El Morya, April 30, 2006 189

Messages from the Ascended Masters between the third
and fourth cycles of Dictations

> Let your consciousness go beyond the limits of
> your family, your city, and your country and take
> the whole Earth as your native home
> *Lord Maitreya, June 5, 2006* 195

> About the forthcoming day of the summer solstice
> and the Divine favors connected with this day
> *Lord Maitreya, June 15, 2006* 199

> You are those who should make changes
> on Earth according to the Divine models
> *Lord Maitreya, June 18, 2006* 202

Book 4
Cycle 4: Messages of the Ascended Masters
from July 1 to July 21, 2006

> You are forming the new reality in
> your consciousness
> *Sanat Kumara, July 1, 2006* 207

> Your level of consciousness is determined
> by the Divine qualities that you gain on your Path
> *Beloved Great Divine Director, July 2, 2006* 211

> I offer you this method in the hope that you
> will be able to use it in your everyday spiritual work
> *Lord Shiva, July 3, 2006* 215

> The success of your evolution on your beautiful planet
> depends on the development of the quality of
> Divine Love in you
> *Beloved Surya, July 4, 2006* 219

> Only the ignorance and limitations of your consciousness
> separate you from accepting in your consciousness
> your unity with every particle of life
> *Lord Maitreya, July 5, 2006* 223

The expansion of the understanding of the Law of Karma
Beloved Kuthumi, July 6, 2006 227

There will be those who manifest their consistency
and devotion and can help us attain our goals
Master Morya, July 7, 2006 232

I am looking for heart-to-heart commune with those
who are ready for such communication
Beloved Jesus, July 8, 2006 236

A Teaching on the karmic responsibility for your actions
in the sphere of translating the texts of the Dictations
and in the sphere of managing cash funds
Sanat Kumara, July 9, 2006 241

A Teaching about Happiness
Gautama Buddha, July 10, 2006 246

Do not rush searching for truth that is coming from
the human consciousness; strive for the Truth that is coming
into your world from the Higher octaves of Light,
and then you will manifest a bright future for planet Earth
Beloved Cyclopea, July 11, 2006 250

A Teaching about the Path of Discipleship
Beloved Lanello, July 12, 2006 254

A Teaching on prophets and prophecies
John the Beloved, July 13, 2006 259

I wish that an increasing number of people become
aware of our Path and enter the steps of the Hierarchy
Beloved Serapis Bey, July 14, 2006 264

My angels and I are ready to come at your first call!
Saint Michael the Archangel, July 15, 2006 268

It depends solely on you yourselves whether you will be able
to provide your Higher Self with auspicious conditions for a
conversation
Beloved Hilarion, July 16, 2006 273

> I wish you to manifest only positive qualities in your lives
> and to be constantly striving for the glorious
> summits of the Divine World!
> *Beloved Lanto, July 17, 2006* 278
>
> We give you the Living Word, the Living Teaching,
> and expect you to bear our Word and our Teaching into life
> through concrete work in the physical plane
> *Sanat Kumara, July 18, 2006* 282
>
> About the dispensation of the 23rd and other opportunities
> being given by Heaven
> *Beloved El Morya, July 19, 2006* 286
>
> Do not miss your chance, and try to stay in the corridor
> of the evolutionary opportunity
> *Beloved Zarathustra, July 20, 2006* 291
>
> The summer cycle of Dictations that we have given
> in Bulgaria through our Messenger is over
> *Beloved El Morya, July 21, 2006* 295

Messages from the Ascended Masters between the fourth
and fifth cycles of Dictations

> The quality of changing consciousness is
> the most important quality
> at the present historical period of time
> *Lord Maitreya, September 13, 2006* 301
>
> I have come to affirm the qualities of joy, aspiration,
> and victory in your consciousness
> *Lord Maitreya, October 9, 2006* 305

Book 5
Cycle 5: Messages of the Ascended Masters
from December 20, 2006 to January 10, 2007

> All efforts of your will are required of you not
> to take the bait of the energies of the past
> but to aspire to the new day!
> *Sanat Kumara, December 20, 2006* 311

**Now, at the change of the annual cycle,
it is especially beneficial to make the decision and free
yourselves from everything that is unnecessary in your
consciousness**
Beloved Surya, December 21, 2006 315

**Take our hand and hold it until Faith returns to you
and your doubts clear away like an autumn mist**
Serapis Bey, December 22, 2006 319

**The time is ripe not to speak about God,
but to act in your lives in obedience to the Divine Law**
Babaji, December 23, 2006 323

**We come to tell you about the principles on which
the Community is established**
Master Lanello, December 24, 2006 327

**One more vital point is added to the dispensation
on the 23rd of each month**
Gautama Buddha, December 25, 2006 332

**You must constantly analyze the consequences
of your actions and stop trying to teach
in those places where your teaching will be immediately
dragged through the mire**
Beloved Kuthumi, December 26, 2006 336

**Now, before the New Year's Eve,
we hasten to bring home to your consciousness
the new tasks that need implementing**
Beloved El Morya, December 27, 2006 340

We make your consciousness ready for The New Age
I AM THAT I AM, December 28, 2006 344

**I came to remind you of your Divine origin and the necessity
to overcome your unreal part**
Cosmic Being Powerful Victory, December 29, 2006 348

Let us focus on implementing our tasks together
Lord Lanto, December 30, 2006 352

The sooner you change your behavior and yesterday's habits, the sooner the whole world will enter into the New Age
Beloved Zarathustra, December 31, 2006 356

A Message at the beginning of the year
Gautama Buddha, January 1, 2007 360

A talk about God
Lord Shiva, January 2, 2007 365

A piece of news from the session of the Karmic Board
The Great Divine Director, January 3, 2007 369

A talk about the healing of the soul and the body
Beloved Hilarion, January 4, 2007 373

A Teaching on the substitution of fear with Divine Love
Saint Michael, the Archangel, January 5, 2007 378

A Teaching on your soul
Beloved Kuthumi, January 6, 2007 382

The time for choice
Sanat Kumara, January 7, 2007 386

A Teaching on genuine Faith
Beloved Jesus, January 8, 2007 390

An admonition for those on the Path
Lord Maitreya, January 9, 2007 395

A Teaching on Devotion
Beloved El Morya, January 10, 2007 399

Message from the Ascended Masters between the fifth and sixth cycles of Dictations

About the current situation on Earth
Gautama Buddha, March 7, 2007 405

Book 6
Cycle 6: Messages of the Ascended Masters
from June 20 to July 10, 2007

Joyous News
Sanat Kumara, June 20, 2007 411

Recommendations to humankind of Earth
Beloved Surya, June 21, 2007 415

Exhortations for the current day
Master Morya, June 22, 2007 419

A Teaching on the Initiation of the Crucifixion
Beloved Zarathustra, June 23, 2007 423

Instructions for the current time
Beloved Serapis Bey, June 24, 2007 428

About the spiritual mission of Russia
Beloved Mother Mary, June 25, 2007 433

Guidance for every day
Beloved Kuthumi, June 26, 2007 437

A warning about the danger of contacts with the subtle world
Lord Maitreya, June 27, 2007 441

On protection against the lowest levels of the subtle plane
Saint Michael the Archangel, June 28, 2007 446

A Teaching about the actions on the physical plane
Gautama Buddha, June 29, 2007 450

A Teaching about our Path
Babaji, June 30, 2007 454

The time for choice
Master Nicholas Roerich, July 1, 2007 458

A Talk about the Law of Karma
Beloved Lanello, July 2, 2007 463

A Teaching on the change of epochs
Beloved Jesus, July 3, 2007 467

A Teaching about the necessity to keep your lower bodies pure
Beloved Kuthumi, July 4, 2007 471

The last warning
Beloved Alpha, July 5, 2007 476

A discourse on the aspiration to Victory
Cosmic Being Mighty Victory, July 6, 2007 479

A discourse on the change of the physical plane through the change of consciousness
Beloved Surya, July 7, 2007 483

A Teaching on the Transition
Lord Shiva, July 8, 2007 487

A Teaching on Buddha Consciousness
Gautama Buddha, July 9, 2007 491

The final Message of the summer cycle of Dictations
Beloved El Morya, July 10, 2007 495

Appendix to Cycle 6 of the Messages

Appeal from the Masters to the people of Russia
Part of a speech given by Tatyana N. Mickushina in Moscow, March 27, 2007 501

Explanation to the "Appeal from the Masters" 505

Book 2

Cycle 2: Messages of the Ascended Masters
from December 12, 2005 to January 7, 2006

We would like to incline you to fulfill new tasks

Sanat Kumara
December 12, 2005

I AM Sanat Kumara. I have come in order to open the new cycle of Dictations that we wish to give through our Messenger.

You know that we have already given the Dictations through our Messenger this year. And it has been an important condition to spread these Dictations widely enough among the people of Russia and all over the world.

We are glad that our condition has been met. Thousands of people, not only from Russia but also from all over the world, could become familiar with our Dictations and receive from the Ascended Hosts the information so necessary for many at the given stage of the evolutionary development.

We are pleased to state that our efforts and our energy have not been wasted in vain. You have completed your portion of the work, and now we can continue what was planned and give some more information related to the events of this year and the following year, concerning what you should prepare for, what you should care about, and what measures to take.

Therefore, I come again, and I wish to declare that no matter how difficult it may be, we will fulfill the obligations given to mankind of Earth and render all necessary and feasible help that mankind needs at the given stage of the evolutionary development.

Every time we will be giving our instructions, we will place a particle of the Divine energy into our Messages. And you will drink and enjoy the nectar of the Divine energy again. Like last time, we are asking our Messenger to ensure the appearance of these Dictations on the website the same day they will be given. It will give you an opportunity to be virtually present at the reception of these Dictations, no matter where you are on the globe. All you will have to do is turn your computer on and get on the Internet.

For those people who do not have access to a computer, we will give an opportunity to read these Dictations a little later through the printed edition.

Now I would like to get to the main thing that we have again come to you for. It concerns the turn of the year and the beginning of the new yearly cycle. We would like to incline you to fulfill new tasks and new goals that you must set for yourselves and fulfill the next year. Therefore, take the information that will be given to you now and in the following Dictations seriously.

So, it is necessary to sum up the results of the past year of 2005. We are doing it with great joy because despite all the twists, turns, and disasters of this year, we were able to achieve the main goal — the transition of the consciousness of many people to the new, higher level. And that has taken place; it has happened! Therefore, the results of this year are impressive, and these results will impact the physical illusion surrounding you without delay.

You will be able to feel those blissful changes that you deserve from your hard work, your prayer vigils, and your deeds that you carry out on the physical plane.

I should say that you have come to your world in order to act. You have come primarily to carry out specific actions on the physical plane. Therefore, you should take care of and be concerned about the environment around you. Leave alone everything that happens outside your planet and in other worlds and spaces. Believe me, there are enough Beings of Light in space that are performing their work at a proper level. I suggest that you concentrate on the needs of your planet, particularly on the needs of the people who are around you. Take control of everything that you can take under your control. Strive for the Divine patterns of behavior to be manifested in everything that surrounds you. This concerns not only the cleanliness of your homes and workplaces but also the cleanliness of your thoughts and your behavior in everything. You are those people who are making an impact on the whole world. With your help will we be able to change this world. Very few people in relation to the total number of people inhabiting Earth read these Dictations. Though you may not believe me, if only just several thousand people in every nation get access to these Dictations, and with the help of these Dictations they change their consciousness, then that will be enough to change the situation in their countries and in all countries on the planet. It is important to have points of Light and the support through which we can carry out our actions. And I must tell you that we have received such support this year.

Fortunately, it applies not only to Russia but also many other countries of the world, especially Bulgaria, Ukraine, and some other countries that have an opportunity to read and understand the Russian text. Therefore, the primary task at this point is the translation of these Dictations into other languages of the world, and first of all, into English. Since those hurricanes and disasters that America has gone through this year are a direct consequence of its inability to have kept the focus of Light, we have been forced to move it to Russia. Therefore, the extent to which America will be able to able to perceive our information that we are giving through the Russian Messenger, depends on whether America will be able to keep itself as a civilized and highly-developed country in the near future.

Therefore, I am appealing to everyone who reads these Dictations and has an opportunity to translate them into English.

It is your turn to serve the world. In your hands are the destiny and lives of millions of people who cannot receive our energy and our information, and that is why their countries are exposed and will be exposed to those terrible natural disasters that they could not even imagine in their consciousness before. I am also asking those people of America who can overcome a bias and perceive the information being given by us through our Russian Messenger: Cast away all prejudices and dogmas of your consciousness. Trust your hearts. Do everything that is in your power to spread the information that is being given by us, in English-speaking countries.

The time for specific practical actions on the physical plane has come, and you must realize that all you have to do in the nearest future is carry out our plans for the physical octave. Do not search for anyone to be found on the other end of Earth to guide you. You will receive all the guidance, all the support, and all the necessary energy from the inside. We are giving you the knowledge of the Internal Path for that; the Path that all the devotees of all times were following; the Path that you must follow because there is no more time left to wait and postpone the realization of our plans for planet Earth. Start doing something specific right where you are now. It may be a small thing, it may be the knowledge that is contained in these Dictations that you can give to only several people living in the same town as you, or it may be lectures that you will read at school or at work. Use any opportunity to distribute our information, our energies, and our vibrations into your world.

That is what you must do right now, and that is what your main service next year will be.

Therefore, do not waste time on grand preparation for the forthcoming Christmas and New Year's holidays. The best service that you can render to us will be manifested in your deeds, which you will carry out under our guidance coming from within you.

Learn to listen to the voice of silence coming from within you and giving you an opportunity to experience all over again the bliss of Fatherly love of the Heavens, which the Heavens are tirelessly pouring into your world.

**I AM Sanat Kumara,
dwelling in the infinite Love for you.**

New Divine Mercy

Beloved Surya
December 13, 2005

I AM Surya, and I come to you again through our Messenger.

I have come in order to set you once again to the perception of the information that will be given today and on the following days. You know that the situation on planet Earth escalates every time at the end of the year. This is connected with the annual cycle that the planet is going through. And every time, the last days of the year are very tense in terms of the energies that have not been transmuted and seek manifestation on the physical plane.

This release of negative energies may cause the next cataclysm, or it may not if the transmutation of the major part of the negative energy on the plane of thoughts and feelings takes place.

That is why it is so important to keep internal harmony and reverential awe toward the Creator at the end of the year.

Are many people on planet Earth capable of it?

How can we make as many people as possible think about their responsibility for the whole life on planet Earth? We come again and again in order to remind you of your responsibility, and we hope that you will manage to deliver our information to as many people as possible.

Do you remember the horrible cataclysm that happened last December and took lives of hundreds of thousands of people?

Can you imagine that a similar cataclysm strikes again? And how realistic is it to prevent such a cataclysm?

I have come to tell you about the opportunity that Heavens are giving you on this December day. Today, before the beginning of the session of the Karmic Board, we have decided to alleviate the karma of planet Earth if only a few hundred of people spread across the world take the burden of the karma of Earth for the period until the end of this year.

What is required of you, beloved? Who will take the burden of the world karma for that difficult period of time?

The task that you must fulfill may seem very easy to you. However, do not delude yourself with the external simplicity of the assigned task because even the simplest actions undertaken by you will provoke such strong resistance from the side of the forces opposing us that every action of yours will be accomplished with great effort. And yet we are asking you to dedicate exactly one hour every day until the end of this year to a praying practice according to a certain method that I am about to give you now.

Thus, your whole task is to reach the most harmonious possible state of your consciousness.

You engage in various spiritual practices and belong to different religious groups and schools. We have taken that into account.

Dedicate exactly one hour every day to the praying practice you are used to. It may be reading of prayers, Rosaries, commands, or simply a meditation.

The main task that you must achieve during your praying practice is the harmonization of your inner state. You must find the state of complete harmony and oneness with God.

At the end of your spiritual practice, I am asking you to do one simple thing. Imagine that your aura expands and becomes the size of a house, and then it expands more and covers your whole city, your country, and the entire globe. And every living creature that gets in the field of your aura experiences its impact.

Every living being becomes filled with the state of harmony and peace that you have managed to achieve during your spiritual practice.

It will be enough if only several hundred people assume that obligation and carry out our request from today until the end of this year; and I guarantee you that Earth will avoid that horrible cataclysm that happened at the end of last year.

Let's all unite our efforts in this direction together, no matter which confession or religious group you belong to.

Let this simple step become the first step toward your unity on the earthly plane.

I was glad to come to you today and announce the new opportunity and the new dispensation that will work during this dark time of the year.

I am sure that with your help we will effortlessly overcome any inharmonious manifestations on the planet that usually develop into various cataclysms and natural disasters.

The first step that I have provided to you is waiting for your efforts to be applied.

Now, I would also like to give you important information that requires your immediate action.

The Karmic Board session will take place at the end of this year starting December 23rd. So along with your annual letters to the Karmic Board, do not forget to present those helpful elaborations of your mind that Lord Shiva asked you about in his Dictation of November 27, 2005.

The larger the number of important projects you will be able to establish during the time remaining until the end of this year, the greater the probability that the Karmic Board at their session will be able to consider your wishes and exert efforts to eliminate those karmic obstacles that may be in the way of manifesting your projects.

You see, beloved, how Heavens care about you. May we hope that you as well make those efforts we are asking of you?

I hope so very much.

We are asking you for such a small thing; and the time that we are asking you to spare to work for the good of humankind of planet Earth is even incomparable to the time that you waste on watching television programs and meaningless chatting every day.

As always, there is Common Good and well-being of the planet on one scale, and there is satisfaction of your ego's desires on the other.

Think about your choice and make a firm choice in favor of the eternal Divine reality by giving up any illusive choices within yourselves.

I was glad to see you again, and I was glad to announce the new Divine Mercy to you.

**I AM Surya,
and I have been with you today.**

I come in order to ask you for the help that your ill planet needs.

**Beloved Alpha
December 14, 2005**

I AM Alpha. I have come to you today in order to give you a small Teaching on how you should act in the nearest future and how you should get ready for the future.

Every time during my communication with the incarnated people I feel an incomparable bliss. I sense your needs, and I treat you so tenderly and lovingly as no father of your world can treat his children.

That is because I am your Father, your real Father, who cares about you and uses any opportunity to come and give you my guidance and Teaching and caress you.

The reason I have come today is to do my fatherly duty to all mankind on Earth.

Your native planet needs your care and guardianship. Imagine that Earth is your Mother, and your Mother is sick and needs your help.

If you are loving children, then you must respond to your Mother's calling no matter how carried away you are with your life's problems, or how hard it is for you. Because this is your Mother, and she is sick and she needs your help.

The reason I have come to you today is to call you to your Mother and tell you that she needs your help and your care, and your guardianship now as never before.

You have reached the age when you can assume the responsibility for your Mother who is now in need of your help.

There was a time when you were getting help from your Mother. There was a time when you were getting everything you needed: food, heat, care.

Now the time has come to pay your dues, to thank your Mother — your native planet — for everything she has done for you.

Your Mother has a lot of children. And not all of her children are able to respond to the call. For they have lost the connection with their parental home. For they have chosen a path that leads nowhere.

Those of you who can hear me and are able to perceive my vibrations, you will not leave your Mother in trouble.

Can I count on you? Can I? That is why I come, in order to ask you for the help that your sick planet needs now as never before.

You know that the illness of your planet is related to the consequences of those thoughts, feelings, and deeds that the children of Earth admit. You know that your Mother Earth worries about her unwise children. And that is why she is sick. That is why you must give Mother Earth the help that she needs. And she needs your Love. There is no more valuable medicine that you could offer your Mother than the Love of your hearts.

Please, make it a rule, starting from this day, to spare at least several minutes a day to send Love to your native planet. Please remind yourself of the best minutes you have spent in nature, in the mountains, at the river, in the forest. Remember the minutes of joy you have been experiencing from communicating with nature.

Remember quiet summer days and evenings. Remember sunrises and sunsets.

Remember a clear hot summer day and a cool evening. Remember everything that is connected with your best memories.

Thank your Mother Earth for everything that she has given to you in the past. And now, if you can send Love to your Mother, she will be able to recover her health and her life forces, and become a shelter and a sanctuary for many generations of people.

Do not treat your planet as something permanent and given to you once and forever. Your planet, the state in which it is now, is a reflection of your thoughts, feelings, and the level of consciousness that you have now.

That is why the future of your planet and the climate of your planet and everything that surrounds you on your native planet, your Mother, depends on you and nobody else.

I have come to give you a clear understanding that Earth needs your help. And now you know how to provide this help.

I have come to remind you of your duty; and I have come to say that the time to carry out your duty has come. The Cosmic opportunity is not exhausted yet. But you must be continuously feeling your responsibility for everything that surrounds you.

For everything around you was created with your consciousness. And along with the rise of the level of your consciousness, the illusory reality surrounding you will be changed because it will become more Divine, closer to the Divine reality.

I have come. And I have said.

**I AM Alpha,
your Father in Heaven. Om.**

A Teaching on responsibility for the received Divine energy

Lord Shiva
December 15, 2005

I AM Shiva! I have come to you through this Messenger today.

I have come to remind you once again of the dispensation I have given you this year on the 27th of November.

You must consider once again the opportunity that Heavens are giving you and apply it in practice. Do not think that opportunities like that will be poured on you as manna from Heaven. We grant an opportunity, and then we carefully observe how you use the given opportunity. And if you are so deep in your illusion that you cannot appreciate what is being granted, then there is no sense to keep giving you opportunities, knowledge, and information.

Understand that the fact that Heavens once again decided to address mankind of Earth through this Messenger is not an ordinary event similar to situations where many people appeal to God and receive some directions and guidelines. In this particular case, we intend to work for the whole world. And we are once again giving our knowledge and our information through our Messenger.

I want you to learn the difference between the way some people have a chance to receive a particular type of information by taking it from specific levels of the subtle plane and the way we give you information through our Messengers.

There is a big difference. This difference is connected with greater authenticity of the transmitted information as the transmission of the information is carried out not spontaneously or occasionally, but quite purposefully. A great amount of the Divine energy is spent on the transmission of this information. Therefore, appreciate what is being given and do not forget about the responsibility that you assume as soon as you have received this information.

If you do not apply what is granted to you in your lives and if you do not follow the advice and recommendations that we are giving in these Dictations through our Messenger, then you automatically create karma because you do not use the given Divine energy that is contained in these Dictations according to its intended purpose.

The goal for which we are giving this energy is definite. We wish to raise the consciousness of humankind and prepare it for the transition to the new level that will correspond to the new stage of the cosmic evolution.

Therefore, think about it very carefully one more time. Probably, you should not read these Dictations at all, and this will be a better solution for you than if you take the energy of these Dictations and follow none of the recommendations that are given to you. In this case you will create the karma of inaction, which has been described in detail by Beloved Kuthumi in his Dictation on June 24, 2005.[1]

You cannot take the energy without using it for the purposes it is given. In this case, for the purpose of raising the consciousness of humanity, and by that, preventing the cataclysms and natural disasters connected with the imperfect human consciousness.

But I must tell you that if you have had access to these Dictations and have read them, then it is your turn to serve

---

[1] Refer to the Dictation "A Teaching on the karma of inactivity," Beloved Kuthumi, June 24, 2005, in *Words of Wisdom Volume 1*.

humankind of Earth. And if you give up reading them now in hope of avoiding the karma of inactivity, then by doing so, you will make a choice that will take you away from the Path. And you never know which kind of karma will be heavier for you.

Understand that there is nothing in Cosmos that does not obey the Law existing in this universe. And humankind has reached its limit of using the Divine energy too freely. We told you that free will, which was granted to humankind, is limited with the time frame. And if humankind, having reached the limit that was allowed for the experimentation with free will, cannot on its own return to following the Law existing in this universe, then humankind will be strictly redirected and guided even if the whole Earth will have to be turned upside down for that. Therefore, be sensible. And finally take a stand on those steps of the cosmic Hierarchy that correspond to you at the given stage of your evolutionary development.

The more you doubt or return to the behavior associated with abusing your free will, the more rigidly you will be put on the way that has been prepared for you and is in accordance with the forthcoming stage of the cosmic evolution.

It may seem to you that I am too tough and that I am trying to scare you.

Yes, I am a very determined and uncompromising Master. I do not like to joke around and I do not like it when someone doesn't obey me.

I am doing what I have to do because my status in the Cosmic Hierarchy allows me to speak to you in a very strict way. The period when we could allow ourselves to persuade you and give you compliments has come to an end. Now we will speak more rigidly, and this rigidness and determination are justified with the approaching cosmic deadlines. It will be better for you if I reprimand you in the most rigid way, rather than if a global cataclysm falls upon you at the most inappropriate time.

If not for the probability of this terrible choice that increases with every minute, then I could continue giving you compliments and granting you all of our attention and signs of our attention.

Now I suggest that you take very seriously those opportunities that have been given to you in the previous Dictations by Beloved Surya on December 13, 2005, and Beloved Alpha on December 14, 2005.

It may seem to you that what is offered to you is insufficient for keeping the balance on the planet and avoiding the cataclysm. But if only several hundred or thousand people respond to our call sincerely enough, then I guarantee you that the result will be manifested very soon, and it will allow the removal of the imbalance on the planet that still keeps escalating. It is especially important to do that now, before the end of this year.

We started the new cycle of Dictations. And you can see that we warn you about the threatening danger in every Dictation. Don't you think that this is strange? Is this not a clear evidence of the fact that, finally, it is high time to break out of your illusion and do real work? Choose whether to get ready for the holidays or with all the determination and firmness fulfill what the Masters are asking of you. There are enough other people who will rock the boat during these holidays. Some people have to keep the balance. And you are the ones who must do it. There are no coincidences in this world. And the fact that you read these Dictations means that you are those people on whom Heavens rely at this crucial period.

I AM Shiva!
And I hope that hardly any other Master could tell you about the vital tasks in a more definite and strict way.

A Talk about the Path of Initiations

Lord Maitreya
December 16, 2005

I AM Maitreya. I have come to you in order to give an important Message for mankind of Earth. I have come today with a specific purpose that has to be carried out exactly at this time when the change of the year cycle takes place. You know that when I came last time, you had an opportunity to get an idea about the Path of Initiations and about my School, which I invite all volunteers to; however, not all volunteers are able to study at that school and even more so graduate from it.

The secret is very simple. People aspire toward initiations as something mysterious and unreachable. Studying at the School of Initiations for them is like attending a prestigious educational institution, a famous university, or an educational center on Earth, and getting an education that opens a path to a career.

There is a fundamental difference between The School of Initiations and any prestigious educational institution of Earth. This difference is related to exactly losing any career in a standard earthly meaning. Moreover, not only do you lose a career, but you also lose everything that may be dear to you and that you still have purely human attachments to.

Therefore, even at the early stages on the Path of Initiations, very few people interested in continuing their education stay, no matter how prestigious the education at my School of Mysteries may appear in the eyes of the uninitiated and profane in the field of esoteric knowledge.

According to an old law unknown to a wide audience, initiations at schools for the initiated were held behind closed doors, and access to our Schools of Initiations was thoroughly guarded. And even those of our disciples, who had already gotten up on the Path and had received initial initiations, were not allowed into the most secret sacraments and mysteries. Why? Because the level of consciousness of the majority of the disciples is not able to perceive many things that occur behind closed doors and that a small number of people have access to.

If you, with your unprepared consciousness, accidentally entered the room where initiations of the highest level were given, then you would most probably leave the School of Initiations that very minute and would never peek beyond its doorstep again. Moreover, you would tell everyone that the School is just a limb of the devil and that no one should even think about crossing its doorstep.

Well, it is in our favor that failed disciples spread such ignorant rumors about us. For, indeed, when a person is getting liberated from his unreal part, this process is so painful and sometimes goes so dramatically that a feeling may arise that you are in a torture room.

Indeed, when you meet your unreal part face to face you get a sensation that you have come across the devil himself. But this devil, contrary to a common belief, does not reside somewhere in the underworld but within you.

Yes, beloved, both God and the devil exist within you. This is the innermost secret that was revealed to the initiates while they were going through their tests. During the preparation they had an opportunity to face their unreal carnal part, and then they had a full feeling that they had an encounter with the devil; and they had an opportunity to meet their Divine part, and then they felt their Divine eternal nature.

After they realized the duality of their nature, they had to make their final choice and completely surrender themselves to their Divine part, to God residing within them and to God within their Teacher.

This choice is so difficult because this choice is the fundamental choice that every incarnated person makes. Each of you intuitively supposes that the most important question you have to solve for yourself is the question of your choice between God and devil, between your real and your unreal parts. You know about this choice and therefore, you are afraid to make a mistake. There are many people who abuse your desire to serve and your aspiration to follow the Path of Initiations. And it is very easy to come under their influence, but it is much more difficult to break away from. All of that truly resembles staying at the real School of Initiations; only the choice that you make makes you serve not God within a man but a human ego. So do not hurry to get under the influence of any person, no matter how pure and gracious they may seem to you.

Our task is to show you the most subtle facets of distinction. While you are moving further and further along your Path, you have to make a distinction at a more and more subtle level. If at the beginning of your Path everything was clear to you — you only had to follow the Ten Commandments that were given in the time of Moses, and your salvation seemed guaranteed to you — then, as you advance along the Path, the observance of these commandments itself becomes your test.

If I tell you now about the most subtle facets and shades that are possible to get lost in even following the Ten Commandments of the Bible, you would not be able to comprehend.

Therefore, the Divine science is very complicated, and studying that science must occur under the guidance of an experienced tutor.

The first choice that you make is the choice of the tutor, the authority whom you will follow.

Many of you are at such a low level of consciousness and perception of reality that what I am trying to tell you today will just go past your consciousness without leaving a slightest trace. However, there are people who will perceive everything that I have said as very important information, without which their further journey along the Path will be merely inconceivable. I am speaking for these few. And those of you who don't understand what I am talking about will remember my words when your turn comes, and you will encounter those circumstances within you and outside that you will not be able to deal with. And you will remember these tips that I have given you during our conversation today, and you will return to them and reread them. And you will understand that nothing was said in vain. Everything said contains very important information for those who are able to perceive it.

I am coming with my instruction at the turn of the year cycle because the time is coming right now when you can evaluate the results of the year without any hurry and realize what you should aspire to next year. The change of the year is a very important phase, and the stereotype of how most people celebrate the change of the year is one of the main stereotypes that you should overcome in your consciousness.

For the change of the year cycle requires actions from you that are directly opposite to staying in a loud and drunken company.

You can acquire much more for the development of your soul if you stay alone or with your family for the celebration of the New Year; and instead of deafening yourself with music and alcohol, you should try to calmly contemplate on the past year and make plans for the future.

All of the great achievements started in silence, during a quiet calm talk at a family hearth.

No sensible idea was born among a crowd at a loud celebration.

I have been speaking with you today from the point of great love that I feel for those of you who have become my disciples, who have made that decision after my Dictation in which I invited you to my School of Mysteries,[2] and who haven't even for a day forgotten about me and their intention to get through studying under my guidance.

I have been closely observing whether your aspiration is firm enough.

Many of you forgot about your request to enter my school the next day. But there were those who still remember their intention. And with them I will continue my work.

Half a year is a sufficient period for you to be able to feel the seriousness of your intention. And now we will move forward. Those who fell behind will be able to analyze their intention again at a more serious level and ask to be accepted to my School again.

**I AM Maitreya,
with Love to you.**

---

[2] Refer to the Dictation "I invite you to enter my School of Mysteries," Lord Maitreya, March 28, 2005, in *Words of Wisdom Volume 1*.

You must prove your level of Christ consciousness every day.

Beloved Lanello
December 17, 2005

I AM Lanello, and I have come to you again through our Messenger. I have come in order to remind you once again of the responsibility that comes to you simultaneously with the energy and the information being received by you. You could notice that this cycle of Dictations differs from the previous cycle.

Indeed, we had the right to expect something greater from you, after all that information and energy that you received during the previous spring-summer cycle of the Dictations.

There is something we managed to change in people's consciousness, but these changes are negligibly small in comparison with those changes that we had the right to expect.

Yes, quite a large number of incarnated people have acquired a level of Christ consciousness, and we had the right to expect more actions on the physical plane from them.

However, inertness and dullness of matter instantly affected their level of consciousness as soon as we finished the cycle of the Dictations. Having lost constant replenishment that came to them together with the energy of the Dictations, many people who had already achieved Christ consciousness allowed their level of consciousness to decrease again. I can tell you, beloved, how the person who has reached and is keeping the level of Christ consciousness differs from the rest of the people who have not achieved this level yet. The main and basic difference is that this person cannot live anymore as he has lived before; he can't help acting, and he dedicates all his life and all the circumstances of his life to the manifestation of specific actions on the physical plane in order to realize our plans.

You cannot achieve a level of Christ consciousness and rest on your laurels up to the end of your incarnation. No, you must prove your level of Christ consciousness day after day every day. It is hard daily work.

To our regret, we saw that as soon as the cycle of the Dictations that we gave through our Messenger was over, gradually, many of those whom we counted on and put our hopes in lowered their consciousness to the previous level.

And this is a very saddening fact.

None of the achievements in the spiritual area that you have achieved while being in incarnation can be kept for even several months if you do not maintain your level of consciousness with your everyday efforts.

There cannot be any rest in the physical octave, only everyday work and everyday efforts.

I will give you an example with a sportsman who has achieved an outstanding result and got the world champion title. But if he stops training every day and rests on his laurels instead, then very soon he will not be able to keep his physical shape. And others will come who will beat the world record achieved by him.

If you are satisfied with the champion title that you have achieved and now you wish to rest on your laurels, then we, the Ascended Hosts, do not wish to have anything in common with you, and you cannot count on our support anymore.

Understand that daily efforts are required from you.

There are many light-bearers in incarnation, but how difficult it is to find those among them whom we can fully rely on.

We see how the hearts of many have lit up after they read the cycle of the previous Dictations given by us through our Messenger. And it was so painful for us to observe how the flame burning in their hearts gradually faded until it began to smoke and blacken and finally went out.

You cannot imagine how grieved we are to witness your poor "achievements." It is similar to how you see many people around you; your cities are literally overcrowded with people. But when you go out in the street, you feel complete loneliness because even if these people speak the same language as you, you are not able to understand each other. And it happens exactly because your levels of consciousness differ so much.

When you allow a fall in your consciousness, the information that brought joy to you and inspired you starts to be perceived by you as something uninteresting and not requiring your attention.

You embark on a search for new information and new sources of information and forget about that quiet joy in your heart and that excitement when you were drinking the healing balm of the Divine energy contained in our Dictations.

Because the level of your consciousness has fallen, you are not capable of distinguishing the authentic vibrations anymore, and you are compelled to consume the surrogates that the shelves of your shops are stuffed with.

Now you have a better understanding of our sadness and the reason why the tone of our Dictations has changed.

We expected more. Now we are forced to rely only on those who have not lost the spark of the Divinity within them, who have been able to keep burning the flame that lit up in their hearts after reading our Dictations.

Well, each of you has the right to make your own choice. We can only regret the choice made by you, but we cannot help you in any way.

The state of your consciousness can be maintained at the needed level only with your daily efforts. Every day you must relentlessly force yourself to work not only on your body muscles but also on your spiritual muscles. Otherwise they will simply deteriorate.

If you have not experienced blissful delight from contemplating the nature, a child's smile, if you have lived through a day without love, you have lived that day completely in vain.

Every minute of your stay on Earth you must remember your true Home where your souls have come into incarnation from, and you must be constantly guided by the advice of your Higher Self in all your daily choices.

How can you determine if you are residing in God?

It is very simple, beloved. You simply observe the state you are in. And, if you are subjected to any negative feeling, whether it is judgment, worry, depression, or irritability, then you are not in the Divine state of consciousness.

Only when you experience incomparable quiet joy and peace, you are residing in God, in the Divine state of consciousness.

Therefore, learn to observe yourself. And learn to identify your inner states.

The state of consciousness you are in leaves a mark on everything you do. And, if you are irritated, then you act literally as a generator of irritation. You are contagious, and you infect everyone around you with your irritation even if you are simply sitting at home at that time. There are no borders for your thoughts and feelings. And any one of your negative thoughts and feelings is instantly spread by you over the whole globe.

Miracles of heroism demonstrated by a handful of our devoted servers are required in order to offset and neutralize the consequences of your thoughts and feelings.

You only need to watch your inner state and constantly keep harmony and peace within you.

There are certain recipes for each of you on how you can maintain your harmonious state. There are none and cannot be any common recipes. And we cannot make you all pray or meditate. But you must use some measures that help you reach a harmonious state.

It is usually enough for the majority of people to simply be alone in nature in order for inner harmony and peace to come to them. But maybe you need interaction with children or animals or engaging in something that you love doing.

Learn to constantly control your inner state and take measures to suppress any imperfect state within you.

You can ask the Ascended Hosts for help but sometimes you forget to take even that simple action.

I am ready to render my personal help and support to everyone who will turn to me at this dark season. Here is my hand. Take it and hold it tight during any hard situations you go though in your life.

It is necessary for as many incarnated people as possible to be able to keep the balance on the planet right now. And if you are not capable of keeping the balance on the planet, then at least keep the balance within you. And with that you will render your invaluable help to the Ascended Hosts.

**I AM Lanello,
and I have come in order to give you
my helping hand again.**

Leave your holiday fuss. Start doing the real work on balancing the planet

Beloved Maha Chohan
December 18, 2005

I AM Maha Chohan, coming to you through our Messenger.

I AM the one who you know as the Master who was working with many Messengers.

That is why I came to you again through this Messenger in order to perform my part of work and give you the Message that I have to give you today.

I was trying to understand what I should start with. First, I should greet those representatives of mankind of Earth, who read our Messages not out of curiosity but to take our Messages as an unquestionable guide for action. Reading our Messages just out of human curiosity without implementing our requirements and requests given in the Messages, is the manifestation of human imprudence in the highest degree.

It is so strange to watch and see that people perceive the Masters' appeals at the same level that they get information from purely human sources as if there is no difference whether ordinary people talk to them or those who have taken control of the planet at this hard time.

This unwise attitude toward our Messages is typical for undeveloped human consciousness. A child in kindergarten also cannot distinguish the information that comes to him from different sources. He perceives a tale and everything that he really sees around him as events of the same kind. The same happens to you. But you perceive events of life surrounding you as real and the things we tell you about as a tale.

You will grow up when you are able in your consciousness to distinguish the Divine reality from the fairytale illusion of your world. And moreover, your world resembles a scary fairytale.

I have come on the eve of the change of the year cycle, which is celebrated at this time of the year in most countries of the world, in order to remind you once again of the responsibility that lies with you at this hardest time.

I have to admit that events on the planet are not developing in the best way. And if you have forgotten about that horrible cataclysm that happened a year ago in the South of Asia and didn't touch any other countries of the world, I have come to remind you of the possibility of just the same cataclysm.

I don't want to scare you, but if you got used to listening to scary fairy tales, then listen to another one.

Not only in Heaven is it determined whether the next cataclysm happens or not. Heavens can always hold back any cataclysm. But the energy that is spent on holding back that cataclysm should be justified and compensated.

That is why we come and appeal to you again and again, and we remind you of your responsibility and your duties that you should perform while keeping the balance within you and thus maintaining the balance on the whole planet Earth.

The decision on whether to allow the next cataclysm or not hasn't been made yet. We are waiting for your reaction to our warnings and those efforts that you are ready to make in order to prevent the cataclysm.

Understand that you cannot be irresponsible anymore. You can't keep on pretending that nothing is happening on the planet, and even if something is happening, then you have nothing to do with it. Sooner or later you will have to come out of childhood and assume full responsibility for your native planet.

I am coming to you not with a request but with a requirement. Leave alone your holiday hassle. Start doing real work on balancing the planet.

If I were incarnated with you, during the time remaining until the end of this year, I would be directing all of my energies to praying for the balance on the planet and bringing to their senses those careless children who do not want to come out of the state of irresponsibility and irrationality.

We have the right to expect that, in anticipation of the next human races to come, people of Earth should finally become mature and let go of those manifestations of their egos that become unsafe for further existence of life on Earth.

You know that there were a lot of such periods in the past when the situation on the planet was critical; and every time, Cosmic Beings or the Masters came to help the planet and sacrificed their causal bodies and saved the planet.

Now the situation has changed, and saving the planet must be accomplished with your efforts.

The time has come to examine the maturity of those souls that are incarnated on the planet now.

That is why I come, and I address you not simply with a request but with a requirement.

You may not follow my recommendations and advice. However, I still hope that a sufficient number of incarnated souls will be found on Earth who will realize their responsibility for the planet and will fulfill their duty.

No matter what spiritual practice you engage in and what religion you belong to, I am asking you until the end of the year to spend as much time as you can on exercising your praying practices. Read decrees, prayers, and Rosaries.

Do it for as long as it doesn't burden your family and performance of your current duties at work and at home.

We cannot make you pray, but we cannot stop asking and begging you to do it using every opportunity.

It is your turn to act.

Take the trouble to tell about the worry that we pass on you to all those people who are ready to perceive this information and spend their personal time on implementing the balancing of Earth.

Try to do your best, and I hope that we'll be able to meet with you at the beginning of next year and sum up the results of your efforts.

**I AM Maha Chohan,
and I have been with you today at Heaven's request.**

A Teaching on Karma descending at the end of the year

Beloved Kuthumi
December 19, 2005

I AM Kuthumi. I have come to you through our Messenger.

I have come to give you a Teaching on how you should regard the karma that descends upon you at the end of the year, what this karma is, and how you should treat its descending.

You know that your four lower bodies contain energetic records about wrong, dishonest, and non-divine acts that you committed during your present or one of your past lives. These can be records of lasting negative conditions that you were experiencing in the past and have not been able to get rid of up to this day.

You are aware of the karma that returns to you. You are aware of the karma that is activated within your aura in accordance with the Law of Cosmic Cycles and arises in front of you in the form of some situation, feeling, or poor state of your consciousness. This return of karma happens continuously and gradually during the year. But when the annual cycle is nearly over, you come up against a slightly different situation. It might happen that the karma, which has been returning to you during the year in accordance with the Cosmic Law, has not been worked off by you as much as required by the Law. Imagine that during this particular one-year cycle other people have also not been able to work off their karma by making right choices, praying, or committing good deeds.

In this case, at the end of the year an accumulation of surplus karma takes place that looms over humanity and is ready to descend in the form of various states inherent to humankind: diseases, depression, hunger, or in the form of various cataclysms and natural disasters.

In any case, at the end of the year, even with your inner sensation you can feel that you experience some increased heaviness. This is just the extra karmic burden that lies on humanity in the form of non-transmuted negative energy.

That is why it is so important to maintain increased discipline of your consciousness at the end of the year. It is very helpful for you to consciously impose limitations upon yourselves (such as fasting, practicing silence, prayer vigils, or helping the poor and underprivileged) that you can bring as a sacrifice to the altar of Service.

In this case, you create additional good karma that in the most extreme circumstances can be used for the purpose of balancing the situation on the planet.

That is why we come to you during this new cycle of Dictations and remind you again and again about a probable cataclysm or a natural disaster. Not because we want to scare you and make you pray. No, we come to explain to you the current heavy situation on Earth and offer those of you who are ready to act as co-creators to God and to the Hierarchy of Light existing in the Universe.

If your consciousness is not ready for such service, it is rather possible that you will perceive our requests as an unreasonable intimidation.

However, let's reason upon this together. What is the alternative? How else to liquidate the excessive masses of negative energy accumulated on the planet? Do you think a miracle will happen and all the energy that you have not been able to work off in the given one-year period will just miraculously vanish?

All such miracles, even if they did happen in the past, always required a great amount of additional energy. This energy was granted to your planet either from the cosmic reserves or from the causal bodies of the Ascended Masters.

Now picture a company that shows a net loss from year to year. The owner of the company borrows funds from other companies — profitable ones — and covers the loss, and that can last for some period of time. But there comes a time when the owner realizes that the loss is not a random occurrence but is connected with the negligence of the employees of this company.

So, a good owner can either make his employees work better or close the company.

The measures being taken by the Ascended Hosts now are aimed at encouraging the best representatives of mankind to work better. You do not want to lose your workplace — your planet if using the above analogy — do you?

Therefore, it is necessary to have a clear understanding of the alternative the planet is facing at the present moment. You will either be able to take responsibility for the situation on the planet, or you will be deprived of the opportunity to continue the evolution on this planet because it will be recognized as a dead-end.

Of course, all this won't happen right away. You will be given a chance to gradually realize your responsibility. In order to make our persuasions more convincing, you were warned earlier[3] that we would no longer restrain the karma that is being created by people living at particular locations. And this karma will almost immediately return in the form of one or another technogenic or natural disaster. The probability of such cataclysms increases by the end of the year. That is why you are strongly recommended to

---

[3] Refer to the Dictation "Each of your acts of service to all the living creatures reduces the probability of the next threatening cataclysm," Lord of the World Gautama Buddha, May 2, 2005, in *Words of Wisdom Volume 1*.

approach your spiritual practices, prayers, and meditations more consciously right at the end of the year.

There are people whose consciousness is at such a low level that it is useless to speak to them about such things. But luckily for them, their extent of karmic responsibility is low in comparison with those individuals who realize all the complexity of the situation, but due to their inherent imperfections, laziness, and shortsightedness they do not take those actions that we ask them for.

Depending on the level of consciousness reached by people, the Law of Karma operates in different ways. And what can be forgiven for some people is unforgivable for others. You should not care about the fact that somebody's behavior is improper but still no karma descends upon them to teach them a lesson.

Purely and simply, this person has either enough time for his evolution or a sufficient supply of good karma. Do not worry. The Karmic Law operates impeccably. And everyone will receive an opportunity to encounter the karma that they created in the past.

Do not think about others, think about yourself. Think about how you personally can mitigate your karma, your family's karma, and the karma of your country and planet.

You may not have a clear understanding about all the details of how this universal Law operates, but you should have a general idea about it, and you should tell about it to those who are not yet familiar with the Law of Karma. The more people who know about this Universal Law, the greater is the probability that they will avoid committing improper deeds in their lives.

When karma descends upon you, most commonly you are unable to observe the cause and effect relationship between the actions you committed and their consequences that descend upon you in the form of different misfortunes and illnesses. And you exclaim: "Why, Lord?!" instead of accepting with humility everything that God sends your way.

Believe me, God is very merciful. The karma that descends upon you returns to you in the easiest possible way. If you had an opportunity to understand which of your actions burden you with this or that type of karmic responsibility, then you would thank God for allowing you to so mercifully work off what you deserve from what you yourselves committed in the past.

There are several ways of working off your karma.

The first way is not to create karma at all.

The second way is to work off your karma by making right choices.

The third way is to work off your karma by accepting with humility any situation that you get into.

And, finally, you can mitigate your karmic burden by praying and true repentance. This is what we suggest you should do intensely during the time remaining until the end of this year. Now you have an opportunity to realize that everything that the Masters ask of you is justified and reasonable. None of us has an intention to scare you and make you do something.

We speak to you as sensible people who are standing just slightly lower on the steps of the evolutionary ladder.

**I AM Kuthumi, and I was happy
to share a seed of my knowledge with you.**

Create selflessly, strive for the Divine world without looking back, and you will receive what you deserve.

**Beloved Jesus
December 20, 2005**

I AM Jesus, and I have come to you through our Messenger. I have come again and like half a year ago I intend to give you the eternal Teaching on eternal life. Now I have come before Christmas, which is celebrated in the Christian world as a holiday honoring the day when I came into this world about 2000 years ago.

Then, as well as now, I am feeling the discomfort and the darkness of your world.

Oh, if you could only take a glimpse beyond the curtain out of the corner of your eye and feel the bliss of Heavenly life, I think that you would forever keep in your external consciousness the image that you should aspire to and that you must manifest in the life around you.

The whole problem of your consciousness is connected with its instability and lack of aspiration. You cannot manifest heavenly patterns in your earthly life until you gain that state of aspiration and highest faith, in which you will be able to dedicate all your earthly life to manifesting Divine plans in your physical octave. Only in this way you will be able to become the co-creator to God and manifest His Will for your octave.

Your world does not totally meet the requirements that it must satisfy at the given stage of evolutionary development. That is why the concern of the Ascended Hosts is so great, and that is why the nature of our Dictations has become so tough and uncompromising.

Believe that our love has not gone anywhere. We continue loving you as we have always loved you. But our love is manifested as caring about your souls' development and creating the conditions in which this development can be realized in the future.

Just as loving parents do not force their children to eat sweets all day long but vary their food so that they could grow healthy and active, the same way we try to provide you with the best spiritual food. And at the present time we are giving you the exact spiritual food that you need. And, even if it seems hard and not sweet to you, it does not mean that it is not good for you.

In our practice of teaching we constantly resort to alternating the carrot and stick method. When you get too much used to our affection and care, then we sometimes allow ourselves to show you that excessive care is not always useful. And the time comes when you must start acting on your own instead of expecting the whole Cosmos to continue spoon-feeding and cherishing you.

Had you not once in your life made the first step, you would have never learned to walk.

That first step for you is the realization of your responsibility not only for your life and the life of your family but also for the realization of your responsibility for the whole planet.

This is the next stage of the development of your consciousness. It would be unreasonable for you to continue relying on your nannies and parents when you have already reached that age at which you are capable of taking care of yourself. Moreover, you must assume the responsibility for the destiny of those livestreams that fell behind in their development and without your help are not capable of further development. And precisely the same role that we are playing in relation to you, the role of careful nannies and teachers, you must assume in relation to those representatives of mankind who are still playing childish games and do not wish to grow up.

From now on, education and upbringing of these unwise children lies with you as your duty and karmic responsibility. If you do not care about the younger generation and guiding those grown-up individuals who need your guardianship, then there is a high probability that too many livestreams on planet Earth will not touch the Divine Truth in this lifetime and will not be able to reach awareness of the eternal life.

I do hope for your care. When you choose to help other living beings, then you receive Heavens' help, and you receive the knowledge and the Divine energy that you need. If you do nothing, then you will not be able to fulfill your Divine plan and your Divine purpose, and you will not be able to help others.

This is a very ancient and wise law, and this law works impeccably. Never care for any reward that you expect to receive for your good deeds and help. Let God decide what you deserve. The more selfless your service is, the bigger the treasure that you save in Heaven will be.

And that is the very same choice and one and the same choice that you are making during your entire life. You either try to receive something tangible for yourself in the illusion surrounding you, or you think about the eternal life. Eventually you receive what your attention is focused on. And if from life to life you continue chasing the things of this world, then you are compelled to come to your world again and again and work off your attachments.

Therefore, create selflessly, strive for the Divine world without looking back, and you will receive that what you deserve.

I was glad to meet with you today, and I was glad to present you this short Teaching as a Christmas gift.

I hope that you will also remember me with love during these Christmas holidays and give me the love of your hearts.

**I AM Jesus,
and I am standing in the flame of Love.**

Faith is the remedy that you need

Beloved El Morya
December, 21, 2005

I AM El Morya Khan and I have come to you through my Messenger.

I have come to bring to your attention an important offer that I am empowered to make this afternoon.

Just as during the previous cycle of Dictations, I am now very determined. And if anyone of you doubts my determination and seriousness of my intentions, you'd better not read our Messages, because you create in your consciousness an impassable barrier and block not only the stream of the Divine Truth but also the stream of the Divine energy.

Your consciousness belongs to your dual world, therefore only those things happen in your world that you allow in your consciousness. That is why we will never fully tell you what kind of catastrophe you are probably facing, irrespective of the complexity of the situation on the planet. That is because if you only conceive the idea of a forthcoming catastrophe in your consciousness, this idea will be multiplied, and instead of extinguishing the existing fire you will be putting more and more wood into it.

That is why we will never fully tell you the information that we possess. But we will never cease to warn you and ask you to do all you can in order to harmonize the situation on the planet.

You have noticed that from the moment of the beginning of the new cycle of Dictations through our Messenger there was not one joyful and optimistic Message. That is not because some changes have happened to our Messenger and she is intimidated by impending cataclysms. All is well with our Messenger. And I can assure you that our Messages are transmitted with a sufficient degree of accuracy. No, the thing is that the situation is actually tense. And no matter how hard we try, we have not yet been able to encourage you to assume those responsibilities that we are asking you about. The law of free will that is operating in your physical octave does not allow us to intervene and force you. That is why we can only ask you or, as a last resort, require of you. But it seems that the only thing that will make you take actions is the threatening circumstance that we are talking about.

Well, you seem to prefer acting in accordance with the Russian proverb, "One believes in wonder when hears a sound of thunder."

There are very few people who seriously perceive our information and are ready to sacrifice much in order to comply with our requests.

We have not yet been able to enlarge the circle of people capable of specific actions. However, think about the fact that no matter how widely and promptly we give our warnings you are still unable to answer our call.

The problem is not even in your laziness and neglect. The whole point is that you are so captured by the illusion that you can differentiate neither what source contains the Truth nor the vibrations inherent to the true source.

Therefore, all your practices and all your actions should be directed at learning to make a distinction. In reality, staying in the illusion will come to an end only when you learn to make a distinction between the events that take place on the illusive plane and the events that belong to the real Divine world. Your task is to acquire a distinct vision and learn to give an evaluation to every event and fact that you face in life.

It seems to you that your life is running smoothly, and at times you don't even have an idea that in this silence and smooth flow of life there are hidden pitfalls that are capable of turning the peaceful flow of your life upside down in a moment. Therefore, try to resist this soothing calmness. You are constantly getting your lessons. Sometimes one small stone lying on the rails is enough to make the huge train of your life derail at a great speed and turn over. However, you yourselves prepare your own future by making your everyday choices.

When the critical mass of your wrong choices reaches the limits of permissible karma, you encounter the situations in your life that literally destroy everything you are used to, and you exclaim in surprise, "Oh, Lord, what have I done? Why has it all fallen to my lot?"

It is a familiar picture, isn't it? And at the next step, ninety percent of people start cursing God and the Masters for what has happened in their lives. They blame all the people around them and the whole world instead of humbly accepting all that has happened as a punishment or as a karmic retribution that overflowed the edges of the permissible limits and spilled in the form of a horrible punishment.

Thus, on one hand, in the course of the entire history of its existence, mankind has been guided and warned. On the other hand, only when something terrible happened to people were they able to think even if for a short time about the reasons things fell upon them.

No matter how much we speak and give you the optimal advice in order to avoid the expected, you are not able to believe that everything you are told is true. And the reason for your disobedience and shortsightedness is the lack of the true Faith.

That is why I, the Master who represents the aspect of God's Will, am addressing you this afternoon. I can help each of you who will turn to me with a request to strengthen their Faith.

Faith is the remedy that you need. I am speaking now not about blind faith based on ignorance and intimidation. I am referring to the Faith based on the exact knowledge of the Law that exists in this Universe.

This Law is the Law of cause and effect relationships, or the Law of Karma, or retribution. This Law operates regardless of your wish or your will. This is what is real. And that is what your aspiration to assert your free will, regardless of any circumstances, stumbles upon. If this natural barrier provided by the Creator did not stand in the path of misuse of your free will, the question of existence of not only your planet but also the Universe itself would be put into challenge.

That is why the first thing you should accept within yourselves is the supremacy of the Law governing in this Universe and in your lives.

You may appeal to me with the request to strengthen your Faith. And I will gladly provide you with this aid as it is the most important and immediate remedy that you need.

**I AM El Morya Khan,
with faith in your victory!**

On letters to the Karmic Board

Gautama Buddha
December 22, 2005

I AM Gautama Buddha. I have come to you through our Messenger again. I have come to you at this dark time of the year when the whole northern hemisphere, where the majority of the population of Earth is concentrated, has very little sun energy at its disposal. It is truly a dark time of the year. And you can feel in your inner state that even the approaching holidays aren't facilitating your well-being.

I have come to you to give one more Message, at the heart of which there is concern that we have about the planet and the very existence of life on this planet.

However hard the Ascended Hosts were trying during the past year, they did not succeed in achieving the balance on the planet that is necessary for its steady progression. With great attention and alertness we are anticipating the decision that will be announced after the session of the Karmic Board that is beginning now. You know that at this dark time of the year an annual session of the Karmic Board begins. At this session important decisions are made according to which the planet will be living during the following six months until the next session of the Karmic Board, which takes place during the period of the summer solstice.

Therefore, you can also take part in this session of the Karmic Board and thus influence the course of the planet's development during the next half year. Of course, you will not be let in the hall where the session of the Karmic Board takes place. You will not be able to be present there either in your physical bodies or your Higher bodies. But you may appeal to the Karmic Board with your letters, and I assure you that all of your letters will be thoroughly considered.

One letter written by a passionate soul can be enough in order for the decision of the Karmic Board to be changed. That is why I highly recommend you to use the granted opportunity and write letters to the Karmic Board.

I can even tell you where exactly you can apply your help.

If a sufficient number of souls assume, in the name of I AM, the responsibility to read the prayers, decrees, or the Rosaries for a certain amount of hours during the next six months, and if they direct the energy of their prayer vigils at the stabilization of the situation on Earth, this will help the Karmic Board adopt a decision that will allow use of the cosmic reserves for the stabilization of the situation on Earth.

We must be confident that the energetic expenditures will be compensated with your prayer efforts. So, please consider and evaluate your abilities one more time.

I ask you to use this opportunity that is granted to you by Heavens.

In exchange, you may ask in your letters about those leniencies for you and your relatives that can be granted if the Law of Karma permits.

For example, you may use the offered opportunity to free from a part of karmic causes those of your relatives who suffer from chronic illnesses or bad habits.

But do not forget that first and foremost your energy will be directed at the restoration of the energy taken from the cosmic reserve for the stabilization of the situation on Earth, and only after that will the energy be directed at the realization of your requests.

Do not assume such obligations that you will not be able to fulfill. Let your obligations make up only fifteen minutes of praying, but you will fulfill your obligations daily. And this will be so much better than if you undertake a responsibility to read prayers or the Rosaries for an hour or two and are not able to fulfill the assumed obligation even for a week.

Correctly evaluate and distribute your resources.

The session of the Karmic Board is beginning any minute now. But you may still send your letters to the Karmic Board during the next two weeks.

I am happy that my fortunate duty is to remind you about the opportunity granted to you on these days when the Karmic Board is holding a session on planet Earth.

Ahead of you is the next cosmic cycle that will last until the next session of the Karmic Board. And I hope that with our combined efforts we will be able to keep the balance on the planet.

At least the Ascended Hosts are determined to exert every effort necessary for this. And if at least a one thousandth part of this determination were inherent to just a few thousand of representatives of humankind of Earth, then I would feel absolutely secure about the situation on planet Earth during the next few months.

It may seem to you that every time, during many hundreds of years, you are frightened about the end of the world coming, but the end of the world still won't come. And you fall into disregarding our reminders. In reality, the maintenance of the balance on planet Earth requires great efforts. And this near-destructive situation on the planet has already lasted for many hundreds and even thousands of years.

You know that planet Earth is at the lowest point of materiality now. That is why the influence of the spiritual world on the planet is greatly restricted at this lowest point. And since this lowest point of materiality takes many thousands of years, this state of uncertainty has lasted that long. But you, those who are incarnated on planet Earth, are able to provide a lot more impact on the physical state of the planet at this lowest point of materiality.

That is the reason for our relentless appeals to you.

I remind you once again that not so much of your effort is required in order to change the situation on the planet, because the efforts you apply have a thousand times greater influence on the situation on Earth than the efforts of the Ascended Hosts.

Think about my words, consider everything one more time, and write your letters of obligations to the Karmic Board.

The task that we are entrusting you with seems to be burdensome to you. But think over the fact that the salvation of the whole planet lies on one scale while on the other scale your momentary egoistic interests rest.

Doesn't this situation with the choice you sometimes make remind you of a situation with a man who keeps on watching television when his house is on fire?

We hope that within your minds the Divine rationality prevails over your purely human attachments and habits.

**I AM Gautama,
and I have been with you this afternoon.**

I have come to warn you that this Dictation may be the last

Beloved Serapis Bey
December 23, 2005

I AM Serapis Bey. I have come to you again through our Messenger on this day.

I have come to bring to your perception some information that is useful to you. As you can notice, all of our Dictations are imbued with our caring about you. We are trying to reach your hearts and minds. Sadly we haven't yet succeeded. Our appeals resemble more of a monologue than a dialogue. We are making attempts for you to get imbued with our concerns and problems, but you cannot or do not want to understand us.

I will tell you a secret: During the session of the Karmic Board that is taking place now, among other questions, the question of whether to continue or stop the transfer of our Messages through this Messenger is being decided. We spend a lot of energy in order to transfer our Messages, and we do not yet feel that our energy expenditures have produced any positive effect. In other words, we have made a certain investment of funds, and we would like to receive some energy gain in return. Agree that it is unreasonable to spend energy and funds without getting any positive effect from our investments.

At the present moment, all those efforts that you make trying to carry out our requests do not cover our energy input. And today we are giving this Dictation from a lower energy level because we have exceeded the energy limit that was allowed for giving this cycle of Dictations.

Therefore, I have come to warn you that this Dictation may be the last. And in this cycle of Dictations, we have not given even one-fifth of what we were going to provide. So, no matter how sad it is, I am giving you this information and informing you with regret that probably today or tomorrow, the decision about the termination of this dispensation will be made. We cannot waste the precious Divine energy unreasonably.

Think it over. Consider everything one more time.

You can't use the grace of Heavens endlessly.

The only thing that can extend the given dispensation is your letters of request to the Karmic Board and the responsibilities that you can assume.

Understand that everything has to be balanced in this world. And we create karma in the same way exactly when we pour our energy into leaky bellows.

I should note that we do not have any complaints about Tatyana as our Messenger. She has performed and continues to perform her part of the work impeccably. However, the effect that we were counting on when starting this new cycle of Dictations has not been received by us. Too few people are following our recommendations and are ready to join the implementation of the Divine opportunities given by us.

I cannot say what today's decision of the Karmic Board will be but it is probable that starting tomorrow we will have to stop our Dictations through the given Messenger.

The purpose of my visit today has been to notify you about that possibility so the untimely termination of our Messages won't be sudden to you.

I say goodbye to you now.
I AM Serapis Bey.

We are joyful that our appeals have found response in your hearts

Great Divine Director
December 30, 2005

I AM Great Divine Director. I have come to you through our Messenger on this day.

I have come. You know me as one of the members of the Karmic Board. And I hurry to give you fresh information from our session, which is practically over.

You know that our session began on December 22, and it has been going on all this time.

We will be holding the meeting for some more time in order to consider the letters that you have written and continue writing to the Karmic Board. But the main thing that we have gathered for is already over.

We have considered the opportunity of providing a balanced existence of the planet for the upcoming half year.

I have to tell you that our session has been very intense, and you, the most sensitive individuals among you, should have felt the tension that existed on the planet only several days ago.

We have been waiting for your reaction to our appeals through our Messenger. We have been waiting on what your reaction would be. It is because how you react to our requests and respond to our offers tells us a lot. And, in particular, it tells us to what extent you are ready to cooperate and to what extent we can count on your help.

To our greatest joy, such light-souls were found on Earth who, realizing all the fullness of our worry and the urgency of our requests, spared all their personal efforts and gave all their free time and abilities to serve the planet and the existence of life itself on planet Earth.

We are thanking you for the rendered help. Believe that we are joyful not as much because of your contribution to the process of stabilization of the situation on Earth but more because of the determination, selflessness, and devotion that you have responded to our requests with.

We couldn't help responding to the impulse of your souls. For our part, we have done everything possible and taken all the measures that have allowed us to save the planet from the next devastating and destructive cataclysm, the danger of which seemed to be inevitably looming over the planet. We have managed to painlessly dissolve those negative energy clusters that covered Earth so densely that they would not allow the penetration of our rays and vibrations, which could solely have beneficial influence on the planet and those individuals who were in a critical situation and expected our help.

Therefore, we are joyful that our appeals have found response in your hearts. Of course, the number of those who have responded to our appeals is insignificant in comparison with the total population of the planet. However, according to the impact of the efforts of those few, you can judge how quickly the situation on the planet could change if millions followed our instructions.

Therefore, ahead of you, you have a wide range of activities related to carrying the Light of our Teachings to the widest possible audience of those who need these Teachings and for whom the vibrations contained in our Messages are similar to a cup of cool water on a hot afternoon.

I cannot tell you that the danger of various cataclysms and natural disasters has been completely eliminated, and nothing will be threatening the planet in the near future. But I can tell you that the danger of that cataclysm that we warned you about has passed.

We managed to destroy the cause of that cataclysm on the Higher plane, and consequently, on the physical plane, the descent of the reasons for that cataclysm will happen in a much smaller and local magnitude.

I think that the cooperation that began so successfully at the end of this year between you, our incarnated collaborators and us, the Ascended Realm, will continue next year. I make no secret of the fact that many members of the Karmic Board were not sure that we would be able to find a sufficient number of incarnated light-workers who would respond to our appeal and spend these last days of the passing year in reverential prayer and humility.

We were waiting and preparing for a much worse situation, and the fact that you managed to mobilize all your resources and assume your obligations gave us the opportunity to involve those reserves that we could engage in helping planet Earth.

You know that there are a sufficient number of Beings of Light in space who are ready to sacrifice the momentum of their achievements in order to render their help to mankind of Earth. But the Cosmic Law does not allow rendering such help until there are a sufficient number of incarnated individuals who declare their readiness to cooperate with the Ascended Hosts and make certain commitments. It is similar to your putting something as a security deposit before obtaining a credit in a bank. And only after something has been put down as collateral, can you count on getting some financial resources at your disposal.

Therefore, I can tell you now that your commitment and selfless service have allowed us to distribute the energy that you had already given us in the form of your prayers and your praying commitments that you have made for the next half year, for the purpose of receiving the necessary help in the form of energy from the cosmic reserve.

Therefore, now I am authorized on behalf of the Karmic Board to declare to you that we are happy with the achievements of those of you who have made commitments based on a sincere impulse coming from the bottom of your hearts.

I am taking a bow before you. And let me shake your hands. Truly at such moments, realizing oneness with these currently incarnated devoted collaborators, tears of joy well up in the eyes. And that allows us to hope that the situation on the planet will change and our plans will be carried out!

Thank you, and let me congratulate you on the beginning of a new milestone that I hope will open for us the opportunities for further, even more fruitful, cooperation!

I AM Great Divine Director.

Let your holiday resemble the visit of the Higher, etheric octaves

Beloved Melchizedek
December 31, 2005

I AM Melchizedek. I have come to you today.

Fortunately for you, today I will not be saddened or left out of the holiday spirit.

You are used to celebrating your earthly holidays. And this holiday is one of the favorites. As a rule, even those people who do not believe that much in God and Higher Hosts feel some mysticism on this day.

You know that the Ascended Masters do not celebrate earthly holidays; however, we are with you during your holidays. That is because every time we see that people celebrate the change of a year according to our recommendations, it gives us an opportunity to join your holiday.

You know that the requirements that we have for an earthly holiday differ from the ideas that the major part of humanity associates with the idea of a holiday.

The fundamental and most important requirement that we would like you to take into consideration is to fill your holiday with the Divine mystical meaning. Anything that helps you raise your consciousness and enables you to take a glimpse behind the curtain at least out of the corner of your eye or with the help of your imagination is good from our point of view.

Therefore, we do not welcome all the holiday fuss that you are used to during your holiday. It will be good to remember about your Divine purpose during your holiday, about the reason for your incarnation. And you know that your Higher Self is always aware of where you have come from and where you are going. And those forces that try to hold you in the illusion aim to inculcate you those stereotypes of a holiday that in no way correspond with the Divine patterns cultivated by us. And the only thing that you achieve when you habitually and blindly follow the mass models of a holiday is that you strengthen the illusion prevailing around you instead of making efforts and breaking away from it.

I am speaking with you in a very clear language, but the majority of you hardly understand what I mean.

Still, I hope that among the people who read these Dictations, there will be a considerable number of individuals ready to break away from the habitual stereotype of a holiday existing in the mass consciousness and follow the pieces of advice that we give.

May your holiday resemble the visit of the Higher, etheric octaves that you sometimes happen to penetrate during your night sleep. Try to remember those impressions and feelings that you have during your presence in our octaves of Light. Have you seen drunken companies or any kind of inharmonious groups of people anywhere in those octaves?

No, there is no place for any kind of such manifestations in our world. Try to remember the smooth atmosphere reigning in our octaves. Soft, non-irritating but at the same time bright enough illumination so that you can see everything around you. Remember the sounds of the etheric octaves: very subtle chimes of little bells, calm rhythm of mantras, or choirs singing.

Remember the love and harmony that reign in our octaves. And even when you meet silent beings from the Higher Worlds who do not speak to you, their presence is anyway pleasant for you as you feel the flow of endless love from them. You literally bathe in this love, the mystic power of love that cloaks you like incense.

There is nothing that would irritate you. Everything is very harmonious. And you do not want to leave our octaves. And after those nights when you get lucky and reach our etheric temples and palaces, you especially do not want to wake up and return to your world.

Therefore, your task is to maximally bring the atmosphere of your place where you celebrate your holiday to the etheric octaves, to the extent your outward conditions allow you to. Oh, I understand very well that it will be difficult for you to overcome the resistance of your friends and families when you try to bring our patterns into your world.

And not all of you will succeed in it.

Therefore, I would like to warn you against excessive and futile waste of energy. You know that in your world everything is attracted in accordance to vibrations. And if you have reached a definite high enough level of consciousness, then during the holiday you will automatically get into the company that will allow you to realize your aspiration to the etheric octaves manifested in the physical world. At least you will get an opportunity to stay alone and experience the magic of the etheric octaves around you during your earthly holiday.

The evolution of the human consciousness is very gradual. And if you decide today that your holiday should be exactly like I have just described to you, it doesn't mean that your holiday will be exactly that kind. That is because the stereotypes in your consciousness are very strong. But now you have an image in your consciousness that you should aspire to. And you know that if a seed has been sown in good soil, and you regularly water this soil with our Divine energy, sprouts will inevitably appear.

We are very patient. And we are ready for many of your earthly lives to witness how the seeds that we have sown gradually arise from under the ground and stretch out to the sun of the Divine consciousness.

If your aspiration is strong and your faith is firm, then those patterns and images that we place into your consciousness in the course of these Dictations will certainly sprout in your world. And the stronger your faith and aspiration, devotion and love, the sooner the changes around you that we are waiting for will occur.

It will not take long for the accumulated information and energy to manifest in your lives. And even the inner resistance that many of you feel while reading these Dictations is, anyway, the first step that you are taking in the right direction. Your resistance makes you think and analyze. And the most capable students will be those people who do not accept everything we say as an unquestionable fact but try to check the credibility of what is given with their consciousness and life experience.

Therefore, take our information, our energy. Test everything with your consciousness.

I am sure that from all the material we give, you will be able to extract exactly those golden grains of Truth that are vital for you in your lives at this very stage.

I AM Melchizedek.

You have come to this world to learn a lesson of distinction

Lord Shiva
January 1, 2006

I AM Shiva, and I have come to you again through my Messenger.

For the topic of our conversation today, I would like to use a well-known parable about a horse: You can lead a horse to water but you cannot make it drink.

Our conversations sometimes resemble this parable. We lead you to the river of the Divine energy and give you a chance to obtain priceless knowledge, the wisdom of ages that is contained in our Messages. However, you and only you can make a decision and start drinking. Nobody can do it for you. And exactly the same way, our Messenger cannot force anyone to take the nectar of the Divine energy contained in our Messages.

Wise people do not hurry to touch the information that comes from an unfamiliar source. And this is right. If you absorb everything indiscriminately, you may get indigestion in your brain. You should very efficiently select that information, which deserves your attention, in the reality surrounding you and separate it from the garbage that is located on the shelves of your stores and in the Internet in excess supply.

Not a long time ago, each book that we gave through our Messengers represented a wonder and was perceived as something incomprehensible and confusing. But now the time has changed and a lot of such confusing information and literature has spread around.

The problem is not in obtaining new information anymore; the problem is in protecting yourself against the flow of information that, with all its seeming novelty, presents poison in a beautiful package.

But, unlike the poison that you buy to get rid of pests, which clearly states on the packaging that it is a poison, it is not written on the covers of your books that they represent any kind of threat to your consciousness.

Therefore, we are changing our tactics. And from this moment our task is not to simply give you the information but to give you the knowledge on how to distinguish between the genuine information and the false one in the sea of information around you.

You know that there are no distinct criteria. And always, when it comes to distinction we suggest that you enter your heart and entrust your Higher Self with making a choice and evaluation. Your Higher Self always knows the Truth. However, the thought of the necessity to appeal to your Higher Self doesn't always come to your mind. Not to mention the fact that the purity of your lower bodies can be insufficient in order to feel and distinguish the voice of your Higher Self. That is why it will be appropriate to present external criteria on the basis of which you will be able to make a distinction in the flow of information surrounding you.

First, pay attention not to the quality of the binding or the cover of a book but primarily pay attention to the quality of the presentation of the material. And if the information is not given at the level understandable to you, then stop reading.

The fact of the matter is that there are many levels of presentation of information. And what is accessible to the consciousness of one cannot be accessible to the consciousness of another.

There is not always the truth behind a complex text.

However, if you have achieved a high degree of initiations, then you will always find on the shelves of the shops those keys that will allow you to recognize the Truth in the most intricate text.

We have intentionally resorted to making our Messages complex before. In that case we tried to scare away from us those who attempt to use our information for their selfish purposes. Now we are not inclined to complication. It is always possible to make the given information more complicated, but the essence of the given information is very simple, and as a rule, it is understandable even to a child. Therefore, no matter how long you would wander through the wilds of the so-called esoteric literature, we advise you to look up over the essence of what is given and answer a simple question on how the things that you read help you in your real life.

Does that information that you receive help you free yourself from the unreal part of yourself and strive for the eternal, everlasting reality? What does the information that you read give for the development of your soul? How does this information help you in your life?

You can obtain pieces of advice concerning many very skillful practices but these practices lead you either to the multiplication of the illusion surrounding you or lead you away from your predestination and create the illusion that you are a very significant being on the cosmic scale.

In both cases you lose the point of support in your consciousness. You either go deeper into matter or soar in sky-high heights. As a result, the common thing is that you only generate illusion and create this illusion either on the physical plane or on the astral plane.

Your task is to constantly maintain the real viewpoint on your position in this world. And your real position is to stand with your feet firmly on Earth and at the same time to remember your cosmic origin and aspire to God.

The aspiration to God should not be confused with the desire to occupy a high position in the cosmic hierarchy.

Yes, it is possible that within many of you there are Higher Cosmic Beings who have come to Earth and are using every opportunity to help the civilizations of Earth. However, you should never forget that your soul is going through Earth's evolution. And that evolution is very gradual. Therefore, you cannot become a Great Cosmic Being at once during one lifetime. You can offer a Higher Cosmic Being to act through you, but it is more often that you give an opportunity to an astral plane being to act through you.

What is the criterion? How can one understand and make a distinction?

You know that in order for the Higher Cosmic Beings to act through you, you must say goodbye to the most part of your ego and undertake devoted service to the Cosmic Hierarchy.

In order to give yourself away as a slave to a being of the astral plane, none of your achievements are required at all, except for the desire of your ego to exalt itself.

Having read various kinds of superficial literature, many people consider themselves great beings who occupy a high position in the cosmic Hierarchy.

These people have been playing their games for so long that they are already incapable of making a distinction. Moreover, they do not even worry about making any distinction because they are confident in their exclusiveness and greatness.

However, after several minutes of a conversation, it already becomes clear to people around whom they are dealing with. Therefore, we are asking you to develop the gift of distinction within yourselves. That is why we are telling you first and foremost to get rid of your ego. For your ego obstructs your distinction, your vision, and your service.

We feel sorry for those individuals who have gone along the path of self-exaltation. However, it is their choice. And they have made the choice they wanted to make. Your world of illusion is different due to the fact that everyone gets what they strive for. And if you want to become a Higher Cosmic Being, you will definitely become one. And you will receive all the signs from the subtle plane that you are in fact this Higher Cosmic Being. The whole problem is that your motive was wrong from the very beginning. You desired to become a powerful being.

The true motive would be to become the most humble being, the servant to all living beings, living on Earth. The true motive would be to liberate yourself from the ego and help all living beings.

Therefore, it is not even necessary for you to turn to other people for the confirmation of your, as you think, cosmic achievements. You simply need to answer the question what your motive was when you started studying esoteric literature. Did you desire to get something for yourself, or did you wish to give everything for serving life?

The Divine science seems to be very simple at first sight but many go so deep into labyrinths of false concepts and knowledge that it becomes problematic for them to receive our very help.

Therefore, here is my advice to you: Before going deep into any teaching or following any practice or an external teacher, always analyze attentively the motive that drives you. For you will be attracted according to your vibrations and inner desires that are driving you to that group of people and to that teacher who will simply supply you with that which is necessary for you in order to achieve your goals. And never blame anyone outside of you that you have gotten into a cult or under someone's influence.

For you and only you yourselves are responsible for everything that happens to you.

You have come to this world in order to get a lesson of distinction between the Good and the Evil, the illusion and the reality.

Learn your lessons by yourselves. And remember that we can help you only when you ask us for help.

**I AM Shiva,
and I have come to give some very important instructions.**

You should learn to evaluate your deeds and thoughts on your own and get rid of all those vain and human things that impede your advancement on the Path

Beloved Zarathustra
January 2, 2006

I AM Zarathustra. I have come to you through this Messenger. The length of time that separates us from our previous meeting is not that significant.[4] However, the distance that you have overcome in your consciousness, those of you who regularly read the Dictations given by us through this Messenger, is so significant that it can only be compared to a flash of a supernova, the star of reason and Divine consciousness, which has illuminated your minds and hearts since our last meeting.

I am observing your state of consciousness. I have such an opportunity. And I see you, those who have risen to the new level of consciousness with the help of reading these Dictations, exactly as flashes of new stars in the darkness that continues to cloak Earth.

Each of you illuminates a small space around you, shining for those people who you meet in your everyday life. However, the larger the number of the big and small stars that flash on Earth,

---

[4] Refer to the Dictation "The carnal mind has to give up its place to the Divine Reason," Beloved Zarathustra, March 30, 2005, in *Words of Wisdom Volume 1*.

the more luminous and joyful the overall atmosphere reigning on the planet will be.

In the everyday hassle, you don't notice the changes that occur in your consciousness. Therefore, trust me. If we manage to maintain the same growth rates of your consciousness in the nearest future, you will feel the favorable shifts on the planet even in the lifetime of the current generation. Not the shifts driven toward technological progress, which the planet has been following all that time, but the shifts driven toward spiritual progress, the development of the soul. As you acquire more and more consonance with the Higher Worlds, the penetration of those worlds into your world will be more and more tangible. That is what we are trying to achieve, and that is why we call upon you.

When you are constantly submerged into the atmosphere of faithlessness, where negative energies and qualities predominate, it is hard for you to feel our vibrations, and it is difficult for you to feel the connection with the Divine world. However, more and more of you, even being in big cities, are capable of raising your consciousness so much that they get an opportunity to touch the subtle worlds, even if for a short period of time. And the larger the number of you who are able to raise your consciousness and travel to the subtle worlds, the quicker the rate of changes on the planet toward the Divine Path of development.

You are at the lowest point of materiality at this time. And that is why the impact of the dark energies on you is so great that you are literally wrapped in those energies. They have swaddled you, and you cannot get obtain enough freedom to move in space and time. And it is difficult for you to imagine in your human consciousness those opportunities and prospects that can open at any moment if only you demonstrate qualities of aspiration and faith.

Therefore, no matter what state your souls are in and how burdened you are with your current affairs and human problems you should always remember that it is all temporary. As soon as you manage to take the first, though uncertain, step toward comprehension of the Divine reality and make a call for help, all of the Ascended Hosts and angels will rush in to help you. Do not be bewildered by the fact that help won't be given immediately. We need time to create external circumstances and clear the karmic blockage. But as a rule, what you ask us for in your prayers and letters manifests to some extent. You only have to make small daily efforts. Your prayers are sometimes not important on their own because you do not yet have that momentum of reading prayers, which is necessary in order to bring the real impact. But your daily efforts will certainly be rewarded, because we appreciate and understand how hard sometimes it is for you to spare at least a few minutes to pray. For it seems that everything around opposes you as soon as you seriously start fulfilling the obligations that you have assumed in your letters to the Karmic Board, or you have just demonstrated the aspiration of your heart and decided to selflessly dedicate some time to the sacred work.

Do not be afraid of any obstacles that get in your way in your world because obstacles indicate only that it is necessary to overcome them. If you overcome obstacles every day, and every day fulfill the assumed obligations, then the momentum of aspiration that you accrue during all that time will help you in your prayers later on. For your prayers will gain more and more power with time.

You pray not even with words; you pray with your hearts, with the impulse of your hearts. And we always see you when you perform your prayer sincerely. At that moment you sparkle like a huge flash of light; and that flash serves as a sign for us and for angels; and we rush in to help you.

You know that the prayers that you say sincerely and selflessly in your heart work best.

Therefore, when Jesus said that you have to find a place to get alone and close the door in the room where you perform your prayers, that is completely correct advice.[5] That is because any public prayer bears a seal of hypocrisy.

And many of those who visit churches or houses of prayer every day do that more because of their sanctimony and hypocrisy than from the point of true faith and devotion.

You should be able to recognize that state within you. Do not be insincere and hypocritical with yourself. There is no other judge in your world besides yourself. And you have to learn to evaluate your deeds and thoughts on your own, and get rid of all those vain and human things that impede your advancement on the Path.

On a large scale, you do not need any outer leader because your main judge always resides within you. That is your Higher Self, your conscience, your Christ Self.

It will be useful for you to analyze all the deeds you have performed during the day. Make it a rule to spare just a few minutes before your sleep to analyze the day that has passed and the deeds you have performed during that day. Do not judge yourself strictly for the mistakes you have made. And do not allow your carnal mind to involve you again and again in those improper situations that you have gotten into during the day. Just give your evaluation to the situation and make a firm decision in your heart never to get involved in that negative state or improper action anymore. Ask your Higher Self for help so that it gives you a hint about that moment when you are at the threshold of a similar situation next time and helps you make the right choice.

---

[5] "And when you pray, do not be like the hypocrites, for they love to pray standing in the synagogues and on the street corners to be seen by others. Truly I tell you, they have received their reward in full. But when you pray, go into your room, close the door and pray to your Father, who is unseen. Then your Father, who sees what is done in secret, will reward you. And when you pray, do not keep on babbling like pagans, for they think they will be heard because of their many words. Do not be like them, for your Father knows what you need before you ask him" (Matthew 6:5-8).

Never allow yourself to be focused on any negative events of the day longer than a minute. It is enough for you just to give evaluation to an event. When you think and analyze a negative situation for too long, you are feeding it with your energy. And in the end you create a cluster of negative energy, which will wander in space and be attracted to those people whose vibrations coincide with the vibrations of that cluster of negative energy. Thus, you will be literally creating causes for your future problems and situations.

Your consciousness should maintain the purity that is inherent to small children. Detach yourself from any poor negative states.

Imagine that you take a knife and cut off of you these thoughts and obsessive states you cannot get rid of. Try to replace those negative states with positive images and feelings. Contemplate with your inner view beautiful flowers, sights of nature; listen to calm quiet music. It will be very useful to submerge into contemplation of stars and galaxy pictures before going to sleep. Listen and try to hear the voice of silence that comes to you from the depths of Cosmos and space.

I have given you food for reflection. And I am leaving you today in hope that you will follow my advice and remember it when it becomes necessary.

**I AM Zarathustra,
and I am standing in the flame of Divine harmony.**

A Teaching on humility

Beloved Surya
January 3, 2006

I AM Surya. I have come to you again!

The situation on planet Earth has been normalized and I am ready to get back to the regular pace of giving the knowledge and information that you need.

As we come to talk to you, you have an opportunity to broaden your consciousness and perception of the world. And even if sometimes it seems to you that you haven't learned anything new from a Dictation, don't be deluded. It is typical for you to overstate the level of the achievements you are at now. That is why one of our basic demands of you is the feeling of humility. The feeling of humility doesn't mean that you should humiliate yourself and cringe. No, that would be the wrong understanding of humility and the wrong understanding of service.

It is because the feeling of humility presumes the state where you feel your unity with the Creator. You start perceiving the Creation, the world around you so clearly and in such an exalted way, and you feel such a reverential awe and overflowing love, that you are ready for anything in order to maintain this state of your consciousness as long as possible.

You are ready to sacrifice everything you have, sacrifice even your physical body, your soul, all of your essence. That is because on a large scale you understand that there isn't any sacrifice on your part. You have such a feeling of oneness with life around you; and you have such a deep feeling of oneness with Creator that the barrier of your ego, which separates you and me, you and God, you and every part of life, ceases to exist. And in that state you feel infinite gratitude for Creator's mercy. And there is nothing in your Earth world that could be compared to the state of calm joy and unconditional happiness that encompasses you. And in that state you finally become able to feel that reverential awe that allows you to assume any responsibility and any test if it be God's Holy Will.

No, that feeling has nothing to do with slavery. Every slave deep within his soul hates his position and his master. And he never loses hope for freedom. Your humility comes from the feeling of entire freedom, infinite freedom. You feel that you have true freedom as an individual starting only when you enter in the relationship of complete obedience to the Divine Law existing in this Universe. You obey the Highest Law, and at the same time you gain unlimited freedom to act within the limits of this Law.

It seems to you that my words contain some inner contradiction. I am not hurrying you or making you accept my words as the absolute Truth. Just think about my words. Analyze what you have in the world around you and the attachments that you have to the things of your world. Try to understand that, actually, you have slavery dependence on the things of your world. You are in such dependence that in fact you are a slave of your things and as a consequence, a slave to circumstances of your world. Sooner or later you will face the question of which freedom to choose: the real freedom, the Divine freedom that releases you from slavery dependence on the things of your world, or will you still prefer to stay in illusory freedom with only one inherent quality — the freedom to disregard the Law existing in this UniverseConsider and evaluate what you have now and what you can have, should you only express the wish and take the path of liberation from your ego, take the Path of Initiations commanded to you by all prophets and founders of all religions that ever existed on Earth.

As distorted as those religions later became by zealous followers, the main quality of Divine humility could not be withdrawn and removed from the sacred books. The only thing that could happen and did happen was that the people who misappropriated the right to speak on behalf of God started demanding the quality of obeying the laws existing in human religions and churches instead of the quality of Divine humility and obedience to the Will of God.

You remember that we have told you that any quality and any circumstance existing in your world can be distorted and has a dual character. Today we have touched the quality of humility in its true meaning and the distortion of this quality by earthly leaders.

That is why every time you contemplate on any quality, try to analyze to what extent this quality that exists in your world corresponds with its Divine nature. And if you think about and analyze the accordance of every quality you face in your life to its Divine pattern and remove and cut off everything that is not of God and everything that has stuck to this Divine quality and distorted it, you will be able to reach perfection by removing everything useless and keeping only the Divine in everything that surrounds you.

This process will not last for a single or several lives. That is because all your existence on planet Earth, all thousands and millions of your incarnations, are intended only for separating and dividing within you everything that is of God from the things created by your human consciousness. You are similar to Gods, and just like God who created the universe, you create the illusion of your world with the help of your free will and consciousness. But later the turning point comes, the starting point that the illusion must be folded from. In your consciousness you rise to the level of understanding your Divine purpose, and you start in your consciousness the process of separating the real from the unreal, the Divine from the illusion.

I have shown it to you with the example of the quality of Divine humility and its human counterpart. And in the same way you may take and analyze other human qualities: love, devotion, perfection, and faith. In every quality, as you understand it, there is God's origin and an illusory additive.

With the help of your consciousness you are able to start the process of recognizing and separating the Divine from the illusionary.

In this way you become the co-creators to God. And in this way you become able to create the Divine reality around you.

So, don't postpone; begin your fundamental predestination and separate the real from the unreal in your minds and hearts.

I dare assure you that this is a much more entertaining thing to do than any of your human things. And most important is that any of your human things can also be considered from the point of combination of the Divine and the human within it. And the higher the level of consciousness development a person achieves, the more able he becomes to distinguish the finer sides within his activities that separate the reality from illusion.

You literally take off the illusion cover by cover; and those covers become thinner with each new step toward the reality.

Today we have been talking about humility, and we have been talking about freedom and any quality of your world to which you should give the Divine sounding.

This is the miracle of God and the predestination that you should follow.

I am leaving you alone with your thoughts.

**I AM Surya,
and I have come to teach you the Eternal Law.**

We are waiting for you to grow up

Beloved Vairochana
January 4, 2006

I AM Vairochana, and I have come to you again.

To start with, I would like to greet those of you who, thanks to your efforts, have the opportunity to receive our Messages again. You know that the transmission of the Messages takes a lot of energy. If your efforts had not made the continuation of the process of receiving the Dictations possible, then we would have had to stop. Everything in the Cosmos obeys rationality and feasibility. If we do not see that the teaching being given by us is perceived by you and that you are ready to take the necessary actions in the physical plane so that our Teachings can be widely spread, if we do not see that you are ready to render assistance with your praying vigils, then we close the window of opportunity until better times.

Therefore, the fact that you have an opportunity to receive this Teaching indicates that your efforts were sufficient, and they were considered sufficient in order to continue the Dictations through this Messenger.

Every time when the question arises whether or not to give another Teaching, we carefully weigh all the pros and cons. Jesus gave the Teaching that one shouldn't pour new wine into old wineskins.⁶ That is why we evaluate the quality of a vessel before giving knowledge and energy. This applies not only to the Messenger but also to each of you who have touched this Teaching. You can render your support slightly simply by sharing the given Teaching with your relatives and friends. You can give the energy of your prayers to support the cycle of these Dictations; you can take part in publishing these books, spreading them, or translating the Dictations into other languages. All of these efforts of yours are summed up and analyzed by our celestial computers. We compare the energy that we have spent on giving the Teaching to the energy that you have spent on adopting and spreading the Teachings in your octave.

The balance was a little bit in your favor. Therefore, we are now trying to balance the scale and give you the necessary quantity of the Divine energy and knowledge in order to keep the balance of energies.

I will tell you a secret: Not so long ago, before the Karmic Board began its session, and you know that I am also a member of the Karmic Board, the scale with the energy given by us outweighed yours. Therefore, beloved Serapis Bey⁷ said that his Dictation could be the last one.

Today I am happy to talk to you again and give you my Teaching and my energy.

I AM Vairochana, Buddha Vairochana. And as a Buddha I must give you knowledge and energy. You know that the balance on the planet is maintained by people who have reached the enlightenment of Buddha. It does not mean that these people

---

⁶ "Nor do people pour new wine into old wineskins. If they do, the skins will burst, the wine will spill out, and the skins will be ruined. Instead, they pour new wine into fresh wineskins, and both are preserved" (Matthew 9:17).

⁷ Refer to the Dictation "I have come to warn you that this Dictation can be the last one," Beloved Serapis Bey, December 23, 2005, in *Words of Wisdom Volume 2*.

differ much physically and even mentally from the majority of you. The degree of the consciousness expansion and the level of consciousness of Buddha are not much related to any outer qualities but rather to your inner state. These very people are able to keep the balance on planet Earth thanks to the degree of their achievements.

Your achievement of the level of Buddha consciousness is the task you are to fulfill. All of you will become Buddhas, although not all of you will become Buddhas in this incarnation. But achievement of the level of Buddha consciousness is as inevitable for you as the fact that the development in this Universe will continue.

You are getting access to the knowledge that is not contained in any books lying on the shelves of bookstores and libraries. You are getting access to the knowledge that is contained in the cosmic treasury of knowledge. In order to get access to that knowledge you have to gain Buddha consciousness.

Therefore, we keep repeating that you should leave the part of you that is unreal and prevents you from getting access to the cosmic treasury of knowledge and energies.

You can continue playing your earthly games but still gradually free yourselves from these games — you know: the same way children play with their games and their toys up to a certain age. And then, several years later, previous games do not interest them anymore. Why? It is because their level of consciousness has changed. They have grown up. In the same way, we are waiting for you to grow up and stop playing the games typical for humans in childhood.

If I came to a kindergarten and started talking to children about the structure of the Universe and the structure of complicated information systems, they would not understand me. They would not be interested. But to give the children, at their level of consciousness, the understanding that there is another world beyond the world of children's games is the duty of all good instructors and teachers. Therefore, I cannot give you the cosmic knowledge and the knowledge of the structure of this Universe, but I can tell you that there is another world full of cosmic beings that are at another stage of their consciousness development. And there are other kinds of relations between various life forms.

Maybe when you learn it, you will acquire the impulse of intention inducing you to aspire to distant worlds and Higher states of consciousness.

When you were little, many of you wanted to become adults to get access to the world that adults live and act in. Why now have you withdrawn into your world and lost your aspiration toward other worlds, the worlds corresponding to another level of consciousness, the Buddha level of consciousness?

Just as you are not able to enter the world of adults until you receive certain training and education that will allow you to act in the world of adults, similarly you cannot get into our world and start acting there until you have completed certain training and your consciousness ascends to the new level of development.

The first step in the right direction will be your wish and your aspiration to follow our instructions and advice.

Today I have given you the understanding and the methods that we use when dealing with humanity on Earth.

Maybe many of you will find it offensive that we consider you children.

And yet you will remain children until you are able to overcome your childish wishes and aspirations within you.

Therefore, I wish you to grow up as soon as possible, and finally, take upon yourselves the entire responsibility for your planet and all living beings on planet Earth.

I AM Vairochana, and I have been with you today.

We are looking for those who, in their consciousness, are able to go beyond the limits of the surrounding illusion

Lord Shiva
January 5, 2006

I AM Shiva, and I have come to you again through my Messenger.

Keep up your care about peace in your hearts. Consider the meaning of this phrase. This phrase is telling you about the peace or serenity within your hearts; this phrase is also telling you about caring for everything around you. Actually, everything that surrounds you depends on what is happening within you. Your dependence on your inner state is absolute. There is nothing outside of you that can leave a trace on your inner condition if you reach perfection in controlling your thoughts and feelings.

What a big difference in levels of consciousness there is on Earth. You know that what I mentioned above makes no sense at all for many people living on planet Earth. The deep information that is contained in these phrases goes past their consciousness without leaving any trace.

Why? That is because the level of their consciousness and the level of their vibrations do not give them the opportunity to catch the meaning of these words. Only those people whose vibrations are at the highest level possible in your octave are able to respond to these words and be inspired by their meaning.

Actually, everything around you represents a great illusion that is supported and exists only due to your consciousness, only due to your staying in your world and your interest in what is around you. Your energy flows where your attention is directed. Your energy flows toward what you are thinking about, what you are interested in.

Imagine that all people simultaneously lost their interest in the surrounding reality. All of you would simultaneously lose the desire to possess things of your world and own these things. You would lose interest in getting pleasures of your world. It does not mean that you would lose the meaning of your existence. The meaning of your existence would simply shift to other octaves, finer and more subtle.

What would happen to the world surrounding you in this case?

This world would cease existing and would gradually dissolve as a mirage.

I AM Shiva. I come to you because one of the functions that I perform in this universe is contracting the worlds. I am the destroyer of the illusion. I control the process of contraction of the illusion.

The moment has come when your consciousness must be expanded and face the reality so that the illusion can cease to exist.

You think that my visits to you and my talks with you through my Messenger are accidental. No, it is just that the moment has come when in the beginning, a small number of incarnated individuals and later, more and more people will be able to perceive this new information that we give.

Your world is similar to a big pile of firewood. It is enough to bring a match and light up a few dry logs, and then the entire pile will be on fire. Now we are searching for those of you who are able to burn. It is because not all the logs are ready. Lots of them are still wet. But when more and more people are able to perceive our vibrations and the new information that we are giving, your whole world will be taken over by fire, and there will not be any trace left from your illusory world. This process will not take much time in terms of cosmic measures.

Therefore, we are searching for those among you who are able to carry the flame, the Light, the energy, and our vibrations.

That is why we are saying that those who, with their consciousness, still continue holding on to the surrounding world belong to the past.

There are always people who prefer the Old due to their conservative thinking and the backwardness of their consciousness. And there are always people who look forward to the New. We are looking for such people. We are looking for those among you who are able to perceive the new thinking and the new consciousness. We are looking for those whose consciousness is able to go beyond the limits of the surrounding illusion.

Go up high, toward the Higher worlds — the celestial worlds.

Leave the limited world of your native planet and fly out of your nest into the expanse of the Universe.

We are searching for the brave and the striving, the ones who are not afraid of the new and the unknown.

Who among you are able to step into the unknown mystery? You know that only those people who in their consciousness are able to overcome the limitation of the three-dimensional world surrounding you, can advance to learning about the Higher Worlds.

Life does not end. Life is infinite. Life just shifts into new forms.

This process is similar to perpetual motion, an infinite spiral that never ceases and never stops.

Only the one who has never gone through a winter cannot believe that after winter, spring will come and then summer.

Now your existence on planet Earth resembles existence in the conditions of a very severe winter that you have generated with your consciousness.

You have to understand that this state of yours is temporary. It will change.

That is why we are calling you to change your consciousness, to be ready for a change, and to aspire to Higher states.

It does not mean that you will lose those joys that you are used to receiving from life around you. Your perception will just gain refinement. Pleasures that you will be able to experience will surpass all your expectations. It is because none of earthly pleasures can be compared to those pleasures that you are able to experience in the finer worlds.

The gradual changes in your consciousness are the guarantee of the fact that the difficult stage that your civilization is currently experiencing will be surmounted as smoothly as possible.

But you know that if a baby bird does not hurry to leave the nest, then the careful mother pushes it to the new life, to find the freedom of flight. But in order to do it, it is necessary to take the first step and come out of the limits of your human consciousness and learn to think in categories that are not connected with your world and the limitations of your world.

**I AM Shiva.
I have come to teach you how to destroy
the illusion in your consciousness.**

I am giving an opportunity, and I am opening a perspective

Beloved Alpha
January 6, 2006

I AM Alpha. I have come to you again today for a talk or a conversation that will direct your thoughts and create the mood for you to contemplate and make a decision in your hearts. Your intention is actually very important: what you aspire to and what state of heart you do it in, to what extent you are sincere, and to what extent you are selfless. Depending on that, you attract from space one or another opportunity or one or another perspective. If you continue living as if nothing has happened in these days at the end of the old year cycle and the beginning of the new one, as though there weren't any of these Dictations and meetings with the Masters, then with that you doom yourselves to the delay in your development. And vice versa, if you have accepted the information contained in the Masters' Dictations given through our Messenger with all your hearts and souls, then you create a window of opportunity for yourselves. You give yourselves an opportunity to act within the limits of that corridor of time and energy that we open for you.

I am giving an opportunity, and I am opening a perspective. As always, while you dwell in the matter and are subjected to time and space cycles, you choose whether to take advantage of this opportunity or continue to live in misery.

Your aspirations will be filled with energy, and your affairs will get the necessary support if you make a choice to act in accordance with the opportunity given to you. This opportunity will give you acceleration and development and will allow you to overcome all obstacles on your Path.

It is important that you, in your consciousness, are able to adjust to this opportunity, to our vibration. That is because our vibrations are not audible to your physical hearing, and they cannot be perceived with your physical senses. It is a call that rings deep within your heart, it is the longing for the Fatherly Home that you left, and it is the desire to return Home.

Listen to the call of your heart.

Stay alone in silence and listen to what your heart is whispering to you.

You can't help hearing this. Remove all unnecessary things from your life, everything that does not give you an opportunity to stay alone and listen to the voice of your heart, to hear its tender whisper, and to feel its Love.

You love. No matter how hard you hide your Love or pretend that you do not remember your Love, it is present within you all the same. Your basic quality is Love. Remove all unnecessary things from your life that prevent you from feeling the Divine Love in your heart.

You choose on your own, and you create all the circumstances of your life.

Haven't you gotten tired of giving in to those stereotypes and habits that envelop you? Hasn't the time come to give up all the fuss around you and turn with all your being to the Eternal, the everlasting?

I have come in order to remind you once again of that place from which your souls have come into this world. I have come to remind you once again of your Home and call you Home.

Can you hear me? O, my children.

I am ready to render all the care of my Fatherly heart to you. I am ready to give you the Love of my heart again and again. I just need your decision, your firm decision that you will make in your heart, and will never walk away from the taken decision anymore. And that decision is to return Home and to complete everything that is necessary in order to come back Home, the Fatherly Home that you left and where you are to return.

All of you represent the parts of the One. Your separation and wandering in your cold and uncomfortable world are coming to an end. All of you will return home. I am waiting. I am looking forward to seeing each of you, my beloved but not always obedient children.

Accept my Fatherly Love.

I am sending the gift of my Love to each of you, straight from my heart to your hearts.

Hold up a cup of your heart, and I shall fill it with my Love up to the brim!

When it gets hard for you in your world, you will remember my Love. You will be able to say a prayer-call, and I shall come to cover you with my Love and help you overcome your troubles and misfortunes and go through the most difficult part of the Path.

To do that you should simply say in your heart: "Father, I'm yours. Come, help me."

And I shall come at the most difficult moment of your tests.

I cannot leave you in trouble, and I cannot help loving you — each of you... with my Love — with the Love that does not require anything in return.

I AM Alpha, your Heavenly Father.

I have brought you two pieces of news — one is sad and the other one is joyful

Beloved El Morya
January 7, 2006

I AM El Morya; I have come again through my Messenger.

Just as the last time when we were giving the previous cycle of Dictations through this Messenger,[8] this time I have come to announce the ending of this cycle of Dictations.

It does not mean that we have stopped working through this or any other Messenger who has prepared his or her temple to become a pure vessel and enabled us to work through him or her.

Simply, a certain stage has been completed, a cycle has been finished, and new cycles are ahead. I hope that the Dictations received by you this time will be useful for your development and advancement on the Path.

One thing I have to announce today has remained incomplete and unrealized. This concerns the new information about the dispensation of the 23rd day of each month. You remember that

---

[8] Beloved El Morya is referring to the cycle of Dictations from March 4 until June 30, 2005. At that time, in his Dictation from June 30, 2005, beloved El Morya announced the completion of the cycle of Dictations and said, "I congratulate you on the successful completion of this unique experiment on the transferring of the vital and timely information to the physical plane." Beloved El Morya also announced the completion of the cycle of Dictations. Refer to *Words of Wisdom Volume 1*.

in my Dictation from June 27, 2005, I gave you a dispensation related to the 23rd day of each month, and this dispensation was active until the end of last year.

Now the yearly cycle is over, but I have to announce to you that the dispensation will be active for a period of another year. I have succeeded in persuading the Karmic Board and have received their assistance in the extension of the period of this dispensation because the energy we were receiving during the operation of the dispensation last year has been acknowledged as satisfactory.

We are happy that you have taken advantage of the given opportunity. Many of you have. I hope that during this year new light-bearers will join this dispensation.

Do not forget that on the 23rd day of each month until the end of this year you have a chance to transmute the karma of the next month. Your efforts will be multiplied by the number of light-bearers who will take part on that day in the action granted to you by Heaven.

I will not repeat to you all the conditions of this dispensation. I will only say that all the conditions stated by me in the previous Message dedicated to the action of this dispensation are in force.

This is a great mercy shown to you by Heaven. I hope that this year will become a year of great achievements in the spiritual field on planet Earth.

All of us are hoping for that.

I can honestly say that we do not feel like ending this cycle of Dictations. But the Law does not allow us to spend more energy than has been released. Therefore, we hope that the next opportunity is just around the corner and will still come this year.

This is all for today. I have brought you two pieces of news — one is sad and the other one is joyful. The sad one concerns the ending of the cycle of the Dictations, and the joyful one refers to the extension of the operation of the dispensation of the 23rd day of each month.

Everything should be balanced, and everything should be harmonized.

I am saying goodbye to you, and I hope for future meetings.

I AM El Morya.

Messages from the Ascended Masters between the second and third cycles of Dictations

When a chalice that we can fill with Light appears in the physical world, we always do that

Beloved Shiva
January 23, 2006

I AM Shiva, having come again through my Messenger.

Shiva I AM! I have come. And this means that I have a wish to say the Word to you and to bring home to you the knowledge and the information that you need.

This means that we continue the work through our Messenger, and she meets our requirements we demand of her at this stage.

Now, after I have come and have made this small introduction, I would like to get directly to the purpose of my visit today.

My purpose is connected with the forthcoming event that was announced in the physical plane but was not announced by us through the Dictations.

I am talking about the seminar that will take place in Moscow in March of this year.

You know that this seminar is held by the people's initiative. We, the Masters, will be able to pour our Light and our energy into a group of people who expressed their wish to serve as a chalice in the physical plane.

You know that when a chalice that we can fill with Light appears in the physical world, we always do that.

However, your physical world is characterized by its unpredictability and duality. Therefore, it is very difficult for us to make any predictions, even for a few days ahead. And still, I have come and am authorized to declare that this seminar will be held under my personal guidance and under my personal patronage, which I already provide for this seminar.

You will be surprised that Shiva, a god worshipped in Hinduism, provides his patronage to a seminar that will take place in Russia, a country where Hinduism is not an official religion.

However, I must give you the understanding that we cannot adjust to a concrete religious situation existing in one or another country. We are guided by the interests of Heavens when carrying out all our events. And in this case, I will come to Russia through my Messenger Tatyana. And I will come with a particular aim that I must announce for you now.

I intend to give a blessing of the chakra of the third eye to all the participants of the seminar who will find it necessary for them to go through this blessing. What is this blessing and why do I intend to give it now in Russia through the Russian Messenger?

The fact of the matter is that the situation is such, as it is. And you know that we act though the one who is ready. Therefore, since Russia is the country that has given shelter to our Messenger, it is exactly Russia where we are coming to give the blessing that will provide an opportunity to accelerate the manifestation of the gift of distinction, the gift of the Divine vision.

As soon as you acquire the manifestation of this gift in accordance with your achievements, you will not nuzzle up like blind kittens anymore from one preacher to another or from one church to another. You will obtain the distinction, and you will be able to see and distinguish between the true and the false in any church and in any religious organization.

For this is the requirement of the time. We will act through everyone who is ready, who is capable of rising to the new level in his consciousness, through those who can give up all unnecessary and moribund dogmas characteristic of old religions and recognize the wolves in sheep's clothing among the numerous new religious preachers who have appeared like mushrooms after the rain.

The only Path that we have chosen and that is possible at this stage is the path of direct contact with many people who are ready.

Do understand that you are reaching the new level of your development. And for this level, communication with the subtle world becomes natural and achievable much easier. There is nothing difficult in establishing contact with the subtle world. But the difficulty, as always, is in your consciousness. And if in your consciousness you do not correctly perceive the contact given to you, or you evaluate the contact incorrectly in your consciousness, then instead of acquiring a Divine achievement, you subject yourself to the torment of those forces that inhabit the subtle plane and which have chosen to disobey the Divine Law of this universe.

Therefore, you need the gift of distinction as never before. And together with this gift, you must receive the knowledge of how you should behave at this stage of the evolutionary development, where to aspire, and what principles to follow.

We can make a long list of the imperfections of one or another religious teachers and religious movements. But in this way, we will learn what one should not do and how one should not behave. We have chosen the other way. We are giving the right patterns, and we are giving the right direction. And as always, it is up to your free will which path to choose and follow.

You are making your choice and you are deciding.

Our work is to offer you the right patterns and to show you the right direction.

Therefore, I am waiting for those who have made a decision to go through my initiation. I am waiting for those who wish to meet me at the seminar that is under my patronage.

I am asking you for help. Even if you do not have a possibility to participate in this event of the Masters due to some karmic circumstances, but with all your heart and soul you wish to help us to realize our plans, make the call:

"Shiva! Come, destroy all the opposition and remove all the obstacles that lie in the way of the successful realization of the seminar in Moscow on the 24th - 26th of March 2006!"

Repeat this call three times every day up to the end of the seminar.

I will hear your calls, and I will know those devoted hearts that have already risen in their consciousness to the new level but, due to karmic reasons, cannot break out of the cloaking external circumstances. And when I know about you, I will be able to give you help and to set you free from a part of your karmic burden.

I AM Shiva!
I have been with you today.
And see you at the seminar!

Use the help that Heavens give you, and do not disregard this help

Lord Shiva
March 13, 2006

I AM Shiva, having come again through my Messenger. The state of affairs is that I have come to give the next Message that will allow you to understand the situation and to make clear those guidelines for yourself that you may choose to follow in your lives.

As soon as the previous cycle of the Dictations had been over, we had a sense of great relief that, using the incarnated conductor, we managed the realization of the plan and gave the information which humankind needed.

However, we then encountered absolutely unpredictable resistance to our actions. That resistance passed through many incarnated people's minds, and many of them consider themselves light-bearers. Therefore, I have come to assure you once again that we will continue giving our Messages, no matter what efforts it will cost us. And we will do that according to our plans and our terms that come as provided by space opportunities and a necessity.

Therefore, I have come today to give you an understanding once again that no matter how the situation is developing on planet Earth, we, the Ascended Masters, will work with mankind of Earth and will continue our attempts to change humanity's consciousness.

It seems that there is very little information in our Messages, though each time we keep wondering how the people are found who are ready to respond to all of our propositions and remarks at our first summons and do those things that are necessary now.

You know that one of the most important things that humanity faces is the change of consciousness. And thus, everything that favors the change of earthling's consciousness is good. Of course, we mean the change of consciousness that we try to manifest in your octave, but not the change of consciousness that you think should take place.

Therefore, all the ways of spreading the knowledge contained in the given Dictations are good. Also, good are the ways of communicating the information to people, including private meetings, training classes, seminars, organization of schools for parents and children to learn the foundations of the law of karma and the principles of behavior, based on the Divine Law.

All that is genuinely from God needs your help to grow and widen.

Therefore, when you are surprised that not everything around you looks like you would like it to be, we say: "So much the better! You have seen where to apply your efforts, your abilities and your talents!"

Look around and analyze thoroughly what you personally can change and what you think should be changed, relying on your opportunities and your abilities.

Once again I would like to remind you of that Dictation, which I gave last year on the 27th of November.[9] As soon as you turn your thoughts in the necessary direction and imbue the images

---

[9] Refer to the Dictation "Every effort of yours will be multiplied unprecedentedly because that is the call of the time and such is the situation on the planet now," Lord Shiva, November 27, 2005, in *Words of Wisdom Volume 1*.

emerging in your mind with the Divine energy, I will have the opportunity to help you and to imbue your imageries with my energy.

There is a Divine opportunity, which is given for the planet at a certain moment. That opportunity is being given now through our Messenger. Sometimes nothing is required from you but the acceptance of our Messenger. And as soon as you recognize the Messenger of the Hierarchy, you automatically stand on the steps of the Hierarchy. And all the Hierarchy has an opportunity to help you in your affairs and in the realization of your plans.

I would also like to stop at one important moment. Our Messenger is the person who keeps our vibrations, constantly carrying her devotion to the Hierarchy through all living situations and realizing our plans on Earth. For you who are in incarnation, our Messenger is the incarnated master, the Guru. And that means that you must follow the instructions that you receive from our Guru as if I gave you those instructions personally.

Here you will need all your distinction to understand to what degree you can trust the external Guru and to what degree you should be guided by those instructions that you receive from your heart, from your Higher Self.

The Teaching about Guru requires additional deciphering. I think that to some extent we will be able to give that Teaching of ours for you, because there are too many of those who consider themselves a guru or pretend to be a guru, but all of them — or almost every one of them — do not have the main attribute of the true Guru: the ability of self-sacrifice and the ability to sacrifice their entire self on the altar of service.

Therefore, no matter how your human consciousness impedes your understanding of the true significance of the Guru's mantle and the Guru-chela relationship, any obstacle that is within you can and should be swept away with the help of your sincere aspiration and your devotion to the Hierarchy.

Every time that you need to receive validations or refutations of the verity or falsity of any person pretending to be your Guru or our Messenger, please apply to me for help.

Just take the image of me in your hands or come up to my image in the form of a statue and sincerely ask me for help.

As soon as I see your sincerity and aspiration, I will certainly help you. And you will get that distinction, which you need at the current stage of your development.

Therefore, use the help that Heavens give you, and do not disregard this help.

**I AM Shiva,
and I am saying goodbye to you today,
but I hope for the new meetings.**

We invite you to establish a new type of relations between the Guru and a chela

Lord Shiva
March 15, 2006

I AM Shiva, coming to you again to talk about the Path you will follow if you choose the Path that we are teaching you about through our Messenger.

There are many ways and many roads in your material world. Unfortunately, most of those ways and roads lead nowhere. Incarnation by incarnation you wander about the illusion and cannot find the true Path.

And even when at last you discover the Truth on your Path, you begin to doubt whether what you face comes from God or not.

It often happens that you choose the right Way and already follow it, but at some moment of weakness in your heart, you fall under the influence of your carnal mind and begin to doubt. Your doubts are produced by your imperfection. Therefore, when you choose the Path to follow or start doubting the Path that you are following, you should always consider: where do your doubts come from?

Are your doubts reasonable or are they just a result of your fear and your lack of self-confidence?

You should constantly distinguish your inner states. Are you influenced by unreal forces or do you just reasonably analyze the Path that you follow?

And, every time that you analyze your inner work, you have to be guided only by your intuition and the voice of your heart.

That is why we tirelessly repeat to you: "Develop your intuition, your distinction, and your connection with the real world of God."

It is hard for you to do this when you are completely sunk in the illusion. Therefore, we send our Messengers and our servants who show you the Path and help you to orientate yourself in the sea of life.

However, you and only you can choose whom to follow and whose recommendations to be guided by.

The situation is complicated by the fact that however devoted and sincere our Messenger is, she took a human incarnation, and along with the incarnation she had to take a part of the world's karma, a burden that allows her to stay in the incarnation.

Seeing the imperfection of our Messengers, you can be puzzled and seized with additional doubts.

Therefore, we tell you that you should not blindly trust those people who proclaim themselves as messiahs, messengers, and teachers. There is always an element of unpredictability in any situation, and that person who was our rightful representative and who carried our mantles not long ago, can make a mistake and even stray from the Path. So you should carefully watch and analyze all the actions of our Messengers and be able to distinguish between accidental mistakes in their actions, which it is impossible to avoid in your world, and a more serious sin of betrayal and deviation from the principles of the Brotherhood.

This Teaching is new, and we dare give it now through our Messenger with a hope that many of you have achieved that level of development that will allow you not to make categorical judgments and refuse to follow our Messengers at all.

No, now it is not the right time for you to follow the Path and choose the Path on your own. You cannot do without our representatives and our Messengers. But you have to approach your choice of people whose advice you decide to listen to and whose guidance you decide to follow consciously, along with the measures of your inner consonance and your distinction.

If in former times unconditional obedience and strict following the Guru's guidance was demanded of you, now we tell you that you should listen to your inner voice and your inner intuition about everything, and only after that you can follow the outer instructions of any Guru.

The people who are not ready for such new Guru-chela relations will not be able to follow the Teachings being given by us through this Messenger. They need other harder instructions and abidance with outer dogmas and rules. That is why we give this Teaching, but we completely understand that different human individuals are at various stages of their development, and what is good for one might be undesirable and premature for another.

It is well known that if a person had a long stay underground and didn't have access to daylight, a momentary coming out into bright sunlight can totally blind him and do unrecoverable harm to his health.

People incarnated on planet Earth have different levels of consciousness; and now we are giving our Teachings for those who are ready to be in the vanguard, for those who are ahead of their brothers and who are ready to start immediate relations with the Ascended Masters, based on cooperation and mutual respect. However, while you are incarnated, the principle of unconditional obedience to the Ascended Masters and our representatives is fundamental for you.

But, you make the decision about such obedience in your heart by yourself, and you should always be ready to change your decision if you feel that the circumstances have changed.

Therefore, Guru-chela relations typical for the new era will be notable for you to have creative, mutually-enriching relations with your Guru, rather than the relations based on compulsion and diktat as had been accepted before in many of our organizations.

And those relations are more suitable for the spirit of the time and those common democratic reforms that are taking place in the world.

Let me repeat once again that not all people will be able to establish and accept the new relations. And many people are just not ready for establishing such relations because any hint that the teacher can be wrong is a signal for them not to consider their Guru's opinion at all.

We invite you to establish a new type of relations between the Guru and a chela, the relations based on unconditional love, true brotherhood, and cooperation.

We hope that a sufficient number of individuals, who are ready for such relations and already follow them, will be found.

I am glad to give you this important Teaching today, which you undoubtedly need.

I AM Shiva, and I have been with you today!

A Teaching on Divine Gratitude

Lord Maitreya
April 10, 2006

I AM Maitreya, having come to you through my Messenger. I have come for guidance in the sphere of the Divine Knowledge.

The minutes of our communication are sweet and having a physical transmitter that meets our requirements is too rare. Therefore, everything that is being said and everything that will be told is to have everlasting and unconditional value for you, like precious pearls.

We come and grant you one pearl of wisdom after another. And you string these pearls on the necklace that you collect throughout your life.

It is truly an invaluable necklace of Knowledge. And you should treat it with care.

That is why I am giving this long introduction, so you could check the purity of your motives once again and tune to the Divine state. We notice that many of our chelas who have already been briskly following the Path of Initiations, at a certain stage begin to doubt, and temptation starts taking them away from the Path, the True Path that they were searching for in many incarnations and that they found at last.

What is the reason for this situation? And why does it happen?

I will tell you the reason. You constantly feel hunger and lack of Divine Love and Divine energy. But as soon as you get a bit of our Love, of our energy, you immediately forget about those states of hopelessness and despair in which you had been before you found our Teachings.

Human consciousness is very active and unstable. And the quality that you have to develop in yourselves is the feeling of Gratitude for the Teaching being given to you, gratitude toward the Heavens, the Creator, the Ascended Hosts and our Messenger.

It is exactly the feeling of gratitude, because this feeling remains the purest and unblemished in your physical octave.

The feeling of Love is the highest of all, but reaching the purity of that feeling is very difficult in your octave because there is no other feeling that has as many distortions as the feeling of Love.

Therefore, I recommend that you start cultivating the feeling of gratitude for the received Knowledge and Teaching within yourselves.

Without gratitude you will not advance along your Path. Do not be confused by the fact that you will have to express your gratitude and thankfulness in public. Many European people do not have a clear understanding of how to serve God, the Masters, and the Most High, which is inherent in the people of India and Tibet. Therefore, you have to restore within yourselves those traditions of worshipping God, worshipping the Divinity around you, and worshipping the Divinity within you.

You have to find the balance, the equilibrium, in your relationship with God. If you receive everything that is given to you without feeling gratitude and without expressing it, you will voluntarily deprive yourselves of further advancement. Heavens cannot give you more if you do not balance the given energy with your energy that you send to our octaves. There is no money in our octaves, but the Divine energy is the equivalent of money. Therefore, when you get knowledge, you have to give us the equivalent of the Divine energy that is able to penetrate into our octaves. You know that no imperfect energy can penetrate into the octaves of Light. Therefore, I recommend that you start cultivating the feeling of gratitude within yourselves.

You can feel Love and send us your Love. But unfortunately, many people have such a low standard of love in their hearts that such Love cannot penetrate into our octaves.

However, you should constantly watch that your gratitude and worship do not go to another extreme when you begin external worship without having the true feeling of gratitude in your heart. Any external worshipping should only compliment the internal manifestation of your feelings. Contrary to this, many people think that it is enough for them just to have the feeling of gratitude in their hearts without expressing it externally. In this case, carefully analyze your state and your motives because sometimes you are just guided by your pride.

You live in the physical world; and you should manifest your gratitude at the physical level.

Do not forget that you are responsible for taking care of our Messenger.

That ancient Truth is erased from the memory of the current generation. When Divinity predominated in people's minds, those people who heard the voice of God in their hearts and could bring God's Word to the people always prospered.

The way that people treat our heralds, prophets, and Messengers can be seen as fallen morals of the society and how far society is from the Divine ideal.

Therefore, do not hesitate to provide our Messenger with your patronage and care. Always remember that our Messenger is the representative of the Hierarchy of Light on Earth, and it is your duty to show respect and to take care of our representative.

When you are able to accept this simple truth in your consciousness without different stipulations and twists of your minds, we will talk to you in a different way and will give more profound Knowledge and Teachings.

No matter how we try now, you cannot assimilate our knowledge. First, you should restore the return flow of the Divine energy going back to our octaves. Then we will be able to give.

This law is indisputable, and it should be realized.

You stop the flow of the Divine energy yourself. And the reason for blocking this flow is your pride and your unwillingness to pay for what is given, regardless of whether your gratitude is expressed in the material form or it is expressed in your feelings.

The combination of inner and outer gratitude is ideal in your time. And you should watch and control that combination yourself.

I have given an important Teaching for you today. This Teaching is well known and widespread in the East. But the people in the West are not acquainted with it in practice. However, without the realization of this Teaching, the West will not be able to get the wisdom of the East in full.

I AM Maitreya, and I have been with you today.

You have to be ready for constant changes in your consciousness

Lord Maitreya
April 11, 2006

I AM Maitreya, having come to you again.

From this day forward and in the nearest future, something amazing will take place in your lives. You will not be able to live according to the laws and stereotypes typical for you earlier. The laws of the physical world have been changing and have already been changed. Therefore, those of you who think that nothing is changing on the planet and nothing is happening will have to witness the opposite in the nearest future. The planet is moving toward transformation; the planet is changing according to the plans of God.

The more that some of you cling to the old and obsolete, the more painful the process of changes will be for you.

In your consciousness you have to be ready for constant changes and alterations. Every single thing will undergo changes in the nearest future. Your consciousness goes through tremendous changes. If you look at your life with an open mind, you will be surprised to find out how much it has already changed, and it is still changing.

The changes that take place in the world are very significant; and if some time ago those changes took hundreds and even thousands of years, now the process is accelerated to several years. This process is going on regardless of the will of those who wish to continue living within the old limits, no matter whether those are religious limits, moral relations in society, or other spheres of human activity.

Therefore, we come to inform you once again of the changes that are taking place and which have already taken place.

The cycle of the Dictations that we have been giving through our Messenger started just a bit more than a year ago. If those of you, who carefully read and reread those Dictations, look at your lives and at the life around, you will notice the changes. What is more, you will notice that many points from our Dictations, which seemed important and timely a year ago, have become obsolete by now.

The changes in people's consciousness have never been so rapid during the whole history of human development on planet Earth.

The resistance of those forces that stand for the illusion is obvious. They act through everyone who has some imperfection and who chooses to get under the influence of those forces within themselves. Therefore, we are calling you to attentively analyze your actions, your motives, and your reactions to other people's actions.

The point is that the returning of karma is also accelerated. And if earlier you could face the consequences of your wrong actions only in the next incarnation, and you grumbled about why you had been born in such unfair conditions, now you have an opportunity to face the consequences of your wrong choices within a year, and in some cases, literally the next day. Therefore, you can watch the Law of Cause and Effect influencing you, your relatives, and the people around you. You just have to look at what is happening with you from the right point of view and with an open mind.

Now everyone has a chance to get acquainted with the Law of Karma in practice. It is impossible to blame God, saying that some individuals do not have proper behavior but yet they are safe and sound. Look attentively and you will see what happens to those who neglect the Divine Law and pretend to be the master of this universe.

There is a universal Law; and there is a definite order in the Universe. I am happy to inform you that in accordance with the cosmic terms, order will be established on planet Earth in the nearest future. The Divine Law will manifest in people's lives more and more. And it will become more and more difficult not to follow this Law.

It is similar to going up the stream of a tumultuous mountain river. No matter how you try, the stream will carry you away because it is useless to struggle with God. You should obey the Divine Law operating in this universe.

We are carefully watching that the rise of vibrations on the planet is not followed by big cataclysms. We have managed with it so far. But the process of changes will continue more successfully if you take away from your consciousness all those obstacles that impede your changing and your following along the path of changes.

Every time we come and remind you of the transformations and changes that the planet is going through, there are always a certain number of skeptics who say that nothing is changing in their lives, and they do not notice anything. Well, we can only be glad that the changes are so gradual and mild that many of you do not even notice them or pretend not to notice them.

Now, I would like to tell you one more important thing. It is about your moving along the Path of Initiations. No matter whether you wish that or not, your personal advancement is possible only when you assume certain obligations before the Ascended Masters and accept the Laws existing in the universe.

There is a Law that is not well known on the planet, but this Law is unavoidable just like the law of Karma. According to that Law, after passing a certain part of the Path, your advancement along the spiritual Path requires your voluntary subjection to the Higher Law existing in this universe and taking the steps of the Hierarchy.

As soon as you stand on the steps of the Hierarchy, all the Ascended Masters provide you with their patronage and help. The only thing that is required from you is your subjection to the Law, humility, obedience, and the discipline of a disciple.

Do agree that when you enter a certain institute you are obliged to obey its rules. Why do you think that you can master the Divine science without following certain rules and the Law?

So, I am leaving you today, and I am giving you some time to think about how strong your determination is to follow the Path of the apprenticeship and how much you could sacrifice in your life in order to get access to the Divine Wisdom.

**I AM Maitreya,
and see you on the Path of Initiations.**

Book 3

Cycle 3: Messages of the Ascended Masters
from April 15 to April 30, 2006

Give your Light, your Love, and your support to the people around you

Sanat Kumara
April 15, 2006

I AM Sanat Kumara, having come to you again.

When we came more than a year ago to give the Dictations through our Messenger, that event was not noticed by the majority of humankind. And we didn't try to draw attention to that event. The main and most significant events always happen quietly and without being noticed.

We come to speak with humanity of Earth, and every visit of ours becomes more and more natural for your consciousness like sunrises and sunsets.

We come, and the situation on planet Earth changes with our coming because every time more and more individuals can get access to these Dictations and enjoy the nectar of the Divine energy contained in them.

Now I have come to remind you once again of those resolute transformations that should happen and about those changes and alterations that Beloved Maitreya mentioned in His Dictation of April 11, 2006.

And as He did, I make no secret of the fact that the speed of the change depends on each of you who reads these Dictations because everything that is connected with your physical world and any changes in your world happen due to the changing of your consciousness.

As always, I will give you some directions and a short Teaching that will help you in changing your consciousness.

Each time I come with great excitement, and my heart trembles when I have the opportunity to talk to those of you who are incarnated now.

My children, you do not realize and cannot fully realize the whole responsibility that lies on your shoulders.

Quite recently, before you incarnated, many of you had received a huge training and education in the etheric retreats. The best souls were chosen for incarnation in this difficult time.

Therefore, it is very painful to watch these souls, who have already come into incarnation, allow the illusion to take possession of their consciousness to such an extent that they have not only forgotten why they incarnated, but they have also forgotten all about God, and they have lost in their hearts not only the Divine models but also the moral landmarks too.

It is painful to realize this, but it is more painful to watch these souls making a transition and coming again to the fine plane. The heart bleeds profusely when you see the suffering of these souls. When the curtain falls from their eyes and the plan for which they came into incarnation and which they have not fulfilled gets revealed before them, then the stress that these souls receive is comparable to the most terrible stress a soul can pass through in incarnation. And this stress lies like a heavy burden upon the soul. A lot of efforts of angels who are called upon to cure the souls between the incarnations are necessary in order to prepare such a soul before it is able to incarnate on Earth again.

If you treated one another even with a thousandth of the love and care that your soul receives in the period between the incarnations in the etheric octaves of Light, then the world would change unrecognizably after a very short time.

What you have to do is to change your attitude toward the people around you.

If you are an old soul having come to the incarnation for the enlightenment of the less developed brothers and sisters, remember your duty and the responsibilities that you accepted before the incarnation. No matter how difficult it is for you, do not think about yourselves; think about those near you who need your care.

Sometimes a tender look or a good word is enough for the soul again to become full of hope and to gain confidence in the day of tomorrow and the meaning of its life.

Think of all these millions of souls who need your help. Not every soul is capable of understanding the Teaching that we are giving through our Messenger. And not every person is capable of taking the book and start reading it. However, you are able to provide your help and support — not by forcing them to read our Teaching — but simply by being next to them and giving them support with a word, deed, or a look.

Do not be disturbed by the people who will not appreciate your efforts. Simply give your Light, your Love, and your support to the people around you. And do not allow the external consciousness to judge anyone: "Here God has given this person up for lost and he or she is the top of the ignorance and imperfection."

We have provided this Teaching many times and I am repeating it now. Many souls of Light, before they receive incarnation, burden themselves with such large karmic obligations and assume such huge imperfections that sometimes they are not capable in the conditions that exist now on Earth to overcome these imperfections and work off the karma they assumed.

Therefore, never allow yourselves to judge. Remember that when you are judging, you decrease your vibrations and become not capable of making right choices and giving correct assessments.

Be above judgments and gossips and do not allow these negative energies to take control of you.

Forgive everyone no matter how unjust it seems what people do to you. Forgiveness, as well as humility and sympathy, does not have any limits.

There cannot be too much of any of the Divine qualities. Your world is in such a need of Divine vibrations and Divine qualities that throughout the day you can pour out your Perfection, Good, and Love, and the world will be grateful to you.

However, this gratitude is not obligatory to manifest on the physical plane. On the contrary, you may encounter complete misunderstanding and even hostility. Every manifestation of Divine vibrations and Divine qualities immediately clashes with the manifestation of the opposite qualities that are trying to deafen the high vibrations and to postpone the moment when there will be no imperfection on Earth anymore.

It is required from you to manifest Divine qualities, regardless of any reaction on the side of the opposite forces. In no way should you submit to provocation on the side of these forces. You can achieve a lot, but you have to be very firm and brave.

It is in this that the complexity of the given moment consists, and it is this very help that we would like to receive from you.

It is characteristic of the present moment that in the life of every human being there will be situations when he or she will clearly see what forces act through him or her and around him or her. And you will consciously be making the choice within yourselves: which forces you will manifest and where you will direct your energy.

Let the temporary mistakes not disturb you. Do not castigate yourselves because of them. You have made a mistake, you have realized it, you have taken a decision not to repeat it anymore, and continue further.

Do not allow your consciousness to linger on your mistakes for too long. Do not forget that where your attention is directed, there your energy flows.

The most correct thing would be to live in only the moment in which you are present now. The past and the future should not take too much space in your consciousness.

You are living in the present moment, and in this moment you will always joyously meet all of life's difficulties and failures, and you should always keep confidence in your strength so that you can overcome everything, and then you will come out victoriously from every situation.

Remember that the biggest victory is that which you achieve over your unreal part, while the outer world is only an illusion that does not require your attention. When you stop feeding the illusion with your attention, it stops existing.

I have given you a very important Teaching. I think that you will use this Teaching in the nearest future and will appreciate its inner power.

**I AM Sanat Kumara.
Always with you!**

The process of returning to Reality, the process of folding up the illusion, will be accelerated to its maximum

Beloved Alpha
April 16, 2006

I AM Alpha, having come to you again. It has been a long time according to your earthly measures since our last meeting. However, when I look from my Reality, only a few hours have passed for me. As if it was yesterday.

So, I have come to you again, people of Earth. And I have to tell you about those changes that have taken place on the planet since our last meeting. It seems to you that nothing has changed. However, I am sure that there are people who feel the changes that have occurred. There are only a few of them, but there are such people. It is good. It makes us happy and confident. For when we have an opportunity to speak through one person, it means that tomorrow we will be able to speak through many. And when several people feel the changes and they feel the changing in their external consciousness, it means that tomorrow many people will be able to feel those changes.

First, we become understandable and accessible to very few people. We give our knowledge and our information. It is similar to an avalanche that is the falling of only one rock at the beginning. Then gradually, more and more rocks are involved in that process. And then the moment comes when the avalanche becomes so powerful that it can wipe out everything in its way. Now you are at the very beginning of that avalanche moving.

After some time that avalanche will gain power, and it will be able to wipe out everything old that resists the changes.

The new changes have already entered people's consciousness, and these changes are unavoidably spreading around Earth.

I have come to tell you the secret that has not been accessible to you before, but it becomes accessible now because you have reached the new level of consciousness. I will tell you about the secret that is being revealed. So, you know from our Dictations that not long ago we announced the coming of the new stage of the cosmic evolution for planet Earth. You know from the previous Messages that this stage should take many years according to earthly measures — millions of years.

And here I have come to make you happy because it has been decided that the transitional period will take much less time than was planned. And the transitional period will be manifested so rapidly that each person living on Earth now, will be able to watch the changes and admire them.

It has been decided that the process of returning to Reality, the process of folding up the illusion, will be accelerated to its maximum. The highest and the most advanced evolutions of this universe take part in the process of raising the vibrations of the physical plane, including the physical plane of planet Earth. This information seems to you unimportant and having no practical use.

However, you need this information, and it is given to you.

You become older and you become capable of perceiving more subtle vibrations that belong to our octaves. And the process of maturity is reduced for you. You will be able to understand more and you will be able to see more.

So, do not block your consciousness. Allow yourself the highest dreams, and they will certainly be realized. Remain children, dream, use your imagination, and do not allow yourself to become those adults that live on planet Earth.

You become adults within yourselves, but your consciousness remains open for perceiving the Higher Reality. And only when you become children, you become adults for the new Reality.

Unfortunately, what you call being adults doesn't mean being adults for the Divine Reality. You become adults when you accept the limitations of the physical world, and the limitations start directing you.

On the contrary, when you become adults in the Higher Reality, you become free of the limitations of your dense world. But you remain children in your consciousness for your dense world.

Therefore, I wish you to remain children in your world, and I wish that you achieve a state of maturity in the Divine world as soon as possible, which will allow you to become our collaborators, our friends, our brothers and sisters.

And now let me express my Love to you again. I have strong hope that my Love will help you and your planet at this difficult transitional time.

I AM Alpha, with Love to you.

A Teaching on Divine Miracles

Beloved Surya
April 17, 2006

I AM Surya, having come to you today from the Great Central Sun. I am happy to greet you today, children of Earth, and I am glad to meet you again.

Now we leave your Human problems behind, and move to me through time and space to that area of the Universe where I love to dwell.

You will not even be able to imagine the bliss and peace of this place. This place is the cradle of everything that exists in the Universe.

How often many of you have experienced a longing for this place! Sometimes you may feel that anguish and depression take hold of your heart, and you cannot explain that state of yours because you look for the reason outside of yourself, but the reason is actually within you. At this moment your soul is longing for the World that it left millions of years ago, but the memory of it is still with you in your hearts.

Seventh heaven, eternal peace, and all-embracing happiness express the state in which I live and the state in which you used to reside before you descended into the Physical World. If you could escape from the surrounding vanity and dive into that bliss, perhaps you would not bring yourself back into your World. Therefore, such states are only accessible when you reach a certain level of spiritual development. All of you have a chance to reach those states — maybe not in the current incarnation, but in the next ones. However, each of you will certainly experience that bliss and incomparable peace, as if you returned to your Father's Home and you do not have to leave it again.

Now the time has come when you should start to recall the place where your souls came from. It is simply necessary for you in order to start your Journey Home, to that original state of peace and bliss.

I have come to remind you again of that place where you came from and where you should return. It is hard for you to hear me because of your day-to-day vanity and problems.

However, I come and deflect you from your cares and your vanity. You have the right to wave me away like an annoying fly. You can do so, and this is your right. However, I am sure that many of you will take time to listen to my words and to what is behind them.

I have come by crossing an enormous distance. But this distance is not even in the physical Universe. This path lies within you and separates you from the Higher Reality. While in your incarnated state, it is so hard for you to understand which Reality I am talking about. And it is just as hard for me to descend to the level at which you can hear me, even with the help of a specially prepared Messenger who is incarnated with you.

We come to her temple and have the opportunity to give our Messages. This is the miracle that is happening in front of your very eyes because you have the opportunity to read our Messages on the very same day when we give them. Every Divine miracle happens so naturally that you do not even realize that it is a miracle. This is a distinctive feature of those miracles that come from God. Any miracle that is born by human consciousness cannot happen so naturally, and it requires considerable efforts in order to prepare it. You know many teachings that train you to perform miracles. Many of you strive to perform such miracles that may be called "magic" or something else in your language. But if you come across the Divine Miracle, then the first thing that catches your eyes is the fact that it happens very naturally, and in a while you begin to realize that you came across something truly fascinating and noteworthy. But the Miracle has already happened. And this Divine wonder happened without any collaboration with your consciousness.

Therefore, when you are looking for a miracle in your life, there is nothing reprehensible about it. And when you are looking around for miracles, you find them. However, miracles, as everything else that surrounds you in your world, have a dual nature. There are miracles manifested by the Holy Spirit, and those are indeed Divine wonders. But there are also wonders that are manifested by human consciousness and with the help of human consciousness. Those miracles are human and not from God. Therefore, learn to distinguish between them, and be discerning. There is nothing bad in your aspiration for miracles. But when you dedicate too much time to this aspiration of yours, you receive something like miracles from the illusion around you, but God and the Heavenly Hosts have nothing to do with those miracles. Therefore, you should aspire to God and God's Truth only and not just think about miracles. Only when you approach God's Truth in your consciousness, do you begin to recognize the miracles in your life.

Believe me; God gives you His miracles at just the right time without any request on your part because the advancement toward God's Truth inevitably leads you to facing wonders as soon as you carefully look around.

Divine signs of Truth manifested in the form of wonders are unavoidable for those who stand on the path toward God and for those who do not look for cheap miracles that come from humans.

Now I am leaving you face-to-face with your thoughts about miracles and the Divine World. The Miracle of God is always ready to become apparent, but only those who have the eyes of a child will be able to see this miracle. Leave your adult games and cares, and let yourself return to your childhood — at least for a few minutes every day — when you expected wonders and God performed those wonders for you in the form of sunrises and sunsets, snow, rain, and rainbows.

All those wonders you saw through your child consciousness, and you accepted them as God's miracles. Why do you not see them now? What prevents you from seeing the miracles around you?

I agree that you have lots of problems in your life and many duties that you should carry. However, if you look unbiased at your lives, you will understand that there is nothing more important for you than watching God's miracles in your lives. And if you regularly start seeing God's wonders in the surrounding world, your life will change significantly. And you will be surprised how much time you will have to observe the miracles of God.

I have covered an enormous distance to remind you that you should wait for miracles, and they will start to happen around you.

Just to remind you that it is worth covering this Path to you and to your hearts.

**I AM Surya,
staying within your hearts.**

Your consciousness is the key to your future and to the future of the whole planet

Gautama Buddha
April 18, 2006

I AM Gautama Buddha, having come to you this day.

I have come to give you certain knowledge and training. As always, I am using the vessel and the opportunity afforded to me by our Messenger, Tatyana.

Just a short time ago we had no opportunity to give our Teaching so freely on a worldwide scale. No longer than two or three years ago, no one could have supposed that the Teaching could be given in the territory of Russia. Just look how great the changes are.

We are giving our Teaching, and at the same time the situation in Russia and on the whole planet Earth is changing.

You have a chance to observe, and you see how a seemingly insignificant event is capable of influencing the whole world. Probably, you cannot draw analogies to your lives and connect the changes taking place in them with the fact that we now have an opportunity to give our Dictations. Well, we do not expect you to draw any analogies at all. Just try to observe the changes taking place in your lives and in the lives of the people around you.

Some time will pass and you will be able to discern the influence of the Ascended Hosts behind these changes. We are acting straightforwardly, and there is nothing in our actions that we do not reveal in our Dictations. Without keeping anything back, we reveal in our Dictations and in our Teaching the whole mechanism of our influencing both planet Earth and the changes on planet Earth.

The way things happen is very simple. You read Dictations; you attend seminars that we hold with the help of our Messenger and the people who expressed a wish to serve us. You receive energy and knowledge, and you change your consciousness, your thinking, and your vibrations.

You influence every person you meet in the street and at work. In such a manner during this year, we have managed to exercise our influence on millions of people. That is why we can now safely say that the process of changing of consciousness is gaining momentum so successfully that it has been decided to hasten the process of changes on planet Earth to the maximum. This does not mean that in the near future you will be threatened by impending major disasters and natural calamities. Moreover, if the process of changing of consciousness goes on at that successful rate, you will avoid many major cataclysms and disasters.

However, we cannot guarantee that no cataclysms and disasters will occur if the opposing forces, which are ready at any sacrifice to delay the process of changes, take dynamic actions and galvanize many people into them.

Therefore, before you start any activity in your world, carefully debate your motives in your mind, and try to understand the motives that predetermine the people who invite you to take part in these or those actions including prayer practices. The energy of prayers can be craftily used for reaching goals diametrically opposite to the Divine ones.

At the present time your level of consciousness enables us to give these Teachings about the distortion of the energy of prayers. At all times there were people who directed the energy of prayers to the Supreme octaves of Light. But there were other people who used the energy of prayers while having an axe to grind. In that case they did not act in accordance with the Will of God. Moreover, the people involved in their activity created karma.

All actions in your world, all thoughts and feelings, create karma. It is impossible for you not to act, and consequently, not to create karma. However, there is negative and positive karma. Negative karma extends the cycle of your lives on Earth and you have to come into embodiment again and again.

Positive or good karma, in contrast, leads to reducing the cycle of your stay on planet Earth.

The fate of every individual and the situation on planet Earth are influenced by the balance between the positive and the negative karma that was created by humanity in the past and is being created now, at every moment of the present.

That is why we say time and again that the future of planet Earth and the process of changes on this planet depend on each of you.

No matter how grave your difficulties are, you should always remember that your existence does not terminate with the death of your physical body. Oh, you are far more than your physical bodies. Each of you has the potential to become a God. And in the course of time all of you will become Gods, except for those who voluntarily refuse to become Gods and wish to identify themselves with the physical body. You know that everything around you represents a colossal illusion. And in the grand scheme of things your task is to rise above this illusion within your consciousness. When you rise above the illusion and give up your attachments to the physical world, you continue your evolution in the Higher Worlds. However, if you identify yourself with the physical world, then you voluntarily doom yourself to death because in due time the physical world will be no more, and you will be unable to transit to the Higher Worlds because your consciousness does not accept them.

Thus, the key to your future and the future of the whole planet is your consciousness and the degree of your readiness to change your consciousness.

The valuable opportunity, which is being given to the planet, must be accepted by your consciousness. You should realize the fact that the Divine opportunity exists, and you should strive to accept this opportunity and implement it in your lives. In that case the Divine opportunity will be able to manifest itself in your physical world.

I have told you about the mechanism with the help of which we influence the physical world and change the physical world. This is the most natural way of changing, which should be applied first and foremost. Any cataclysms occur because the level of human consciousness does not conform to the level that Heavens wish earthly mankind to have at a given moment. That is why we always warn you when stepped-up work is required of you in order to change your consciousness.

At present I am happy to state that the rate of change of human consciousness satisfies the demands we raise.

Keep it up! Heavens are grateful to you. And you may fairly have high hopes for the new mercies of Heavens.

I am pleased to have met you today.

I AM Gautama Buddha. Om.

A Talk about the Path of Initiations

Lord Maitreya
April 19, 2006

I AM Maitreya, having come to you again through my Messenger. I AM coming for the new directions that I would wish to give today.

As always, I am very glad to meet you. And no matter how difficult it is for us and how much effort we apply to establish our relationship, all our efforts return in those changes of your consciousness that we are expecting of you and that you have already started to realize.

So today, as before, I am coming to give you certain knowledge and information concerning your Path of Initiations. The Path that I urge you to follow differs from many things that you face in your everyday life. This Path differs from the teachings that you face in your daily lives.

I have to tell you that you are aware of the Initiations that you have in your lives only after you reach a certain level of your consciousness. Until that time you are like teenagers, floundering and splashing in the waters of life. They do not realize adult life, and they are not aware of the whole complexity of living and the forthcoming course of life.

There is a moment in the life of every being when it realizes its connection with the Highest and that it should consciously start to follow the Path of Initiations. The state of the society has made conscious passing of the Initiations impossible for the last centuries, especially in the West. People forgot about the Schools of Mysteries and about the knowledge that was given at those Schools.

Therefore, our task, and the task of our Messenger, is to remind you of the Path of Initiations and to recommence the traditions of the ancient Path of Initiations. We will try to give you the necessary knowledge concerning the Path of Initiations, but each of you will pass his own initiations individually without leaving your usual life; and that will be a distinctive feature of our new actions.

We hope that this new opportunity will be adopted in the West at this time. And you won't have to look for teachers overseas or go to the ends of Earth to find them.

I repeat to you once again that precisely those things happen to you that you concede, or allow, in your consciousness. It is not necessary to go to the ends of the Earth in order to enter my School of Mysteries, as a new time and new opportunities have come. Exactly those things happen which you concede in your consciousness. And if you accept in your consciousness that you can communicate with me and the other Masters of Wisdom, it will happen in your life sooner or later. I will come to you directly, or I will come to you through your enemies, your friends, and your relatives; and I will give you the lessons that you need. Everything has become easier. The level of consciousness achieved by the best representatives of humanity allows you to communicate with us, even staying in the conditions of big cities. All that you need is maximal isolation from outer noises and stimuli. You should learn to listen to your sensations. You should discern vibrations. You should listen to those thoughts that come to your mind and distinguish between the thoughts that I send to you and the thoughts that appear within your mind or come to your mind from the mental plane.

You visit my classes within you when you are in a peaceful quiet place where nobody disturbs you. Everything that impedes our communication is at the level of your vibrations. So, I will be able to come to you directly and start communicating with you when you are able to raise your vibrations, with the help of prayers or meditation, to the level where no human thoughts and emotions can disturb you.

You get what you are directed toward. Do not be confused or disheartened if you fail to do it the first time or even the second time.

Your aspiration should not leave you. Sometimes it might take a significant period of time to establish our inner contact. But as soon as you get an opportunity of direct communication with me, it will serve as a sign that you have entered my School and have passed all the necessary entrance examinations. But as soon as you enter my school, your life will start to ruin in terms of usual human logic. It is due to the fact that the only difference between the initiate and an ordinary man is in their level of consciousness. And the deeper your realization that everything around you is illusion, the higher degree of initiations you achieve.

The level of your consciousness is what I am interested in. And I am ready to give you the most difficult tests so you can achieve this new level of consciousness. All the tests are aimed at depriving you of any attachment to the material world around you. When you voluntarily, and with my help, are deprived of your attachments to the material world, you become the initiates to whom I can reveal the ancient knowledge about the organization of the universe.

If you haven't gained the necessary degree of initiations, you won't be able to understand even simple knowledge, no matter how you try. You will hear the words, but those words will not get into your consciousness. There is much knowledge and information in your world. However, only those who have advanced consciousness can use that information. It is similar to giving a computer to a monkey: its level of consciousness will not allow it to use this thing appropriately. Unfortunately, when we give our information and watch how you use it, most of you resemble those monkeys.

The whole world is literally full of information and knowledge. But few can use that knowledge. Only a few have passed the necessary initiations and have achieved a certain level in the development of their consciousness during this incarnation or their previous incarnations. And the degree of your initiations is determined only by your personal achievements. It is impossible to buy this initiation. It is impossible that somebody passes your initiations for you or instead of you.

However, there are people who have passed their initiations and are gurus for you; they are the ones who can give the right direction to the vector of your aspirations.

When a chela is ready, the teacher comes. So, only those of you who are ready within will be able to get the necessary knowledge and to find and to notice those landmarks on the Path of Initiations that can lead you to the right Path.

Therefore, as always, I urge you to turn within and watch yourself, because only your imperfections and your attachments separate you from the knowledge and do not allow you to become my disciples.

I am pleased to meet you today. And I have told you about the new opportunity that awaits those of you who are ready and aspiring.

I AM Maitreya.

Instructions about your attitude to everything around you in your dense world and in the finer worlds

**El Morya
April 20, 2006**

I AM El Morya Khan, having come to you again through my Messenger.

As it has been before, I have come to talk to you and to give instructions concerning your life and your place in the universe.

Like children who come to this world to explore it, you start the process of exploration of the world, but only of that world, which is still beyond the perception of your physical sense organs.

But that world exists; and it represents the Higher Reality in which you will be born and where you will stay in the course of time.

When your soul was in the fine world, before your incarnation, you were getting education and instructions about what you would face in the dense physical world. Now I come to give you directions about what you will face after your transition to the finer world.

The more you are ready for the transition to the finer world, the less effort your soul will have to apply to adapt to our world. We speak for everybody, but not everyone is able to perceive the information contained in the Dictations, and especially, to read the information between the lines. That is the difference between the

Dictations that come from the Higher octaves from those messages that you get from the lower levels of astral and mental planes. The Messages are multidimensional. The information is supposed to be understandable for everyone, regardless of his or her level of consciousness. However, there is something that is hidden behind the general phrases, and it only becomes understandable for those who can read between the lines and hear the voice in the silence of the quiet.

There is information for everyone, but not all can accommodate everything.

Do not be confused with the fact that many things slip from your outer consciousness. There will be the time on your Path when you will suddenly start realizing what you have not been able to realize before. Knowledge will be coming into your head, and you will not understand why you know that. You will try to remember the source of the information but you won't be able to remember it. However, once you remember that you have been reading the Ascended Masters' Dictations, you will realize that you have gotten the information between the lines unconsciously.

You join the certain information and energy egregore through reading these Dictations, and you become able to come out to different layers of the finer world spontaneously and to get information from the Higher octaves directly. You get your education during your sleep, and you get your education in the form of insights and understanding, coming out to a high etheric level spontaneously.

Therefore, it is not as simple, as it seems at first glance...

However, I have to prevent your anxiety. There will not be any information or any connection to the source of information without your consent. You can read these Messages, feeling distrust of the source, feeling doubt, and with that you put an insurmountable energy barrier between you and us.

Only if your soul feels joy and triumph when reading our Messages, and you express your willingness to get further education and further perception of the information, knowledge, and energy with all your being, only in this case Heavens open the opportunities before you, and you get access to our libraries, our classes, and databases.

It is similar to getting a password to access certain information. That password is given to you only when you express your willingness to cooperate with us and to get our information. However, on our side we evaluate the level of your consciousness, and you get access to those energies and information that you can assimilate. We watch carefully that the dose of energy received by you doesn't exceed the threshold that can be harmful for your health and subtle bodies.

Therefore, the process of penetration of the worlds and the process of cooperation of the worlds is under thorough control. A person with mercenary motives cannot get access to the information that he can use to cause harm to anybody. The criterion is always your vibrations. Each of you bears a unique vibration spectrum. You are a unique manifestation of the Divine Flame. And the degree of your achievements puts non-washable traces on your Flame and your vibrations. So we can always distinguish you according to your flames and vibrations, and consequently, according to your consciousness level.

You should not worry that you do not get information directly from us. The process of transmission and accessing information from the Higher plane is a century-old and tuned process. You get as much as you need and only when a suitable moment comes for that.

However, you should always be in a state of constant expectation. If you do not aspire or show your willingness, then the energy will not be able to penetrate your aura, and you isolate yourself from the information that comes from the Higher plane.

On the one hand, you should not worry that you do not get information; on the other hand, you should express constant willingness to receive the information right at the moment when it should come to you.

The combination of these two qualities, which only seems incompatible, becomes the barest necessity.

You get information when you are free of merely selfish desires to possess anything. The information arrives to you according to the extent you can get rid of the unreal part of you, and consequently, raise your vibrations to the level at which you can reach the octaves where that information becomes accessible for you.

There cannot be any standard approach for everybody. Everyone has a unique manifestation of Divinity in the physical world. And the main quality will be your ability to feel Love to Creator's plan and to never stop admiring all the diversity of Divine manifestations around you, not to focus on you and your problems but to watch the variety and diversity of Divine manifestations, to be able to see Divine miracles and enjoy them. That is why it is said that until you become like children, you will not be able to enter the Kingdom of Heaven.

Today I have given you some instructions about your attitude to your relations with each other and the Divine Reality, and about your attitude to everything around you in your dense world and in the Higher worlds.

I hope that the instructions received by you will help your development and enrich you.

And now the time has come to remind you of the dispensation of the 23rd of each month that was given by me in the previous Dictations.[10] Now I have to announce that the dispensation

---

[10] Refer to the Dictations of Beloved El Morya: "About the new Divine Dispensation," June 27, 2005, and "I have brought you two pieces of news — one is sad and the other is joyful," January 7, 2006, in *Words of Wisdom Volumes 1 and 2*.

becomes accessible and is practiced by many groups and separate individuals. Therefore, it is decided that the efficiency of the given dispensation will be multiplied not only by the number of people who participate in the dispensation, the efficiency of this dispensation will also be multiplied tenfold for everyone who will not miss any 23rd day during this year, starting from the 23rd of April 2006.

I congratulate you because this new Divine Grace has become accessible thanks to your achievements on the Path.

I AM El Morya Khan,
and I worship the Light of God within you.

A Teaching on extraterrestrial civilizations

Beloved Zarathustra
April 21, 2006

I AM Zarathustra, having come to you through our Messenger. I have come to give one more short Teaching that, I hope, will be quite useful for you at the given stage of your evolutionary development.

As your civilization has started the cycle of ascension now and is in an ascending spiral, any teaching that has already been known before should be taken in a new way by you. And no matter what new teachings you get through other sources and channels, I have to give a small explanation concerning the fact that there are a variety of different hierarchies in the universe that follow their own way. And many of those hierarchies are related to the hierarchy to which I belong and which our Messenger represents on Earth. Other hierarchies are at some other levels of development and have another structure and implement other tasks.

There are some among those hierarchies with which we cooperate, but there are also other hierarchies with which we do not conclude any agreements. They act according to their laws. It is hard for you to realize that situation now, since everything that we have told you before this moment has been related to the uniform Law of this universe and about the obedience of the lower to the higher.

Now you are getting this information, and it differs a bit from the information that you have obtained before. However, I have to notice that, indeed, everything obeys the Great Law that acts in this universe. However, this Law itself acts selectively, and it is refracted differently in various points of the universe. It is similar to the fact that there are different countries on Earth, and regardless of the fact that physical and mathematical laws act in every country, at the same time, there are certain state laws in each country. Like many states that may live and feel animosity toward each other, there are also other states that are friendly with each other, and their development has been based on friendship and cooperation for many centuries.

If we get back to our universe, you should realize that everything in the universe is much more diverse than everything existing on planet Earth. When you go beyond the limits of one particular planet in your consciousness, you understand that there are other civilizations in the universe that may be formed, in essence, on other principles. And in spite of the fact that there is a general Law of this universe that acts in those civilizations, they still have other principles of development, and even the nature of those beings that inhabit other world systems may differ much from your nature.

There is a moment in the development of every civilization when it starts interacting with other civilizations that inhabit the universe. This process is similar to a stage when some tribe has been living peacefully, and suddenly, at some stage of its development, it discovers that there is another tribe not very far from them where there are other laws and customs.

Now, when you come to another country, everything is interesting for you: laws and customs of that country, people's manners and their view of the surrounding reality. When you meet other civilizations from other world systems, mutual interest appears in the same way. Everything happens at a certain stage of development in any civilization.

The point of my instruction today is to give you an understanding that the civilizations existing on Earth have always met other more developed civilizations throughout the history of development of planet Earth. And in spite of the fact that there is a law that is kept in the universe according to which none of the civilizations can cause harm to another civilization, there were always moments when that law was broken. However, there are higher beings that have an opportunity to interfere and regulate any arguable points that arise.

Now, when humankind in whole moves to the new level of its development, many civilizations from those world systems that have by far excelled the civilization existing on Earth, but which have a bit different direction of development than Earth's, will try to come in contact with the tellurians. So, you should be ready for any unexpected situations that might happen in your lives. But even in that situation, as in any other situation, the law of attraction according to vibrations is in force. If you are anxious about extraterrestrial civilizations, and they occupy too much space in your consciousness, then it can be said that there is a strong probability that you will meet representatives of those civilizations. However, if the problems concerning extraterrestrial civilizations do not bother you, you may go past any extraterrestrial object, not noticing it.

You should not be afraid of anything. However, you should always remember that not all extraterrestrial civilizations express friendliness to tellurians. And if you have doubt about some situation and do not know how to react, remember that there are Higher Hosts that are called upon to help and protect you in all situations of that kind. Not everything in the universe can be understandable and accessible for your outer consciousness. But it will be better if you are ready for any unexpected situations and meetings. That is why I consider it my duty to give you this short Teaching about extraterrestrial civilizations.

As a rule, all religious systems of the past had a negative attitude toward any such intrusions of extraterrestrial civilizations and proclaimed aliens to be demons and devils. It was impossible to take those not always understandable phenomena differently in the existing religious bounds and limitations. Now many religious systems teach that all extraterrestrial intrusions are the invasions of the devil and his henchmen.

I repeat once again that such contacts become inevitable at a certain stage of human development. And as many extraterrestrial civilizations differ too much from the civilization existing on Earth, they can be taken as hostile by your consciousness.

You are moving to the new level of development in your consciousness, so the problem of the attitude to extraterrestrial civilizations cannot be disregarded in our directions. You should always remember that the Ascended Masters are the closest beings to you in this universe, according to their development level and their vibrations. Moreover, many particles of the Ascended Masters are incarnated, and consequently, many Ascended Masters stay among you. You have the Ascended Masters' particles within your Higher Self. Therefore, I recommend that you do not pay too much attention to extraterrestrial civilizations and to relations with them until your consciousness is ready to a considerable degree. When your consciousness gets more information about those civilizations, you will be able to see the situations that occur in proper perspective and to make proper decisions in difficult situations.

Now I will give you one more piece of advice. As soon as you face any confusing situation, you immediately call those of the Ascended Masters whom you know. Call for Jesus, Muhammad the prophet, Michael the Archangel, the Goddess of Liberty, Sanat Kumara, me, or other Masters and ask for their help and support in the situation that you are facing.

You can call aloud or silently, or you can also set out your problem in writing and burn the letter with your request. You should always know that all necessary measures will be taken to answer any of your calls. And never, under any circumstances, feel fear in any situation you face. The vibrations of fear paralyze your will and your connection with your Higher Self.

Today I have given you the outline of the Teaching on the attitude to extraterrestrial civilizations, and I hope that these instructions will be of help in your lives at this stage.

I AM Zarathustra, with Love to you.

A Teaching on the Path of Apprenticeship

Lord Shiva
April 22, 2006

I AM Shiva, having come to you again!

I have come, and as always, I have come to give you the information that you need, and that your outer consciousness and your subtle bodies need.

There have been a number of important events since our previous communication. The result of those events can be briefly described as Heaven's approval of the current situation on Earth. And if earlier, during the days of the winter solstice when we were giving the previous cycle of the Dictations,[11] we expressed our displeasure with the situation on Earth, now we can't stop repeating that the Heavens express their approval and joy due to the changes that are occurring on Earth.

The situation is changing, and if it is still not noticed by the majority of humanity, those who can feel higher energies notice the changes and follow these changes in their consciousness.

As it was at our last meeting, I have come to give a short Teaching concerning the Path of Apprenticeship. The vital need for this Teaching becomes more and more obvious. As soon as humankind of Earth is carried away by the illusion, the connection with the Hierarchy and our Teaching, which we have been giving

---

[11] The cycle of Dictations from December 12, 2005 to January 7, 2006.

for many centuries through different incarnated Teachers and Messengers, becomes lost.

So, every time we have to restore our connection again and again through the conductor that we get in the dense world. At this moment we are talking about our Messenger, Tatyana. You see that we continue using this conductor. We are proceeding with our work because when getting a worthy conductor, we try to use it at full capacity. We do not take into account the state of the person's physical body or their inner state. Nothing can stop us when it is necessary to transmit information and the Law for its application in the physical world.

Having this conductor, we will try to use it not only for the transmission of our Messages but also for creating our outpost, the base, the foundation, and the focus of Light on the physical plane. When we get something on the physical plane that can allow us to fix our focus of Light, we will transmit our information and will influence the raising of the vibrations of many, using the bodies of the Messenger. This is similar to the process that happens when you throw a stone in the quiet water of a pond: The waves from the thrown stone spread around the whole pond. Everything that has gotten into the scope of that spreading wave starts to feel the vibrations.

Therefore, the transfer of knowledge is not always connected with giving information through the Word. There is a certain law that allows the transfer of information from the aura of a Teacher to the aura of a disciple. In order to do that, Guru-chela relations based on complete unconditional Love and cooperation should be established. At the moment when the auras of a Teacher and a disciple touch, the momentum of the Teacher's achievements goes to the disciples on that complete and unconditional feeling of Love.

We try to create the conditions in which we could use the potential of our Messenger at full capacity, not only giving information through her in the form of the Word, but also giving the information to our chelas through her conductors to accelerate their development.

All that we need is to create very comfortable conditions in any place of planet Earth, where people can come and stay for some period of time. You can call it an ashram, a community, or a training center. But the purpose of that place is to serve as a focus on the physical plane where we can fix our energies and transmit our vibrations. The only requirement for the place on our part is its maximum distance from any center of population and the absence of any place where there are people who do not have a significant level of vibrations, so as not to create the state of premature testing in those people. Every person who gets into the sphere of our focus of Light experiences the rising of vibrations. And you know that as soon as you get an additional portion of Light, that Light starts to intensively push out any manifestations of imperfections from your aura. So, the person who is not ready, who has not started Guru-chela relations with our Messenger, will feel different uncomfortable states and it will cause increased tension.

Therefore, the more isolated, quiet, and comfortable the place of our future focus is, the better results we will be able to achieve. I appeal to those who have information about such places at their disposal: Where is it possible to organize our ashram? Would you mind telling our Messenger about that or applying to me personally with your letter?

This is a very important step. In order to make our place safe, to a certain extent, from negative influences and any property arguments, I have informed our Messenger about the conditions on which that ashram ought to exist.

I repeat once again that there is a certain Law according to which we perform our work on the physical plane. And that Law assumes the presence of disciples in the Teacher's aura in order to accelerate the process of advancement along the Path.

Those of you who have attended our events that we have carried out together with our Messenger could feel how the process of changing your consciousness has accelerated after those events.

We will continue holding our events. I think that all of you who wish that those events should continue will be able to visit them in due time.

In the near future Tatyana will have to carry the additional responsibility of creating and fixing our focus of Light. Therefore, I ask you to give her all the necessary help and support no matter what kind of help or support it is. Sometimes it is enough just to express your mental support, to send your Love and gratitude for service. And the impulse of your heart can neutralize the impact of a huge amount of negative energy that is drawn to our Messenger automatically because she is on top of the peak, and all winds and hurricanes hit her first.

I have told everything I have planned to tell during today's talk. I hope that I can count on you and your help in our work.

I AM Shiva.

I am giving you a guaranteed way Home

Lord Maitreya
April 23, 2006

I AM Maitreya, having come to you again through my Messenger.

I have come! And as always, I intend to give you a Teaching and instructions necessary for your advancement along the Path. Your Path is the Path of Initiations. How many of you think about the Path of Initiations, living your life? How many of you have at least the slightest idea of that Path?

You have heard and read in different sources that there is this Path of Initiations. And today I have come to tell you that the Path of Initiations is in fact the fastest and the shortest way that leads you to God. That is the Path of ego rejection. That is the Path of your willing consent to go through certain tests, even the hardest ones, to make your way Home shorter.

That is the Path that you choose of your own free will. That is the shortest way, leading you Home. You can choose another way. And that way will be more pleasant, but it will incommensurably take more time. Moreover, following a very pleasant way that doesn't require any tension on your part, you sometimes risk getting lost and fail to find your way Home, and you also risk not getting back to the starting point of your Path. Therefore, I have come, and I am telling you that I am giving you a guaranteed way Home. However, your way along that Path will require all your strength. You will have to sacrifice much that you have. But the most desirable sacrifice for us will be your ego that you should inevitably leave, following the Path of Initiations. All the tests on your Path are aimed at one thing only, at leaving your unreal part; and you should establish a close connection with the real part of you. Therefore, I come again and again to urge you to take it seriously and to warn you that the Path that I teach through my Messenger is very severe, though your return Home, on condition that you stand all the tests on your Path, is guaranteed. You can choose whether to follow that Path or not. Nobody can force you. I am just giving you the information, and you are making your choice.

There are many different teachings in your world. There are correct ones among them, and there are completely wrong ones that take you away from the Path and contribute to your delusion. So, every time that we get a conductor in the physical world, we give information about our Path of Initiations. It is the Path of Initiations that was taught by Jesus and Gautama Buddha. It is the Path of Initiations that was followed by initiates at all times. Now we invite you to renew the ancient traditions and try to cultivate them in your society at this stage.

First, you should know that there is the Path of I AM. That Path opens for you through those who have already gotten the necessary initiations and have given their temples for Serving. Your way Home can be completed through these people, one of which is our Messenger through whom we give these Messages. You get a guide on the physical plane. And at the moment when you accept our Messenger as your Guru, you stand up on the steps of the Hierarchy, and the whole Hierarchy serves you and helps you in your advancement along the Path. It is a very simple Path. However, it would seem as though that simple step becomes an insurmountable barrier for many of you. You see an ordinary person burdened with human imperfections in our Messenger; and you cannot see the true essence of the Messenger behind the human manifestation, the essence that allowed us to stop our choice at that person. When you deal with the true representative of our Hierarchy on the physical plane, and when you completely and unconditionally accept our Messenger as your Guru, the opportunity that the Heavens give at this historical moment for planet Earth opens for you. Of course, only you can decide whether to use this opportunity or not. But, I am telling you that at this time there is no Messenger living in the West and brought up in Western traditions who represents our interests. Therefore, I urge those of you who have not decided yet to use the given opportunity, weigh all the information thoroughly, and make your decision. The window of opportunity is open for many life-streams now. And if you use this opportunity, you will make your Path much shorter. You choose the shortest way, leading you Home.

However, if you are not ready for such a radical step, do not let that circumstance confuse you. All of you are at different stages of your advancement along the Path.

We drop a rope of opportunity for you. And if you do not feel enough strength to grip that rope and climb the upright rocks, well, then wait for another opportunity. But I do not think that you will have the other opportunity during this life.

You should love severe conditions of tests. You should believe with all your being, and finally, stand up on the steps of the Hierarchy that has been leading you and taking care of you for millions of years. And every time, when the window of opportunity opens, it is similar to our throwing a net, catching some souls, and taking them out of the illusion.

However, others prefer to stay in the illusion, and that is their choice.

Now, when our talk has become so frank, I would like to tell you one more thing; you will decide to what extent it will be necessary for your consciousness. We have made a decision to make one more gift from Heaven to you. And that gift is so precious and so blissful for your souls that only those individuals who are still too deep in illusion will not be able to appreciate it. Our gift is the following. Today we announce the beginning of one more Divine dispensation, a Divine opportunity. I will take each of you, who will write a letter to me today or during the immediate month period and wish to follow the Path of Initiations, to my School. But the condition is that you accept our Messenger as your Guru. Without that condition, neither I nor any of the representatives of the Hierarchy can render you all the help that you need.

You accept our rules of play, and only after that we will start giving you all necessary help and support.

I understand that such a decisive announcement will be a source of doubts and anxiety for many of you. However, that is why our schools exist, so that you can live in a state of constantly overcoming your unreal part. And for some people, the needed decision will be made easily and will not cause any tension within. For others the given condition will become an insurmountable barrier on the Path.

And if you feel a very strong resistance and indignation within, I would advise that you go deep within yourself to find out the reason for the given state of yours. What is the cause of it? For you it is the signal that there is a problem within you.

However, you should know that all your problems are connected with the strength of your ego; it doesn't want to lose its power over you. That is why this step is so necessary. And without this step you lose the opportunity of your advancement at least until the end of your current incarnation.

We have never spoken so openly and so concretely.

We hope that your consciousness is ready for such a serious talk.

And now let me say goodbye to you until our next meeting. And I hope that you will make a wise decision in your heart.

I AM Maitreya, hoping for you.

The natural evolution for your souls is following the Path we are teaching mankind of Earth

Lord Surya
April 24, 2006

I AM Surya, having come to you through our Messenger again.

I have come from the Great Central Sun to give a homily to the people of planet Earth.

For your awareness, we are giving you knowledge and information that are vital for you. We provide you with information, and each time you have a chance to receive a new pearl. After some time passes, you will amusedly discover that the pearls we have given you are enough to make a necklace. And you will be wearing this necklace until the end of your embodiment. It will impart its warmth to you and give you strength at the moments when your mind is filled with doubts about the chosen Path, and the troubles of life tie you tightly up in knots of returning karma.

Don't be afraid of any difficulties you will encounter in your life. All the troubles and all the unforeseen situations are required and necessary for the development of your soul. You will be unable to evolve if you do not come across unforeseen daily situations and do not overcome the hardships of life. Only what is dead is unable to experience the delights of life and to suffer from certain manifestations of life. Thus, be thankful for everything you face in life and do not shrink from the changes.

The better your consciousness is prepared for the changes, the more easily and more quickly they occur. The reason for all your disturbances and troubles is the mistakes you made in the past. So every imbroglio you face in life must gladden you, because for you it is a chance to redeem your old errors and never to return to them.

The knowledge of the Law of Karma will enable you to alter your attitude toward any trouble. And the younger you are when you get access to the knowledge of the Law of Karma, the more easily you will accept even the most difficult situations and come out of them with honor. If you do not encounter difficulties in your life, if your life runs smoothly, then I would think over this fact if I were you. Many people seek peace and aspire to external demonstrations of well-being. However, as soon as you get into such life conditions when everything in your life runs too smoothly, this is like a black ordeal for your soul, because you have no opportunity to evolve through external conditions and you have to descend inwardly.

Very few people know how to be all-sufficient and to contemplate only their inner being. The majority of people, after having lost their familiar surroundings full of difficulties and barriers, simply fall into depression. And this is a sign that you have entered a period of overcoming of the most severe karma — the karma between you and God.

Many people threw out a challenge to God on an impulse of arrogance; they were so bold as to speak out against the Law of this universe. At that moment when they made bold to behave like that, nothing happened. They went on living as before and nothing changed in their lives, for a certain period of time must pass before karma starts to return. And this term is made necessary by many reasons. If you step on the Path of Initiations, the time starts running differently for you, and the process of the return of karma accelerates. For ordinary people the karma of their current embodiment can be returned only in the next embodiment or even after a few embodiments. For that reason, it is very difficult to trace how the Law of Karma operates. But when you consciously enter the Path of Initiations, you receive lessons in life that allow you to trace the action of the Law of Karma during the period of literally one year. In particular instances the return of karma can speed up even more and its result can be returned in a few weeks or days.

At any rate, you receive a chance to look backwards over earlier mistakes and to retrace the action of the Law of Karma. Besides, you receive training unconsciously during the day or in your sleep. You receive information from the Masters or from your Higher Self, and this information enables you to bring into confrontation the mistakes you made in the past, and the fruits (the results of these mistakes) return to you in the form of karma, or energy.

And even then, when you cannot sufficiently trace the link between your actions in the past and the consequences of these actions in the present in the form of returning karma, it is important not only to trace this link, but also to accept the fact that everything happening to you takes place according to the Will of God. And the degree of your humility before the Divine Law and before the Will of God will show you the degree of your merits on the Path to God.

There are many nuances and situations on your Path that are not susceptible to a single-value estimate by your external consciousness. Such situations sometimes contravene the code of conduct and the ethical canon existing in your society. But it is not always the case that the Divine Law coincides with the moral law of the society. So, for example, karma from a murder or any other violent act that you committed in the past must return to you. And for this purpose, God can use any person whom you meet on the Path. For the purposes of the human law existing in your society, this person is a criminal and is punishable. But for the purposes of the Divine Law, this human can simply be a doer of the Law of Karma. For that reason, never judge even criminals and never allow yourself to judge anybody.

At those times when a strong bond existed between your world and the Highest octaves, there were people who were fundamentally incarnations of the Divine and who were capable of retracing the link between the actions of people in the past and the present. Such people acted as Divine judges, and their sentencing decisions or voluntarily pardons were peremptory.

At present there are no people on Earth who represent Divine incarnations in full, for any Divine incarnation in the present conditions on Earth is impossible. That is why there is no chance to accurately trace the connection between your actions in the past and the problems that crop up in your life as the consequences of your past actions.

Only when you step on the Path of Initiations can you allow the Higher world to be manifested in your life. You receive knowledge about the Law of Karma and its manifestations in your lives with the help of your personal mystical bond with the Masters and your own Higher part.

That is why I have come today in order to raise again a question before your external consciousness about the necessity for you to follow the Path of Initiations. I have come from the Great Central Sun, and I have brought you this Message with the aim of helping you understand that the natural evolution for your souls is following the Path we are teaching mankind of Earth. But we cannot force anybody to follow this beaten Path.

We can only give you our knowledge and understanding, our information and energy.

Nevertheless, I am sure that a moment will come when common sense and the internal Divine essence prevail in your life, and thereupon you will gain victory after victory over the unreal part of yourselves.

**I AM Surya,
and I wish you success on your Path!**

We cannot make anybody go, but we call you to take the Path

Sanat Kumara
April 25, 2006

I AM Sanat Kumara, having come to you again!

I have come this day to remind you once again about your duties, which your souls took upon themselves before incarnation. You may not remember these duties because the veil is still very dense and your outer consciousness forgets everything you heard and learned between incarnations. However, there is something more in you, and this something is the Higher part of yourselves. This part of you has always remembered and still remembers your destination and your Divine plan.

To awaken the memory of your soul is one of the aims of the given Dictations. You recall your destination when you experience minutes of unmotivated yearning and despair. It may seem that everything goes without any apparent troubles in your life, but your souls are worried because the time is passing and they cannot accomplish the duties they took on. Therefore, your major task is to establish a connection with your Higher part and to remember your destination.

When you meet something in your life that reminds you of your duties and your destination you tremble, and this feeling is akin to a gentle feeling of first love. This is a very tender, inviting feeling. You cannot fail to notice this state of yours. You may associate this feeling and direct it toward the person who has given your soul the joyful message that reminded you about your stay in the etheric octaves. And after you have felt this gentle feeling you will aspire to get this experience of recognition again and again. Because this feeling does not relate to your physical plane, this state of yours may confuse you. Oh yes, it can be compared with the feeling of first love. And this really is your first love that you felt before your very birth. Enough number of years will pass and you will understand that this feeling is not connected with a particular person in incarnation. This is a more elevated feeling. This is a feeling of Love to the whole Creation, to the whole Life.

Those who understand what I am talking about are on the threshold of a new life. Physical life continues to exist around you, and at the same time it is as though you pass to another world that exists simultaneously with yours and yet differs from everything around you. You should make the discernment in your consciousness of this state of yours, the state of being simultaneously among the familiar people and circumstances, but understanding that you are not attached to those people and those circumstances. You continue existing in your world, and at the same time you understand that you are not of this world, for you have passed to another, Higher world in your consciousness. And you begin to realize that the worlds join inside of you. And thanks to you, the Higher world descends to your physical plane.

At first these sensations are so unusual that they occupy your whole being. You enjoy and at the same time wonder at this state of yours.

However, as you continue to exist in your physical world and still have a physical body, the conditions of your world continue to affect you. And as your vibrations have risen and your sense organs have become capable of perceiving the vibrations of the Higher worlds, some manifestations of the common world and its circumstances strike too painfully your sensitive nature.

You feel the difference between yourself and the people around you. And it hurts you deeply that the people who are the closest to you do not understand you. They hear your words, they see you and the changes you have undergone but their level of consciousness does not allow them to understand and to follow you.

This is a very difficult trial. You lose the connection with the closest people, and you are forced to make a choice. You either stay in your present environment and sacrifice your spiritual development, or continue to follow the Path and sacrifice your relationships with friends and relatives.

Believe me, both things are very hard. And the choice will be different in each individual situation. Only you yourself and your soul know what choice you must make.

If it is a goal of your incarnation to sacrifice yourself and your attainments for the good of the people you love and with whom you are karmically connected, then you will make your choice and will stay with your close ones. And if the goal of your incarnation is to help many but the connections with your environment hinder you, then you will tear all your ties and — as a bird broken free from the cage — soar up toward the sky, clouds, and mountain peaks.

However, I must warn you that if you do not fulfill your karmic duties and do not pay off all your debts, you will very likely create big karma, taking, it would seem, a light and high path. You cannot set out on a long journey not having taken care of the people you are karmically connected with. And no high goal can be a justification for abandoning those who are around you and who need your help.

Therefore, we try not to give concrete recommendations, for it is impossible to give exhaustive and universal recommendations for all the situations in life. Life is too varied and karma is very tangled.

Sometimes a decision strongly denounced by everybody from the human point of view is the only correct one from the Divine point of view, and the correct decision from all human positions contradicts the Divine Law. The Divine Science is the most complex science of all of those that you encounter in your life. And while you may ignore studying all the others of them and calmly pass by the shelves containing the books devoted to these sciences, all of you must master the Divine Science; the only difference is when each will master it.

The time to master the Divine Science has come for many of you. And you cannot do otherwise; you must take the Path of Initiations because you yourselves planned it prior to your incarnation. The others may calmly stay in the thick of life and continue playing their roles and playing with their toys for yet many incarnations. Their consciousness is not yet ready to part with the physical world and to rise to the mountain summits of the Divine Truth cognition. I can only tell you this: Those who have accepted these Dictations that we give through our Messenger with all their hearts, and wait for every Dictation with anticipation and hope, are most likely ready to take the Path and follow it.

Therefore, check with your hearts the feelings you have from this Dictation of mine. We cannot make anybody go, but we call you to take the Path.

**I AM Sanat Kumara,
always with you!**

Expose yourself to the winds of change and do not be afraid to catch a cold or fall ill

Gautama Buddha
April 26, 2006

I AM Gautama Buddha, having come to you today.

I have come, and as always, I am intending to give you a short Teaching that I hope will be good for you. Today I am intending to give a Teaching concerning your relationship with nature and your relationships within human society.

You have a unique essence and nature, and the relationships among you and with everything around are very important. Sometimes you do not bother to think about your impact on everything around you. It seems to you that everything around exists independently from you and without your consciousness; however, the connection that is there between any manifestations on the physical plane is very strong. It is so strong that any element of your interaction with the world around can have a disastrously negative influence if it doesn't conform to the Divine plan.

We apply our efforts to balance the situation on the planet. However, you can do the same thing yourselves. All you need is to be inspired with love toward the whole life, to any manifestation of life, and feel your Oneness with every part of life.

Your Oneness is not something external that you have to gain. Your Oneness is your inner state.

Oneness comes from within you. For that you should allow thoughts about Oneness into your consciousness. Do not tend to criticize anybody. Try to find positive moments in everything around you and focus your attention on that.

You influence everything around you. And as you are Gods in your potential, sometimes that influence is so significant that it can change the future of the whole planet within several seconds. That is why it is very important to be constantly focused on positive things — positive emotions, joyful moods. You should face any problems consciously. For the bigger the number of obstacles and problems that you face in this life and overcome them with dignity, the greater is the extent of your working off your karma and of correcting the mistakes you made in the past. Becoming free of your karma, you gain greater influence on the world because the Light of God, the Divine energy, can freely flow to your world through your chakras.

It is impossible to measure with human instruments the amount of the Divine energy that this or that person lets through to your world, but your higher sense organs always know who the Light goes through, and many aspire to communicate with such people intuitively.

There are also other patterns of human consciousness. The consciousness focused on itself, thinking only about itself and about getting pleasures for itself. Such people represent black holes in space. They consume energy but give nothing in return. Everything is dead around such people; and they represent the living dead themselves. There are also different transitional states of human consciousness between these two opposite manifestations.

In fact, you always decide yourself which way to move. You always move only toward the Light or in the opposite direction away from the Light. You either fill yourself and the people around you with the Divine energy, with Light, or you represent a consumer of the Divine energy.

When two individuals who bear the Light within themselves meet, they exchange the Divine energy and enrich each other. Every manifestation of the Divine Flame is unique. Interaction of the Divine flames in incarnation enriches both of the flames.

Therefore, it will be good for each individual and for the whole planet if there are spots on the planet where people can stay and communicate — the people who have caring hearts and who care not only about themselves and their closest ones but also about all beings living on planet Earth. Their communication will enhance the outflow of the Divine energy to the physical world.

In the course of time, the places where negative energy is spread by people focused only on themselves will turn into leper colonies for people suffering from non-divine consciousness.

The population of Earth will be divided in the nearest future. People who believe in God in their hearts will tend to unite with similar people. There will be new settlements where such people will live. And as every person influences everything around, the rise of such settlements will resemble the Golden Age. That will be included in the Golden Age. And the speed of changes on Earth will depend on the success of that construction.

Getting to a favorable environment from early ages, a person will be able to take the behavior patterns and moral norms characteristic of such settlements.

These towns of the future should start to appear on the planet. And each of you can show that initiative and create such a settlement. You know that the best form of a prayer is a prayer through deeds. And if you feel strength and desire within you, do not wait for any external command. Act and create.

Use the opportunity that has come to Earth.

I will be glad if our suggestions come home to your hearts.

Everything that is from God, that makes people aspire to God, will have support and will be manifested in your world. Everything that has chosen to be divided from God will reap the fruits of the incorrect choice. But every person and every living being always has an opportunity to return to the Divine Path.

Some human individuals just have to learn their lessons. Thanks to planet Earth, everyone has an opportunity to learn their lessons, and everyone has open perspectives of the Divine development.

Now I am asking you to go deep into your heart and to think. What is holding you in the usual environment? What has made you follow for years that behavior stereotype you have imposed on yourself? What is limiting your freedom and the manifestation of your Divinity?

Is everything that impedes your development so significant, and hasn't the time come to leave all your small egoistic attachments and to give yourself to all living beings and to get eternal peace and unlimited joy of serving in return?

Try to analyze in your consciousness everything that impedes you from gaining your inner freedom and to soar up to the mountain peaks of the Divinity.

Only you set your limits, and only you impede the manifestation of your Divine qualities and the fulfillment of your Divine purpose.

Let the Divine energy flow through your being freely; and on its way it will wash away all small and big obstacles in the form of your ego, your fears, limits, and dogmata.

Expose yourself to the winds of change and do not be afraid to catch a cold or fall ill.

**I AM Gautama Buddha,
with faith in you!**

We ask you to act in your lives according to the knowledge and teachings received by you

The Great Divine Director
April 27, 2006

I AM the Great Divine Director, coming to you today. I AM coming to give you instructions and tell you the news from the etheric octaves. And this news is much more joyful than those Messages that we were giving during our winter cycle of the Dictations because the situation on the planet is changing for the better; and this change causes our joyful and reassuring feelings.

Only several months ago our anxiety about the state of affairs on Earth was so significant that we could not miss the chance to warn you through our Messenger about the difficult situation. But now I have come to use the opportunity to tell you that the situation on Earth has improved significantly; and those changes, which had occurred in the consciousness of not too many people so far, have now spread at a truly cosmic speed and reached many people in different parts of the globe. We are very glad that we have managed to spread our information so quickly with the help of our Messenger, with the help of the Internet, and with the help of those devoted and unmercenary hearts that have sacrificed much to give the opportunity to as many people as possible and to acquaint them with these Dictations. We are also grateful to those who have translated our Messages into many languages of the world. The Heavens are truly happy with this state of affairs.

Never before in recent history has the information that we are transmitting to the physical world been spread at such a speed.

And that opens up a new opportunity for us and allows you to receive fresh information from our world. Divine mercy truly knows no bounds. And when the Heavens start cooperating with the devoted collaborators in incarnation, we reach such significant changes within a very short period of time, and those achievements can truly be compared to a revolution in consciousness and an energy breakthrough between octaves.

Therefore, I am coming to you today to express my gratitude to each of you who responded to our call and not only changed your consciousness but also contributed to spreading our information in your physical octave as widely as possible.

Now I would like to give you a short guidance concerning the present situation on planet Earth.

From the previous Dictations you know how difficult the energy situation was at the end of the last year. It took truly enormous efforts to keep the balance and not to allow another destructive disaster. Now we are balancing the planet steadily. However, there is still no possibility for relaxation and celebration of the victory. This is because our success and achievements, the more significant and rapid they are, cause even greater opposition from those forces that do not want and do not welcome the changes.

Therefore, there is no possibility of relaxing. It is still necessary to apply all the efforts and all of your abilities not to slow down the speed of spreading of our Messages, our information, and our energy. You can imagine a snow ball that is still growing in size and volume. But in order to make this happen, it is necessary to apply constant effort to push and roll this snow ball.

That is why I am asking you not to stop but to act according to the impulse that appears within your hearts. Do not allow the burning spark to go out. Constantly get back to reading our

Dictations, especially those that give you strength and the impulse for acting on the physical plane.

We do not even ask you to pray; we ask you to act in your lives according to the knowledge and teachings received by you. The need for concrete actions is now placed in the forefront. You can feel how the energy contained in our Messages literally urges you to do concrete things on the physical plane. Therefore, it will be very important to apply your efforts correctly and not to allow the opposite forces to involve you in futile discussions and disputes. The time for empty talk and gossip is over. You should show the Heavens the extent to which you have learned the lessons that we have been giving through our Messenger for the past year, by your concrete actions on the physical plane.

We are happy with the speed at which our Teaching is spreading, though we are not satisfied with the fact that still very few concrete actions are being taken by you on the physical plane.

We are waiting for your actions of transformation on the physical plane. All non-divine things should be removed from your TV screens, radio airwaves, shelves of stores, and the Internet.

You cannot struggle against non-divine manifestations but you can substitute Divine models for those non-divine manifestations. You are acting even if you refuse to watch non-divine programs and films, or take part in any negative manifestations that are still characteristic of your world. Thereby you stop creating karma, and by your right choices you work off your past karma, and by your right choices you also give an example to the people around you, especially to the youth.

Do not worry about somebody doing something wrong. Show how to act correctly. It is always easy to judge. But when you judge, you create karma and multiply the illusion; but when you direct your energy in accordance with the Divine guiding principles, you create good karma and contract the illusion.

Therefore, I have come to you today in order to remind you that each of you has taken certain obligations upon yourself before this incarnation. The time has come for a favorable opportunity for you to fulfill your mission. Turn to yourself, come into your heart, and try to understand the obligations that your soul has taken upon itself before your incarnation.

You should recall those obligations of yours.

If you work in the sphere of education of children and youth, most likely it is one of your duties to provide knowledge of the Law of this universe, as well as the moral Divine Law in an accessible form meant for the upcoming generation.

If you are successful in business, perhaps the time has come for you to allocate your earnings correctly. Instead of an endless rush for useless things and pleasures, spend the money on creating training centers for children, adolescent youth, and their parents, and on building communities based on the new principles and free from the impact of negative vibrations and factors that are characteristic of your society today.

Therefore, starting any constructive Divine activity depends only on you. Nobody will fulfill your obligations for you. However, on our part, we promise to give you all the help you need. Just ask for that help and do not hesitate to turn to us in your letters and prayers.

It is just the beginning of the commonwealth of Heavens and the physical plane; and very soon you will see how fruitful that cooperation may be.

In the end, I would like to pass you the impulse of my Faith and my Confidence in you and in the maximum efficient fulfillment of your obligations.

**I AM the Great Divine Director,
with Love to you and Faith in your success!**

Only when you receive the Law from within your heart, do you become the executor of the Law

Beloved Kuthumi
April 28, 2006

I AM Kuthumi, having come to you again.

It has been several months since the moment of our previous meeting, and today I am ineffably happy with our new meeting because this meeting will be taking place in much more favorable conditions, and I will be able to give you the Teaching that was impossible to give earlier. This is the Teaching on how you should take life and on how you should take those changes that are occurring in your life. Only some time ago this Teaching would be irrelevant for you. But now more and more people become thoughtful about their life surroundings and about their attitude to all that. This new view of life and the conditions around you has become possible after the Teaching about the contraction of illusion that was given through our Messenger. Therefore, you have subconsciously started to take everything around you in a different way; you have become thoughtful about creating circumstances around you and about your influence on everything around you in the physical world.

This is the new view of the world. The bigger the number of people who realize that the world around represents a gigantic illusion and that the manifestation of this illusion is completely determined by the collective consciousness of mankind, the more conscious your attitude to your thoughts, feelings, and actions will be; for it is you who create everything around you and all the circumstances of your life. The fact that the changes that have occurred in your consciousness take their time to be manifested in the physical world is just determined by the inertness of matter and by the impossibility for it to appear instantly in front of you in its new form. Another braking function is the consciousness of most of the part of mankind that has not awoken yet and cannot have such critical influence like the consciousness of those people who have started to realize the Divine Laws and make attempts to follow them in their lives.

Therefore, it is in your interests and in the interests of the whole of mankind to spread these Teachings and this Knowledge that you receive through our Messages as widely as possible. You can notice that the information, being received by you, does not differ much from the fundamentals of most of religions of the world. Still, there is a small difference and the difference is connected with the individual inner Path to which we direct you, the Path of cognition of the world through your heart. For any outer knowledge comes to you from without; and therefore, you are inclined not to trust that knowledge. When you become capable of getting the information coming from within you, you take that information in a completely different way. Even if it does not contain anything new for you, the whole incoming knowledge is interpreted in a different way, and it comes home to your consciousness.

There are different stages of perception of information. When you realize in your outer mind that you already know this and have heard it before, it does not mean that you have deeply felt this information and this Teaching in your heart and have realized it to the extent that you become one with this Knowledge and Teaching. Only when you become one with the Teaching, do you become a bearer of this Teaching, and you inseparably link your life with it and submit to the Law that you have accepted with your whole being.

There are different stages of the realization of the Divine Law, and only when you receive the Law from the depth of your heart, do you become the executor of the Law, and you become capable of influencing the life around you without words and without actions. You acquire an ability to influence the environment around you by your presence. You just meditate, stay in bliss and satisfaction, and the life around you changes as if by magic.

That is a very high level of achievement to which all of you should aspire. But in order to have the state of a deep meditation in your world, you should think about creating the conditions for such meditations. Your cities and even less populated places are filled with so much negative energy that it is difficult for you to get in touch with your Higher Self, as well as being hard for us to reach out to your consciousness, which is constantly shielded by negative energies. Therefore, again and again we draw your attention to the conditions in which you live. You should have a chance to stay alone and apply efforts to spend some time in places where you can restore your energy. When you gain the standard of the Divine state within yourselves, you will know where to aspire, and you will limit by yourselves the influence of those negative energies on you in which your world abounds. We give you a chance to compare your vibrations with the vibrations of our incarnated representative on Earth so that you do not lose your Path. We drop a saving rope to you, and it depends only on you whether to accept our help or not.

At all times there were incarnated people who were bearing the Divine vibrations of purity. And there are such people among you. If your eyes were open and your ears could hear, every day you would thank God for sending His incarnated Messengers to you. But you go past them, even taking no notice.

Therefore, it is your first duty to note the manifestation of Divinity in the people around you and help such people because they carry the burden of your karma.

Honoring saints and yogis who incarnate to take people's karma upon themselves in order to transmute it, is very common in the East. There are also many people incarnated in the West who are not of this world and who take and carry the burden of your karma. Learn to be grateful to such people. They cannot always adapt to the conditions of your society because your society is like a company of the insane for those people. However, you hurry to announce that your saints are insane. Your world is upside-down. The least worthy have everything while those who bear the burden of mankind eke out a miserable existence. However, it has always been this way over the period of modern history.

Your world is an upside-down world. And when you learn to recognize the manifestation of Divinity in your world and separate it from any non-divine manifestation in your consciousness, you will really be able to influence the world around you and transform it.

But first you should learn to recognize the Divine manifestation within yourself. Then you will be able to draw similar Divine manifestations from space according to your vibrations. The islets of Divinity will expand and multiply in your world, and we will be able to come to you, first in our denser bodies and then in our lighter bodies. And the prophecy about the Ascended Masters walking among you will come true, and you will be able to communicate with us.

Therefore, it depends only on you that the prophecy becomes the reality in your time.

Create the islets of Divinity and move to them at least for a while.

I AM Kuthumi.

Comments on the Path of apprenticeship

Lord Maitreya
April 29, 2006

I AM Maitreya. I have come to you again, and as always, I have come to guide you along your Path. Your Path, as you have already understood from my previous Dictations, is closely connected with the Path of Initiations. This Path is your shortest way Home, to God. And if you are still doubtful about it and take the guidance that is being given to you in this cycle of the Dictations skeptically, well, that is your choice and your time has not yet come. You have the right to wander in your illusion, trying to get pleasure from your physical world.

However, you will feel less pleasure with every incarnation of yours, for your soul comes to this world to find the Path while you are still trying to find the meaning of your existence within your limited world, having no eagerness to raise your consciousness and look up, to turn to God and see the whole limitedness of your world.

You are in a prison formed of limitations of your consciousness. Only you can destroy the walls of your prison. I can help you with that, but you should turn to me for help. I give help to everyone who asks me. My help is connected with the destruction of your ego and of your attachments to the physical world. When you start your advancement along the Path, many of you consider the situation that you find yourselves in as a ruin of everything. You see how your stereotypes and attachments are destroyed one after another; and your ego trembles at those trials and suggests that you are going the wrong way and that the Path to God is only eternal bliss and peace. Yes indeed, you are moving toward bliss and peace, but in order to achieve the state of peace you should reject everything that impedes your advancement and makes you come to this world again and again and endure suffering.

Sufferings and lofty states of consciousness are so interwoven and mixed in your world that sometimes you do not understand anything in your life at all. I try to take you out of your habitual life to make you look at your life from another visual angle.

This Path is inseparably connected with giving up your ego; and simultaneously, you should acquire the state of Oneness with all around you and the state of complete humility before God, before the Higher Law that there is in this universe. Any change, not to mention my fearful stories, becomes an obstacle for many of you, and you feel fear and do not wish to accept the conditions that we offer you. Well, you feel fear, and consequently, the first thing that you should do is to get rid of your fear. That fear is similar to the one that you feel during your transition to the other world. That is what you call death in your language. However, I am telling you that the true death for you is the condition of thoughtlessly staying in your world and your attachment to the world. In that case, you truly risk dying because it is not terrible to change bodies, but it is sad if you lose your soul.

But you do not even understand that, because your consciousness is attached to your physical bodies and to everything around you in the physical world. As this world will soon cease to exist, you will really become extinct if you do not turn your consciousness to the Higher worlds. You choose between the perishable and the imperishable, between the physical world and the real Divine world. That is the whole Path of Initiations. When you enter my School and start following the Path of Initiations, you just start seeing consciously how you have to make your choices between the perishable and the imperishable day after day. When you make the right choices and free yourself from another attachment, you feel joy, causeless joy that overflows your whole being. But if you cannot get rid of some habit or attachment when the time has come to get rid of it, you feel depression and the lack of meaning of your existence.

I change your states, and you have your trials. It is similar to the way you train your pets. Unfortunately, sometimes there is no chance to reach your consciousness directly, and we are forced to influence you through your states. Thus, you have an opportunity to move along the Path and to understand where you move.

Many of you are waiting for me to come to you personally or through my Messenger to announce to you that you have entered my School and to give another examination or a test. Believe me, all of you have been under my intent observation for a long time and have been learning your lessons while being in your usual life conditions.

Your external circumstances and the people who you meet represent the best tests and the best examinations for you.

So, do not worry that you haven't been informed about your entering my School. You will know about it when it is needed. But you should treat any losses and troubles in your life as my tests. You pass your initiations and move up to the next class when you make the right choices and come to the right conclusions as a result of your tests.

Therefore, do not rush to get some super-mystical experience. You will face exactly the situation that you should face in your life to work off another attachment and imperfection. And because all of your attachments are connected with the most ordinary things, it is in your everyday life where you should start getting rid of your attachments.

It is very easy to get rid of your bad habits if you are in a favorable environment. But staying constantly where there are temptations is the most difficult initiation, and none of the

Schools of Mystery of the past could offer you such a difficult test.

So, watch yourself and your reactions to all your life situations that you face every day. And then when you pass all the necessary examinations, you will be cleansed from your attachments to such an extent that you will be able to see me and meet me. Then for the first time you will know that you have been studying at my School and have graduated from it successfully.

It is similar to your distance learning, staying where you are living now, and then the time comes, and you go to another city to get a diploma, and you receive it.

Thus, those of you who have written their letters to me and have sent them with the help of the angels, have entered my School. But if you still treat the situations that you face in your life unconsciously, without making proper conclusions as a result, I won't be able to spare you my time any more. There is no place for lazy and careless students in my School. The time for your education has not come yet.

I have told you everything that you should know by now. However, it doesn't mean that I have left you and will not watch or look after you in the near future. Try to keep your consciousness constantly tuned to the Ray of the Hierarchy because in that case it is easier for us to work with you and lead you. We send our Messengers exactly for you so that you can keep your guiding lines. So, use all of the help that we give you.

And now I say goodbye to you, and I hope for future meetings.

I AM Maitreya.

We are calling you to follow our Path

Beloved El Morya
April 30, 2006

I AM El Morya, coming to you!

I have come to inform you that this is the end of the spring cycle of the Dictations that we have been giving through our Messenger.

We are happy with the possibility that we have had, and we are satisfied with the fact that we have been able to give all that we planned to give in this cycle of the Dictations. Unlike the previous cycle of the Dictations that we gave in Altai in the winter, in this Dictation cycle we have paid more attention to your Path. The time has come to accustom you to the Path that has been planned for you. This Path has always existed, and there were always Schools and Ashrams created in this or that part of Earth where the Hierarchy of Light gave the Teaching for its disciples. The time has come when we see the possibility to resume our practice of working with non-ascended mankind through our outer Schools.

Therefore, we try to give all the necessary knowledge about The Path of Initiations so you can consciously make your choice and step on the Path.

The difference between our Path and many other teachings is that we lead you through your heart and let you come into contact with the true Real world through your mystical experiences and insights. Having that possibility in your outer consciousness, to realize the existence of the other Divine world, you consciously aspire to become free of everything impeding you from entering that world. It is your ego and your attachments to the physical world, to things of this world and to people, as well as your habits and imperfections that impede you. Therefore, you consciously step on the Path and you are ready to sacrifice much in order to get the true knowledge. There are many other teachings that use very similar methods. Yet, there are some differences. Therefore, your immediate task is to find these differences, using the most reliable guide — your heart.

We are giving our Teaching through our Messenger. Every one of you who reads our Messages already gets into the outer circle of our disciples and enters the Guru-Chela relationship with our Messenger as a representative of our Hierarchy on the physical plane.

Therefore, as soon as you choose to read our Messages, you already become our disciples. However, there are many levels of Guru-chela relationships. You mount the next step when you consciously make your choice in favor of our Teaching. In your consciousness you try to understand the difference from other teachings, and you make your choice in favor of the Teaching that you receive through our Messenger. In this case you limit your freedom, yet, in return you acquire better understanding and better awareness of the knowledge that you receive through our Messenger.

At the next level you consciously accept our Messenger as your Guru. In this cycle of the Dictations, we hurried those of you who are ready to make this choice consciously and to rise to that level of your apprenticeship.

The next level begins when the Messenger takes you as candidates for apprenticeship. The difference of that level from the previous ones is that the Messenger partly takes on the karmic obligations and bears responsibility for her disciples. Further relations that you experience are entirely under the authority of our Messenger. She determines how those relations should develop.

Therefore, we are trying to restore the Guru-chela relationships that belong to the Ascended Masters' disciple succession. Yet, those relationships are always built at a new level and are determined by the conditions formed on Earth. We do not need millions of followers who only show their undertaking of obligations, but do not let our Teaching into their hearts. We aspire to complete mutual understanding and collaboration with our disciples. Our Messenger is just like a crutch for you during that period of time until you can go independently and get in touch with us directly. Even in this case, you will need our Messenger as a lighthouse to show you the Path in storms and gales of earthly life.

Therefore, we will go on giving our instructions in the following cycles of the Dictations. We ask you not to waste your time but to take all of the instructions contained in our Dictations not as abstract ones, but as the immediate guiding principles that you should use in your lives.

I am a very concrete Master, and I do not like to beat about the bush. Therefore, I am calling you not to wait for somebody to give you more detailed instructions for your actions. We are giving the general direction. You have to get all the details immediately from your heart.

If you reread the Dictations that we have been giving through our Messenger for the last year, you will understand that there is enough information in those Dictations to start concrete activity. You can start with the environment around you and with the habits that you have. Do try to start — not tomorrow but right now. First, free yourself from your biggest attachment that impedes you most of all in your life. That might be fear, inclination to censure and criticism, smoking, or any other attachment and any other imperfection.

Then you will find another imperfection and then the next one. You will always know only one immediate task that you should implement. Then you will be able to start deciding the next issue.

Do not aim at too much activity at once. Take the issues that you can decide.

Sometimes it is much more difficult for many to get rid of smoking than even to build an ashram.

We are calling you to follow our Path. We are telling you that the way is open. But you make your own choice, and nobody can force you to make this choice.

You are mature individuals, and we talk to you as with our equals who are just a bit behind in their advancement along the Path.

So now I say goodbye to you, and I wish you success on your Path!

I AM El Morya.

Messages from the Ascended Masters between the third and fourth cycles of Dictations

Let your consciousness go beyond the limits of your family, your city, and your country and take the whole Earth as your native home

Lord Maitreya
June 5, 2006

I AM Maitreya, having come to you again. Today I have come on behalf of the Karmic Board in order to tell you the joyful news connected with the transformation that has occurred on the planet these days. Many of you, who are used to reading our Messages and who serve us faithfully and try to spread these Messages all over the world as widely as possible, your efforts were not in vain. Your efforts have been noticed by the Karmic Board. You know that the sessions of the Karmic Board are held twice a year during the periods of summer and winter solstices. But you should also be informed of the sessions of the Karmic Board that are held constantly and between those major sessions.

Today I have to tell you that there has been a session this night at which our Messenger has been present. It is the first time in the history of humankind that at this session the question has been raised concerning the possibility of giving the right to those of you who have taken immediate and active part in the activity related to spreading our Messages and to translating them into other languages of the world, to be present at the next session of the Karmic Board in the finer bodies. You will have an opportunity to take part in the planning of your personal karma descending. You will be able to regulate your karma descending, slowing it down or accelerating it for your life-streams, according to your wish and within the limits of the existing karmic opportunities.

That will help you in your further lives, for the Law of Karma is an impersonal Law, and karma descending does not depend on your willingness or unwillingness. However, the good karma or energy that has been accumulated by you during the spreading of our Messages can be used to regulate the process of your karma descending and even to reduce the karmic burden.

You should not disregard that opportunity, because that opportunity will allow some individuals from non-ascended humankind to cooperate with the Karmic Board for the first time.

It is the first time that this opportunity has been granted; and that means that we try to spread these Teachings as widely as possible, and we even make some allowances to make this process more successful and faster.

It is possible that you will not remember in your consciousness about the events that will take place at night during your visit to the Karmic Board session. However, many of you will perceive the traces of the night events in your outer awake consciousness and will get a perfectly clear understanding of the changes that will take place in your lives in the nearest future.

I am glad to give you that important off-schedule information.

And I am even happier that I have a chance to give that Dictation during our Messenger's stay in the city of Novosibirsk. Some people call this city the capital of Siberia.

And it may be true.

Still, it is important that we are giving this Dictation in Novosibirsk, and thus we have a chance to fix and enhance our presence in this city.

In fact, the receiving of our Messages is always accompanied with a huge flow of Light to the physical plane and to the finer planes that are close to the physical plane according to the vibrations. So every reception of the Dictations at a new place brings its blessings to the country and the city where this reception takes place.

So, I congratulate you, and I honestly hope that you will spend all the Light and all the energy received by you on the Divine purposes.

Now I would like to give you the other joyful news. According to this news, the world is ready for more rapid changes at the moment. And those changes that are connected with the changes of your consciousness are so fast, as never before. However, there is a certain skew of energies. The regions of the world where our Messages, given through our Messenger, are read get very much Light, and people's consciousness changes very rapidly.

At the same time there are other regions in the world that do not have an opportunity to get and read our Messages. The imbalance of energies in those regions results in different natural disasters and cataclysms.

It is a great pity that America is one of those regions.

That country, on which the Masters set their great hopes, lost our focus of Light. And now it is forced to receive the Light from the other country. I clearly understand that it is a very hard step for the proud Americans to accept the Teaching coming from Russia. However, it is exactly this way: By accepting this Teaching coming from Russia that America can restore the energy balance and thus avoid many natural disasters as well as economic failures.

Therefore, I ask you to help spread this Message of mine in the land of America as well as other Messages we are giving through our Messenger.

The geographical locations themselves, of America and Russia, being on opposite sides of the globe, will promote alignment of the situation on the planet as possible changes in consciousness, occur equally in the people of these countries.

I appeal to the daughters and the sons of America through the Russian Messenger. And I am asking you to overcome those qualities of yours that impede your perception of the information coming from the other country.

I honestly hope that there are those among the American people who will respond to my call and will be able to overcome those negative character traits that make Americans feel that they are the only people on whom the future of planet Earth depends.

In fact, it is so. You are those people on whom the future of planet Earth depends. And you do not need to announce your ambitions and the priority of your nation and of your country in order to make that future the most favorable. On the contrary, all that you need is to develop the quality of humility and to be on one level with all people inhabiting planet Earth.

There is not any "most important country" on the planet. But there are people who let themselves overcome their own limitations and raise their consciousness to a decent level: the level of god-man, whom all of you should inevitably become.

Therefore, all that you need is not to consider other peoples' standing on the steps of evolution lower than you. No, every nation is a brother or a sister in the Divine family of nations living on Earth. And the earlier you realize your oneness and unite, despite the difference of your inner world and appearance, the faster the desirable changes will occur on Earth.

I am asking you to consider my words thoroughly and finally, let your consciousness go beyond the limits of your family, your city, and your country and take the whole Earth as your native home.

I AM Maitreya,
and I am sending you my Love.

About the forthcoming day of the summer solstice and the Divine favors connected with this day

Lord Maitreya
June 15, 2006

I AM Maitreya, having come again! I have come in order to remind you once again of your opportunities and the dispensation concerning the day of the summer solstice. As always, the session of the Karmic Board will begin on that day; and you can take advantage of the opportunity given to you annually and write letters to the Karmic Board. The content of those letters can be made up by you independently. However, I shall remind you of the existing general rules. First of all, you thank the Karmic Board for the favors rendered to you earlier, and then you can start stating your request. If that request concerns favors you expect to receive personally or by your relatives, then after listing your requests you should write the obligations that you voluntarily take upon yourself and that you will carry out in the following half a year until the day of the winter solstice and the new session of the Karmic Board connected with that day.

Your requests and wishes should be stated very simply with the surnames and names of those people for whom you are asking.

If your wishes are connected with the general situation on planet Earth or with the requests concerning the consciousness development prospects on the planet, it is not necessary for you to take obligations connected with reading decrees, prayers, or with implementation of other actions. In that case your request will be fulfilled according to the good karma momentum already accumulated by you.

Therefore, before writing your letters, carefully consider your requests and motives.

Do not burden yourself with excessive obligations. Take exactly the obligations that you can fulfill without excessive effort. Many people take such big obligations in their letters that the first problem met in their life forces them to forget completely about the obligations taken and refuse to fulfill them. You may take a very small obligation, but fulfill it with joy and love every day. Do not aim at taking too much upon yourself. Sometimes one prayer read per day is enough for help to be rendered. The purer the energy that you put in reading a prayer, the greater is the effect that you reach. And even one phrase: "Let good befall the world!" said by you sincerely, is enough to ease the destinies of many.

I have come to remind you of the opportunity you have which helps those of you who annually use that opportunity.

And now I would like to remind you of one more dispensation or Divine mercy which concerns the 23rd day of each month. On that day, thanks to Heavens' mercy, you can lighten the following month's karma for yourselves and for your relatives. It is enough for you to dedicate everything you do on this day to the transmutation of the next month's karma.

You make a call: **"I dedicate all my good actions performed by me on this day to the transmutation of the next month's karma."**

You can list the concrete karma you intend to transmute: for example, the karma between you and your children, your husband or wife, or your colleagues at work. Then, when reading your prayers or Rosaries, or when rendering some charitable help, constantly remember that the energy of all your actions is directed to the transmutation of karma. Do not forget that part of energy that you release on this day will be directed by the Ascended Realm to the world karma transmutation and mainly to the part of the world where it concerns the prevention of significant cataclysms and natural disasters.

Now I am leaving you, and I will be glad if my advice and recommendations will help you and you will take advantage of them in your lives.

I AM Maitreya.

You are those who should make changes on Earth according to the Divine models

Lord Maitreya
June 18, 2006

I AM Maitreya, having come to you today!

I AM coming to remind you once again of the fact that now you have a chance to take part in the process of your interaction with us, the Ascended Masters, with greater awareness.

Through our Messenger, who is a Guru for you, we have a chance to establish closer relations with you through our Dictations, which we try to give you regularly. You have a chance to communicate with us consciously. It seems to you that your outer consciousness does not take part in the process of communication. However, you already communicate with us because you raise the level of your vibrations through your connection with us via our Messages. And as soon as the level of your vibrations reaches a certain point, we have a chance to be present in you, in those of you, who find it necessary to welcome me or the other Ascended Masters to your temples. We cannot enter until you ask us about it, but as soon as the call is uttered, we must respond. That is the Cosmic Law. We cannot use your invitation and enter your temples if your level of vibrations does not allow us to do that. Therefore, you should constantly be ready for communication with us. The properties of matter are such that they follow your consciousness obediently. And if you set yourself an objective to establish a connection with us, then sooner or later, you will get a chance for a conscious communication with the Ascended Hosts. The whole matter is in your consciousness. To what extent you concede an opportunity of such communication is in your consciousness. We are giving you a rope in the form of our Messenger. Please, use every opportunity given to you.

We cannot help you until you ask us for help, but when we offer you our help, you should also accept it because any cosmic opportunity has its deadline. And now, when the time has accelerated and the space is ready, your wishes and your thoughts are displayed very quickly by the obedient matter. Remember that. Always remember that, being in the vanity of life and in the midst of the masses of people.

I have come now in order to talk to you about one more opportunity that is approaching and that can be open before you now. I would like to turn your attention to the conditions around you on Earth. You can perceive everything around you as perfect, but believe me; your world is very far from being perfect. But as the time has changed, and opportunities have approached, this is the right time for you in your consciousness to treat everything around you consciously. Notice imperfect patterns in people's behavior and in the life around you, and replace those unsuccessful manifestations with more perfect Divine patterns. To start with, try to do it only in your consciousness. Do dream of how it is possible to replace the imperfection that you see in front of you with a more perfect manifestation, and after that, watch what will happen. The greater your aspiration is, then the sooner that imperfect manifestation leaves your life. You do not have to struggle with the imperfection; you do not need to feel any sense of struggle. You just replace the imperfect manifestation with the perfect one — first, in your consciousness.

If you are impatient and the circumstances allow you, you can take immediate part in the replacement of the outer manifestation with the more perfect model. In order to do that, you can literally roll up your sleeves and get down to concrete work on the physical plane. The most important thing is not to focus on censuring the imperfection. Do not contribute your energy to it; do not send the energy of your attention to it.

And vice versa, if you see a perfect manifestation, send your energy to it, and multiply any manifestation of Divinity in your lives. Learn to create like Gods because in the nearest future, you will have to realize your responsibility for everything around, and the most important thing is to realize your responsibility for the fact that you are those who should make changes on Earth according to the Divine models.

I am glad that I have had that chance to give you this short Teaching, and what is more, I am happy that I have had a chance to give this Dictation through our Messenger during her visit to Moscow.

I would also like to take this opportunity to inform you that now, right during these very days of the summer solstice, your opportunities to change the circumstances of your life and of everything around you are especially strong.

I wish you success, and I hope for future meetings on the Path of Initiations!

I AM Maitreya!

Book 4

Cycle 4: Messages of the Ascended Masters
from July 1 to July 21, 2006

You are forming the new reality in your consciousness

Sanat Kumara
July 1, 2006

I AM Sanat Kumara, having come again. As it has already become a tradition, I have come to give a Message to open the new cycle of the Dictations that we intend to give for mankind of Earth. This time, I am pleased to announce that we are ready to give our Messages in Bulgaria, a country which is no less important than Russia, since it is here that we plan to create the conditions necessary for rapid growth of the consciousness of people living in this country.

We are glad that we are having an opportunity to speak again because it is not always possible to realize our plans on Earth. This is due to the large unpredictability of the situation on Earth, when all of our plans are ruined because of a wrong action by only one person. That is always deplorable. However, we hope that there are still a sufficient number of incarnated individuals who will be able to help us in the realization of our plans and intentions.

I have come to remind you once again of the obligations that you have taken upon yourselves before your incarnation. You have been preparing for your missions for many incarnations, and you have all the necessary skills and knowledge in this incarnation. All that impedes your fulfilling of the taken obligations is your fussy, unruly, human mind. Your carnal mind makes you lose your Path, thinking of thousands of reasons and millions of arguments, while the voice in your heart continues to send gentle quiet signals to you, calling you to the Path, to the top, to the manifestation of the plans of the Brotherhood.

Therefore, think once again about the extent of your attachment to the physical world around you, and how important it is for you to listen to your heart's voice and to leave the fuss of the world in order to implement what is destined for this planet. Your planet should become the planet of the developed consciousness. The vibrations of Earth should allow those beings, who you now call the Ascended Masters, to come into incarnation. They are the Teachers of humankind; and now many of you are incarnated in order to create the conditions on Earth necessary for their incarnation. Think about the important task that you are facing. Try to track the moment when your consciousness starts slipping down, gradually refusing Divine models and replacing them with merely human aspirations. Your carnal mind starts activating in you as your consciousness approaches the idea of serving us. It is very dodgy, and it gives you the arguments that your outer consciousness cannot neglect. You leave everything to get that piece of bread to satisfy your physical hunger instead of taking care of your spiritual food and the daily bread that Jesus talked about.[12]

Do not think much about how to support your physical existence. Do think only about how to fulfill your Divine plan. Or is there so little Faith in you that you cannot believe that God will take care of you?

The Teaching remains the same. It is given over and over again, and only the dullness of your consciousness and the inertness of matter have made you listen to the same Teaching for many thousands and millions of years, incarnation by incarnation. You listen but cannot hear, because every time, again and again, you deviate from the guidelines that you have accepted and at the

---

[12] "Give us this day our daily bread." (Matthew 6:9-13)

moment of the insight again you rush in pursuit of useless things of the physical world.

It hurts to observe that. Lack of Faith is the main disease of humankind. Look at animals and birds. God takes care of all living creatures. No one dies of hunger while living in natural conditions. Only when man interferes in the Divine Laws with his imperfect consciousness and tries to create, replacing God with himself, do different disasters and cataclysms occur.

Therefore, we repeat over and over again that your only enemy is hiding in your imperfect consciousness, in your heart that does not let God in.

Now I would like to remind you again that at times all the Ascended Hosts, holding their breath, wait for your choice, the choice that you may or may not make. And the development of evolution on Earth depends on every choice you make. Believe me; everything you do every day is very important. Consider your everyday activities. Try to analyze how long you have been thinking about God and your Divine purpose during the day. How many of you are really ready to sacrifice something for the well-being of the world?

Too many speak about serving and about the work they do for God. However, when the talk turns to doing even one small but concrete thing, there are thousands of reasons and arguments that appear which make the person forget about God, about serving, and rush for the things and pleasures which should not have been in your consciousness since long ago.

I have come to you today, and I am very glad that I can give a talk again on that ancient Teaching because each of you who are reading these lines can wake up at any moment in order to start acting in the new reality.

You are forming the new reality in your consciousness. And as soon as you suddenly realize in surprise how aimlessly the people around you waist their energy, you wake up to the new reality and become those warriors-votaries on whom we can rely. The whole institution of the Guru-chela relationship is designed to constantly keep your consciousness at a decent level. It is very seldom that an earthling can manage without outside assistance, and go through the Path of Initiations on his own. I can tell you that if you are not a partial or full incarnation of an Ascended Master, you will not be able to go through your Path and reach the top of the Divine consciousness on your own without the Teacher's help. Therefore, we send our Messengers again and again so you could see the Path and remember your obligations and those plans that you intended to implement before your incarnation. You have assumed those plans yourselves in your higher consciousness. Now you have to try and reach the highest state of your consciousness in order to remember everything that you have planned before your incarnation on Earth.

There are many people who read our Messages. There are those who start going along the Path of Initiations. But only a few pass the tests and continue going along the Path. It was always like that. We hope very much that your time will be an exception, and we will be able to come to thousands and hundreds of thousands of incarnated people to communicate with them at the level of their outer consciousness and begin to work toward the transformation of planet Earth so rapidly that all the changes will be observed by the generation that is living now.

I need volunteers who would wish to serve the Brotherhood. I am personally ready to come to you and help you on the condition that your intentions are supported by concrete conscious actions to transform the consciousness of earthlings.

I AM Sanat Kumara, having been with you today, and I hope for future meetings!

Your level of consciousness is determined by the Divine qualities that you gain on your Path

Beloved Great Divine Director
July 2, 2006

I AM Great Divine Director, coming to you today through our Messenger. I have come in order to draw your attention to the current information connected with the session of the Karmic Board, which has just ended. This time, we took part in this session with high spirits because the changes that we had been waiting for started to be realized. The rate of the changes has even exceeded our expectations. Not all, and far from all, have accepted our Messenger and the Messages that we give through her, but there is already a sufficient number of individuals who have started reading our Messages and began working on themselves, their thoughts, and their feelings, so that the changes are beginning to occur in the consciousness of people. And you know that everything in this world is determined by your consciousness, by the level of your consciousness that you are able to achieve and keep with your daily hard work.

Our task as the Ascended Hosts, is to direct your development and help to ensure that you do not go beyond the boundary of the evolutional corridor given to you. Now we are happy to state that you have moved away from that boundary of the evolutional corridor, which could lead to a catastrophe even if there was one more slight deviation from the set evolutional course. We have obtained a stable and balanced state. And mankind is ready to continue its evolution in this state, and we are able to direct mankind and to coordinate the creative efforts of the most advanced individuals. Fortunately, there are more and more of those individuals. Many of you who have found the Path and the Teaching again are able to do great things. You do not realize the work and responsibility that rests on your shoulders. However, not much is required of you. You just have to remember every day that you are not just the physical body that you see as your reflection in the mirror. Your life does not end with the death of your physical body; it continues. You will evolve more and more successfully when you constantly identify yourselves not with the physical body but with your immortal part, and when you constantly think about how your present actions influence your future and the circumstances of your next incarnation. Unfortunately, most of mankind still does not believe in reincarnation and lives as if only death is ahead. Every time you think that way, you limit your possibilities and lose the opportunity to connect with the Higher octaves and with us, the Ascended Hosts. Your world just obediently follows your consciousness. That is why you are being told about the expansion of consciousness and about the ability to allow more expansion and to exceed the usual scope of a single religion or a single country.

That is why we would like for our Messenger to have an opportunity to communicate with representatives of different religious beliefs and of different countries, because the information we can give through her depends on the scope of her consciousness. It is very seldom that we can meet a conductor so diversified and at the same time unconditionally devoted to us, so that we can give the amount of information through her that mankind needs at the present stage. But mostly, we have to use the conductor that we are able to obtain. Therefore, I appeal to you to please render all the help that you can to our Messenger because we might not get another conductor of that kind in the near future, someone who can bring up their level of conscious to work with the Brotherhood. Therefore, do accept our Messages with gratitude. Your level of consciousness is not determined by the amount of mental information that you are able to let into your mind. Your level of consciousness is determined by the Divine qualities that you gain on your Path, and devotion, sincerity, unselfishness, and humility are the most important among them.

Without these qualities, no mental skills will allow you to ascend to a new level of consciousness.

Therefore, each time we come, we keep repeating the importance of the development of the Divine qualities within you. Your aspiration compels you to get what is necessary for your development. Therefore, aspiration and persistence are the next qualities that you will need.

Think carefully about what I have said and about the requirements that our disciples should meet. How many of you are ready to maintain the right guidelines in your consciousness every day? Does your daily fuss and the objectives that you set for yourselves in your world divert you from service? Each of you chooses the extent of the sacrifice that you can make. But I can assure you that the utmost sacrifice you can make is to completely renounce everything that attaches you to the physical world and to achieve that state of liberation from the bondage of matter that will allow you to never incarnate in the physical body.

Thus, there is an evolutionary way of development that we teach through our Messenger, just the same way we taught about this Path through many other Messengers and prophets in ancient times and also not so long ago. You can always catch common things in many Teachings that we gave. And despite the distortions that were introduced by the followers who either did not get the essence of the Teachings completely or deliberately distorted the Teaching, the essence can still be distinguished in many religions, faiths, and doctrines by those with an open and inquisitive mind. There are no contradictions between the Teaching that we are giving through our Messenger now and those fundamentals that we gave through all the founders of all world religions. Do try to catch common things in your consciousness, and you will understand that exactly the same Teaching that we are giving now, also lies behind many dogmas and rules. There is no other Teaching in the world that we would give, but there are many people who try to gain the attention of the masses and invent rather strange practices and doctrines, and what is more, find their followers. Therefore, it is very important for you to raise your consciousness to the level where the veil falls from your eyes, and you can see the nature of each false guru and can distinguish where there is truth in his teaching and where there is a blatant lie. Therefore, we do not hesitate to repeat again and again that your main tool, by which you should be guided when acting in your world, is your heart and the sincerity of your motives. If you are honest, unselfish, and inquisitive in your mind, you will get access to the true sources and will be able to quench your thirst of knowledge, pressing your lips to the cup of cool reviving water of our Teaching that we always give for you, the people of Earth.

The complexity of living in your time is caused by the fact that informational flows are so saturated and littered with different substitutes, that all your attention and intuition are required to sort out these flows. Never aim at trying everything — you can get indigestion. Take only the food that is tested and of high quality, which we give through our Messengers and prophets. Now that you have been warned, you are completely responsible for the choice of literature you read and for the source that you use. This is your choice and you will carry the karma of the wrong choice.

One of the tasks that the Karmic Board performs is to ease the burden of karma caused by the wrong choice of the teaching that you decided to follow. In order to lighten the karma of going along the wrong path, you can apply to the Karmic Board and to me personally, and ask to create such circumstances for you in your lives so that you can understand and realize all your delusions and can consciously overcome the karma from the wrong choices in your lives.

Today we have been talking about many things, and I hope that the talk will be useful for you.

I AM Great Divine Director, always with you!

I offer you this method in the hope that you will be able to use it in your everyday spiritual work

Lord Shiva
July 3, 2006

I AM Shiva, having come again!

I AM Shiva, I have come!

I have come and I am glad to meet you through my Messenger again!

Since we finished the spring cycle of the Dictations, several important events in the finer world have taken place, and the most important among them is that humankind of Earth have started to give in to the efforts we tirelessly applied and to move along the evolutionary Path that was planned. Some time ago, none of the Ascended Masters was sure that it would be possible to carry out the forthcoming transformations on Earth. Now with certainty, we can state the fact that we have managed to do everything so that humankind can return to the evolutionary Path of development and harmonize a part of the distorted energies of the past. Now we should not slow down the pace. Therefore, I have come in order to direct you to your further deeds and provide instructions to those who are capable of perceiving them.

The main and most important thing for humankind now is harmonization. By harmonization I mean a combination of measures and methods that will lead to the levelling of consciousness development rates in different regions of Earth, in different countries and continents. You know that our Messages are spread very successfully in Eurasia. But there are other continents. There, people know very little about our Messages and the new Teaching that we are giving. Therefore, there are two ways to harmonize the situation on the planet. The first way assumes intensive spreading of our Messages to other continents, especially in America. The second way is simpler and at the same time more difficult because it requires of you a particular degree of selflessness and certain spiritual achievements. That way assumes particular spiritual work to be done on the finer plane. Now I will explain to you what it exactly means.

Every time you read our Messages, imagine the people of those continents where our Messages are not accessible so far. Imagine Africa, America, and Australia. And every time visualize that you communicate with the representatives of those countries and give them a notion about the Teaching that we give you in the Dictations. If there are people among your acquaintances who live on those continents, then please, do visualize those people and tell them in your mind about the knowledge you have received, and have a mental talk with them. Try to explain to them in your words, the foundations of the Teaching you have received. Thus, the goal will be achieved, and our energy of changes will touch the consciousness of the people who live on those continents, and the desire will rise in them to read our Messages and to assimilate the information contained in them. Even if those people's external consciousness does not respond to the work you do, their fine bodies will receive the impression necessary for the changes. And again the foundation of the changes will be laid by you together with us.

I am giving you this method, and you can use it for working with the people who have a big influence in the countries where they live. They can be outstanding statesmen, artists, and science and culture representatives. Your consciousness will give you a hint with whom and how you can work. I am offering you this method in the hope that you will be able to use it in your everyday spiritual work. Before you start your visualizations, please do take care about your harmonious state of consciousness so that none of your small everyday home cares can worry you. Take care of the purity of your inner space, for you will transfer your inner state to the people with whom you will be working distantly.

The purer your thoughts are and the more elevated your state is, then the more wonderful results you will achieve.

I have to warn you of another important moment. If your state is not harmonious, and your motives are not pure, the energy that you will put into your work can create your karma, which you will have to work off yourself later. Always remember that karma is created not only by your actions and deeds but also by your thoughts and feelings. Therefore, I turn to you now in the hope that you have already read all the Dictations we have been giving through our Messenger, and your consciousness is completely prepared for this important work we are asking you for.

I am talking to you as to equal beings capable of understanding our problems and of sacrificing small everyday interests for the Common Good, for the prosperity of your mother planet.

Always remember that there are no enemies on your planet, there are only people in poor states of consciousness, including ignorance.

Ignorance and lack of knowledge are the enemies you will have to fight with. Therefore, bring the Light of knowledge to the people of planet Earth. Come up, kindle your torches, and bring the Light to those who need it.

Exactly the same principle can be laid as the foundation of your work with your relatives who need knowledge but for some reason are not ready to apply their own efforts to receive it. Do help them. Tell them about the Teaching. Tell them about it in your mind when you are in a good and harmonious inner state. This particularly concerns your closest relatives with whom you have karmic connections. Try to give them the knowledge at the level of thoughts and feelings. Don't hesitate to send Love to your closest ones. For nothing is as favorable for people's souls as watering them with the energy of Love from your hearts every day.

I was glad to meet you again today. And I hope that this meeting and my talk have been useful for you. I wish you success on your Path!

I AM Shiva, always with you!

The success of your evolution on your beautiful planet depends on the development of the quality of Divine Love in you

Beloved Surya
July 4, 2006

I AM Surya, having come to you today. I have come to you from the Great Central Sun to open another page of the eternal Teaching about Eternal Life and the absence of death. It may seem to you that I am using a very pompous language; however, it is the usual language in the circles and octaves where I come from. Our language does not resemble yours. We speak the language of thought and not even so much the language of thought as the language of energy. We exchange energies, and it is similar to your exchanging your feelings of Love. I have just told you one of the greatest secrets of Space. Everything in this universe is based on the great power of Love, and everything that there is in this universe exists only due to the power of Love.

Love is the essence of this universe. Therefore, your vibrations are solely the vibrations of Love when they are as close to the vibrations of the universe as possible. The more you are able to manifest the quality of Love in your heart, the closer you get to the true reality and move away from your physical illusion. However, there is a big difference between the shades of the quality of Love in your world and in ours. What many of you mean by Love is, in fact, not Love at all. That feeling which you sometimes call love is equal to the sexual instinct or the instinct of a sex, and there is no difference between that feeling and the one which birds and animals have. Therefore, you should think about the quality of the Love you experience. True love has no attachment at all to a definite sex, or to the object of Love. This is an inner feeling, having no attachment to a definite being or an object; it is Love toward everyone, toward the whole of creation, the whole of Life, and the whole universe. Many of you, being in nature, can raise your vibrations to that true feeling of Love. But the power and the fullness of that Love can be even more intense. Your physical bodies simply cannot experience loftier and finer manifestations of this amazing quality of Love. Each of you shows love in your own way, and each of you has your own inherent individual and personal understanding of the quality of love. At the beginning of Creation, God divided his Love into an infinite number of parts, and each of you, being a part of God, received your own little part of Love. Now you have an opportunity to experience that Love and to refine it. That is why you have to get rid of everything in your life that prevents your feeling of Love from growing. Observe your lives thoroughly and try to trace the states you experience most often. You will be surprised that you hardly ever experience the feeling of Love that is inherent in the whole of Creation, the true feeling of Love. And even when the time of your first love comes, it is very seldom that this feeling is not colored with a possessive instinct and the desire to own the object of your love. Therefore, the success of your evolution on your beautiful planet depends on the development of the quality of Divine Love in you.

That is why I have come today to give you this Message based on the feeling of great Love toward mankind of Earth.

And if the other Ascended Masters and I didn't have that feeling of unconditional, perfect Love within, we would hardly be able to come and babysit you, care about you and to give our Teachings and instructions during the whole cycle of the evolution of the material universe.

We know quite well that no matter how you resist, you do not have a choice, and sooner or later you will follow the path destined for you by the plan of the great Creator of this Universe.

And that is the path of the highest Love and the highest bliss. Everything that separates you from that state is subject to gradual refusal and must leave your consciousness and your lives. For such is the Law. You have to make your own choice and to follow this Law — the Law of the highest and unconditional Love.

Now it is hard for you to believe that everything around you is just the manifestation of the non-divine feeling of anti-love. Yes, everything you have created that is not based on the great feeling of Love will disappear in the course of time and will stop existing. What will be left is only what is perfect in God, which is primarily the feeling of Divine unconditional Love, not clouded by human consciousness.

I am very happy to give you this Teaching today. It is a pleasure to talk about Love and to feel Love for you, children of Earth. You cannot even imagine how happy I am.

Now I would like to say a few words concerning our future plans. These plans do not differ from everything you have already heard. We continue to pull mankind of Earth to the level of evolution that it must be at but which it still endeavors to attain. It seems to you that you have made great achievements, but all of your achievements are directed at multiplying the illusion. At the current stage, other achievements are required of you: the achievements in the field of developing the Divine qualities within you, with Divine Love as the main quality. However, there are other qualities that you have to develop in yourselves. In order for you to concentrate on the true inner achievements, you should turn and look inside of yourselves. This is exactly the path that we teach, the path of mystics, the path leading you to your Source.

But in order for you to follow that path, you must renounce your attachments to the world and the achievement of any kind of goals in your world. It is very difficult. In order for you to attain an inner connection with us and with your Higher Self, you need unconditional and absolute Faith. Faith and Love are two sisters, two loving sisters who are inseparable throughout eternity. There is also Hope. Hope alone can expand your consciousness when it seems to you that there is no way out of the deadlock and disorder of the storms of life.

That is why we come, in order to keep you in harmony with the Higher reality and to give you hope for tomorrow, which will no doubt be better than today. For such is the Law of this universe. And with every successive cycle of evolution, you will get closer and closer to the Divine Reality, and it will become easier for you. In the course of time, the awareness of this reality will come, and happiness will overflow in you and will never leave you. The twilight of your consciousness is coming to an end. The new dawn and the awakening in the new reality are ahead.

I am happy to announce the coming of the new reality, the sun of the new reality in your world.

**I AM Surya,
having come to you with a feeling of great Love!**

Only the ignorance and limitations of your consciousness separate you from accepting in your consciousness your unity with every particle of life

Lord Maitreya
July 5, 2006

I AM Maitreya, who has come to you again on this day through my Messenger Tatyana.

I have come in order to remind you that each of you is an inimitable and unique particle of God. In accordance with God's plans, you need to progress — that is, follow the Path of evolutionary development in the way that God had planned it at the beginning of this universe. It seems to you that you are independent and autonomous, that you are absolutely isolated creatures without any connection with each other or with anyone in this Universe. At the level of your consciousness, this belief is almost undeniable. That is because all around you, you see uncontestable proof of this belief, of this viewpoint, of this understanding of the world. Many times you have been given the example that only several centuries ago you thought that Earth was not round and that it did not spin around the sun. Those perspectives and beliefs that you have now will be subject to further change, and in fact, a drastic change. You have mastered your physical world. And because you have mastered your world, you should advance further in your consciousness toward cognizing other worlds, the more subtle ones. And you should feel more and more the connection that exists between you and me, between you and the Ascended Masters, and even between you and each other.

No matter how much it seems to you that you are separated and self-sufficient, with time you will have to feel your unity not only with the One and indivisible Creator of this Universe but also your unity with each of you, your oneness with each other.

Since I have come to you on this day, I would like to use every moment of our meeting productively. Therefore, I am moving on to the main point for which I have come. You know that your planet is not the only planet in the universe. There are other worlds and other star systems. You are not alone in space. Your interactions and your contacts with other cosmic beings, which happen from time to time, cause you to experience different feelings: from fear to curiosity. However, your interaction with other beings that live in the Universe will continue during the process of your development. Everything will depend on your inner state of consciousness. If you continue to insist on your imperfections, you will attract to your planet representatives of similar technocratic civilizations that are focused solely on themselves. Yet, if you try to change yourselves and to concentrate on developing Divine qualities in yourselves, then very soon you will be able to communicate with angels, elementals, and representatives of the worlds that follow the Divine Path of development. That is why we continue to provide more and more reasons in order to convince you that you need to start working closely on your consciousness.

The entire Teaching that we give is inseparably connected by only one thing: the changing of your consciousness, the expansion of your consciousness. We do everything we can so that you are able to go beyond the limitations that are inherent in you — the limitations of religious character, of your nation's culture and interests. Everything that is directed toward convergence, toward integration, and toward the Common Good is beneficial; everything that is directed toward separation is subject to oblivion.

However, the unity that we talk about is only possible when you unite with each other based on common principles. It is impossible to unite when everyone defends only his or her own point of view, and does not want to see the other person's perspective. However, there is a common point of contact, a common position that allows unity when one takes it. That position implies giving up one's ego. The path of giving up one's ego is what we teach you. Your detachment is strong within you only as long as each of you defends your own point of view to the disadvantage of another person. And only when you are able to give up within yourselves that what prevents you from seeing the other person's point of view objectively, only then can you move along the path toward unity and agreement.

Much is said about unity, but little changes. That is because everyone who talks about unity expects that everybody should listen to his or her point of view and share it. However, all you need to do is rise up in your consciousness to the level where all contradictions are alleviated and invisible.

This is the task that we want each of you to resolve in your consciousness.

Try to analyze what separates you from the representatives of different spiritual lineages, and you will understand that the only thing that separates you is your ego, your ignorance. As always, we offer you the path, which by following you will be able to get rid of your imperfections and reach the cherished unity.

In fact, only the ignorance and limitations of your consciousness separate you from accepting in your consciousness your unity with every particle of life.

In the near future, you have to take steps and make efforts directed at overcoming the inner limitations that separate you from each other. Note that I am not saying that you should convince anyone that his or her teaching is false and that yours is the true one. I am saying that you should remove the barriers and limitations within your own consciousness that do not allow you to accept other teachings.

Think this over: All the founders of all the religions of the world taught the same Truth at different times and in different languages. And if you consider yourselves educated, intelligent representatives of mankind, direct your efforts at finding that common thing that lies as the basis of all religions. Do not pay attention to what is different. Concentrate your attention on the common principles and approaches, and you will see the unity of all religions and all moral teachings that have ever been received by humanity from pure sources.

That unification of all religions and the creation of a new religion that encompasses all world religions will happen when you, in your consciousness, become able to respect and accept the viewpoint of another person instead of blindly insisting on your point of view and defending it even with weapons in your arms. All this should be left in the past. There is no place for any and all animosity in the New World. The animosity will leave your world as your consciousness changes and grows.

All the problems of your world are only in your head, inside you. All the Divine perfection is also inside you.

You should make it a habit to go within, to your Higher Self when making decisions on all main questions of your life.

The connection with the Higher Self and the liberation from the ego are the main foundation stones of the Teaching that we give.

Now I would like to part with you.

Until we meet again!

I AM Maitreya!

The expansion of the understanding of the Law of Karma

Beloved Kuthumi
July 6, 2006

I AM Kuthumi, who has come to you today.

During the period of time when we did not meet with you, I had a chance to analyze and comprehend the responsibility that our communication puts on you and on me. That is because if you think about it, you will come to an inevitable conclusion that everything that happens during our communication in the process of receiving the Dictations has an astonishing value and must be treated with respect and care. At first, you may not realize this and attach little significance to our Messages, but as you read our Messages and dive into our energies, you appreciate the minutes of our communication and assess both the possibility of communicating with us and the quality of our Messages more and more. So, I have come today to speak with you as with old friends. Moreover, I can tell you that I meet many of you almost daily during your night's sleep in my retreat in the etheric plane. When the knowledge that you receive from me in the course of our communication in the retreat finds an external confirmation in these Dictations, it germinates within your consciousness, and you start doing many things consciously in the physical plane. Your consciousness begins to comprehend the truths that could not otherwise penetrate your dense world.

So we continue our mutual work on the transformation of your physical world. This work of ours does not presuppose your blind obedience to our advice and recommendations, but it implies a creative application of all the received knowledge in your lives. We do not need blind followers who are ready to do what we tell them to do at our first call. We need conscientious serious-minded disciples who do not just do something thoughtlessly, but consciously reflect the received knowledge in their external consciousness and find the best scenario for the optimal implementation of our plans.

Thus, you join in with the cosmic co-creation. We highly value those of our disciples who do not run from one teacher to another in search of advice on how to behave in daily life situations, but who are able to raise their consciousness above the day-to-day chores and see the perspectives that open up and set them in motion without waiting for the ideal conditions in the physical plane to come. You are able to evolve only through the path of overcoming yourselves and the hardships surrounding you in your lives. You should not be afraid of life problems and the failures that await you. The whole point is in your attitude to these problems and failures. The Teaching provides you with correct approaches. You yourselves, guided by these approaches, create your lives.

You change your consciousness and begin to see the problems that you face in life differently; you analyze the problems and barriers that come up before you, and you thank God that He has given you the chance to understand your past mistakes and to correct them through your right attitude to the arising problems.

You should never give in to disappointment and depression. You receive the Teaching in order to form within yourselves proper attitude to the things you come across and that accompany you in your lives. If some of you, with my help or based on your inner intuition, a hint from your Higher Self, suddenly understand the reason that had karmically brought a certain situation into your life, then you will start giving countless thanks to God for allowing you to work off your karmic debt in such an easy way.

Truly is the grace of Heaven endless, and only you yourselves by your irrational behavior were able to generate the reasons for the problems and disasters that you face in life. Sometimes, these problems are so big that your whole life literally crosses off your chance to render your service to the Brotherhood fully. That is because you are too burdened with your karmic debts. Yet, the wisdom received by you through our communication helps you understand that in your future life you will be able to continue your service, and you will receive such circumstances in your lives that will not be so difficult and burdensome for you. That is because during your present life you have already worked off a big part of your karmic debts. Because you have worked off these debts yourselves, your children will carry a much lighter burden as well. It is because the property of karma is such that sometimes the karmic load that has not been worked off comes down as a heavy burden on children and grandchildren. Therefore, be glad about the misfortunes and miseries that come down on you. By doing so, you prepare a bright future for yourselves in your next life and for your children and grandchildren in their present lives. The proper understanding of the Law of Karma makes you happy even when you carry an intolerable karmic load from the point of view of the people around you.

The whole point is in the attitude of your external consciousness to the burden that you are carrying. Therefore, never be saddened by your problems. Allow yourselves to be happy with the fact that by overcoming your current problems you are preparing a bright future for yourself and your children and grandchildren.

The next generation will be much happier than you because many of you have taken on karmic responsibilities that are too big to work off during this life. You have done this on purpose in order to accelerate the process of changes on planet Earth. Those people around you, who point at you and say that you have probably sinned too much because your load is so heavy, understand nothing about the mechanism of the Law of Karma, and their consciousness is unable to grasp the size of the sacrifice you have taken upon yourselves voluntarily before your incarnation. However, we, the Ascended Hosts, highly value your sacrifice. Moreover, we are ready to respond to your requests and help you as much as the Law allows in order to ease your burden. Sometimes, when the good karma (created by you during your current incarnation) allows, we are able to answer your call and help you in a situation when you seem to have no strength to endure it any longer. Then, after your call, a while later you look back surprised and realize that something that had been lying on your shoulders as an insurmountable burden suddenly disappeared, vanished, fell off your shoulders. In such a case, never forget to glorify the Heavens and send your gratitude. The best gratitude for us will be the service that you can render for the benefit of life on Earth.

Now I will give you a formula that will enable you to get relief from your karmic burden if your good karma allows you to. So, you say:

"In the name of I AM THAT I AM, in the name of my mighty I AM Presence, in the name of my holy Christ Self (or simply in the name of God Almighty), I appeal to the Great Karmic Board and ask you to use the momentum of my righteous achievements for the purpose of neutralizing the karma which has led to... (you should describe the situation for which you wish to receive help from the Karmic Board).

May all the things take place in accordance with the Will of God."

You can write a letter addressed to the Karmic Board, read your call aloud, and burn the letter. If the amount of your accumulated good karma allows, and the Karmic Board decides that your request can be granted, your karmic situation will be resolved to a greater or lesser degree.

In accordance with the opportunity given to you earlier[13] you will be called in your subtle body during your night's sleep to

---

[13] Refer to the Dictation "Let your consciousness go beyond the limits of your family, your city, and your country and take the whole Earth as your native home," Lord Maitreya, June 5, 2006 in *Words of Wisdom Volume 2*.

a Karmic Board session and your soul will have to confirm your request, which you had written in your outer consciousness.

Sometimes there are cases when someone's external consciousness does not want to endure the karmic load any longer, but the soul of that person refuses the help. In that case, the Karmic Board listens to the opinion of your soul. Therefore, if your request is not granted after some time, you can talk to your soul and try to come to an agreement with it on this question.

I highly recommend that you practice talking to your soul and write letters to the Karmic Board only after you and your soul have reached an agreement between yourselves.

You are multilayered beings. You have many bodies. That is why you need to reach harmony and unity among all your bodies. The bodies of the majority of people are unbalanced to such an extent that you cannot even understand how you should act in the best interest of all the bodies. Stop associating yourselves with just what you see in the mirror. You are much more than your physical body. The next stage in the evolution of mankind will be the understanding of your Higher nature and the creation of harmonious conditions for your Higher nature to manifest itself. That is because the conditions in which you are living now sometimes do not facilitate at all your being able to bring your subtle bodies into harmony. That is the next stage of development of mankind. However, you already should be concerned about creating the environment for the harmonious development of all your bodies.

I have given you a lot of new information today. And I am leaving you with a hope of new meetings.

I AM Kuthumi.

There will be those who manifest their consistency and devotion and can help us attain our goals

Master Morya
July 7, 2006

I AM El Morya, who has come to you again through my Messenger in order to give a Teaching and talk to you about vital problems. I am glad to have such an opportunity. Every time when I come, I cannot hide my delight about the fact that there is an opportunity to communicate with you. Therefore, today, in order to save time, I am starting to report what is necessary. It is necessary for you to know about many things. If you could constantly concentrate on the goals of the Brotherhood and carry out our plans, the evolution on the planet would go at a much faster pace. Yet, you continue to reside in illusion, soothing your consciousness with the illusionary manifestations that surround you. That is why I come again and again and try to get across to your consciousness the things that are indispensable for you. You forget everything that I tell you literally right when you stop reading my Messages. I have to come again and give you the same Teaching at a somewhat different angle hoping that there will be those who manifest their consistency and devotion and can help us attain our goals. It seems to you with your agile mind that you already know everything that we talk about and you go off in pursuit of new impressions hoping to occupy your carnal mind. However, you do not need any new knowledge. There is only one Teaching and one Divine Truth. This Truth can be understood only with a mind of a child. Abandonment of excess speculations and intellectual refinement is what you should do. I realize that your mental bodies are not fully developed yet. That is why you are trying to load them with various intellectual twists. You come into the gross world, and one of the goals that you come with is to develop not only your physical bodies but also your subtle bodies: the astral body, the mental body, and the etheric body. Your subtle bodies represent your soul. Your soul needs development. That is why you will remain in the matter until you gain enough experience and until all your bodies are developed. Now the cycle is such that your mental bodies receive an impulse for development. They are curious like children and are trying to find more and more new terrains for their activity. However, in the same way as you give up alcohol, nicotine, and other attachments and habits of your physical body, you need to find the strength within you to give up the attachments of your mental body, of your carnal mind. All of your four lower bodies undergo evolution on planet Earth. You have to achieve harmony and maturity of all your bodies. Until you gain enough experience, until all your bodies gain enough experience, you cannot return to the world from which you originally had come as Divine particles. You will take the experience that you have gained to this Divine world, but only the part of your experience that corresponds to the Divine models.

So, since the mental bodies of a significant part of mankind are now going through their experiences and acquiring the necessary knowledge, you need to take that into account in your development. You have to constantly try to detect when your mind leads you into the deep forest of intellectual speculations and when you are actually coming in contact with the eternal Divine Wisdom. You should try to make your differentiation within yourselves. The Divine Wisdom does not have anything in common with intellectual speculations, which resemble some sort of a drug for your carnal mind.

Many people, when they open another Message and do not see any food in it for their conceited mind, go seek that food in other places, and they receive what they are aspiring in considerable amounts. However, what is not visible to you is visible to us. We can see that what you sometimes receive and consider as being very valuable and indispensable is in the best case useless for you, and in the worst case, it pushes back the development of your soul by years and incarnations.

There are many intellectual traps into which many people of light fall. Those traps are placed so skillfully that at times it is impossible not to be caught in them if you are not constantly maintaining the attunement with our Hierarchy and asking the Ascended Masters for help. Many people rely on their own powers, on the physical muscle, and neglect the help of the Hierarchy of Light. However, this is another manifestation of the intellectual ego. At the modern stage of human development you cannot differentiate between the proper models and their malformed counterparts, between the intellectual speculations and the Divine Wisdom. That is because the difference between them can sometimes be seen only at the level of the Divine intuition and the vibrations that are natural to these manifestations.

Now I have to tell you one more important thing. It concerns your advancement on the Path of Initiations that many are trying to follow and take on responsibilities to follow that Path. Yet, in the same way as they take on the task eagerly, they turn away from the Path, whether because of their own laziness or the lack of Faith and devotion.

That is because the qualities of consistency, devotion, and determination are inherent to a very small number of individuals. As a rule, these qualities have been acquired by those individuals in their past incarnations by means of training themselves in those qualities, either in the communities of spiritual Masters or in hermit's shacks. Do not think that everything that you have in this life has been inherited by you from your parents or that you have attained these achievements yourselves in this life. Many of your attainments and qualities go back into the distant past, up to the times of ancient Atlantis and Lemuria. Only now, in this life, they come out in you, and you are given the right to use them. Therefore, please use your Divine gifts and qualities to serve the Common Good, to serve the Life on Earth, and to serve us, the Great White Brotherhood. We are the Masters of mankind that have been accompanying humanity for millions of years. We were with you during your incarnations in ancient Lemuria and Atlantis and taught you — as less developed individuals at that time — in our schools and ashrams.

Therefore, you should value what you have as your heritage, your achievements that have come to you from the remote past. Use your gifts not to submerge yourselves into the illusion, but to ascend to the peak of the Divine consciousness. Do not think that you are alone on your Path. We are constantly by your side and are holding your hands in our hands. However, we cannot take you by your hand forcefully and lead you if you are like stubborn little children pulling out your hand and running away from the evolutionary path of development. Apparently, your intellectual body is not developed enough yet to conform to the Law and understand all the advantages of the Ascended Masters guiding you and helping you on your Path.

I am parting with you for today, but I am foreseeing new meetings and talks.

**I AM El Morya,
with hope in you.**

I am looking for heart-to-heart commune with those who are ready for such communication

Beloved Jesus
July 8, 2006

I AM Jesus, having come to you today in order to give you my exhortations that I have prepared for you beforehand.

It is not often that we have an opportunity of immediate commune with those who are in embodiment now. However, this chance of direct communication between you and me is inherent in your nature. And if you took the trouble and aspired with all your heart, with all your soul to our commune, then you would be able to hear me. I would come to you exactly as I have now come to the body temple of Tatyana, and we would have a talk with you.

I could give you my exhortations directly, without a Messenger. And this is what I strongly desire — to have direct contact with each of you.

Most people who read these Dictations are familiar with Christianity, but religion is not an obstacle for the commune of ours. People themselves divided faith into different religions, and each religious system is trying to subordinate their congregation and is keeping vigilant watch so that they do not leave the bounds of their church. However, I exist and aspire to communication with everyone regardless of that religion to which you and your family belong. Do try to recognize me in your consciousness as an Ascended Master — not as an idol that is worshiped by most Christians of the world, but as your elder brother, your friend who is ready to respond to any request of yours and to come to the rescue when you are calling me.

I am that Master who is very close to humanity of Earth, and you cannot even imagine how close my presence is. I can be among you during your prayers when you are calling me. And I can come to you in the silence of your solitude when you sincerely intend to meet me and get some advice in a hard life situation. Do not hesitate to appeal to me. I am an Ascended Master and I have been serving humanity of Earth during all that time since I performed a transition in that life when I was Jesus. Since then, I have often come to those who have been practicing genuine Christianity in their hearts. But not to those who have made the religion of Christianity their source of living, and not to those who insincerely follow church dogmas and rules. I am looking for heart-to-heart commune with those who are ready for such communication. For many I am not so much a Christian symbol as a friend. And many incarnations ago I met you and gave you my Teaching during my incarnation as Jesus, and our connection still exists in the subtle plane. You have an opportunity to get your education in my retreat during your sleep. I am urging those of you who have not used this opportunity for our communication yet, to take advantage of this opportunity. If you are in a calm, harmonious state before your sleep, then after your prayer you can aspire with your thought toward our meeting, and we will surely meet during your night sleep. I will answer your questions and give you all possible help. Do not be confused by the fact that after you awaken you may not remember all the details of our meeting or even may not remember that our meeting has taken place at all. This is not important, because you will use the received advice in your life, even if it will go past your external consciousness. Therefore, keep the aspiration to meeting me within you and we will certainly meet.

Do not expect that I will come to you as if I were a human and dropped in to your place. No, our communication will take place in the subtle plane. And you should apply your efforts in order to hear me. I will speak to your soul or to your Higher Self. And you will hear my words in your heart. Those will not be common human words, and they may not even be thoughts. There will be the sense of my presence and your sense of my energy filling you. I will fill the chalice of your heart with life-giving water, and I will give you quietness and the sense of peace and bliss, everything that you lack in your life. And after you drink the nectar of bliss from my chalice, you will realize that everything that has concerned and tormented you, all your problems, moved somewhere aside. And many of them will not return to you, because I have given you a part of my consciousness. And as your consciousness has changed, you will no longer be involved in those karmic situations that have caused your anxiety and trouble.

You are granted according to your faith. If your faith is strong and your aspiration cannot be broken by any life failure, then we will always meet with you. I have strong hopes that we will meet. For the opportunity of our meeting is that help for you that is given by Heavens.

Do not believe those who say that you need a mediator in order to communicate with me. No, I can have a meeting with you in the silence of your heart, and I will help you to solve your current problems. However, that degree of Faith and devotion that allows me to be present in your aura is not a common thing among people. I cannot come to you if you are staying in a big city and if you are too concerned about your earthly things and problems. I cannot come to you if you are burdened with any habits that separate us — by that I mean any of your attachments to alcohol, nicotine, watching TV, bad states of consciousness that haunt you: offence, envy, jealousy, and anger.

I will not be able to be present in your aura if you are burdened with these faults or any other faults, which you can easily list yourself because you know them pretty well and cannot get rid of them incarnation after incarnation.

I am open for communication but you must apply your efforts in order to approach me, raise your vibrations to that level where our communication can take place. And each of you knows very well about those faults that impede your approach to me; however, you do not hasten to part from your faults and problems.

Well, I will wait until you become mature and decide to initiate immediate communication with me. For the time being I am having the opportunity to speak to you through this Messenger. And I also remind you of an opportunity to meet me in your dream.

The opportunity for our meeting always exists, and only you yourselves limit the opportunity of our communication.

And now I would like to wish you to acquire that inner aspiration that will surmount all your faults and will allow you to rise to the summit of the Divine consciousness without stopping or slipping down.

Sometimes one wrong choice of yours is enough in order to close the opportunity of our communication to the end of your current incarnation. Be careful as you go through life and consider every choice of yours and every step of yours.

There are a lot of inhabitants of the astral plane who aim to come in contact with you in order to get in your person to execute their will and their plans. And coming in contact and starting an interaction with such beings is much easier than coming in contact and having an interaction with me. For this you do not need to part from any of your habits.

Therefore, you will always know yourselves with whom you meet in the subtle plane. With me, or my counterpart, who is not from the Light. The key to the answer of this question will be the purity of your consciousness and those habits and attachments that you are not able to give up.

You do not even need to ask anyone about who you communicate with in the subtle plane. It is enough for you to simply make an unbiased analysis of your thoughts, your way of living, and your interactions with the people around you.

Therefore, everything is in your power, and you make a decision yourself concerning who you come in contact with in the subtle plane.

You need the gift of distinction, but sometimes you do not need any gift in order to make a distinction; you simply need to analyze your thinking, your habits, and your attachments.

I don't lose hope for meeting with you. And I look forward to our meeting.

I AM Jesus,
with great Love for you.

A Teaching on the karmic responsibility for your actions in the sphere of translating the texts of the Dictations and in the sphere of managing cash funds

Sanat Kumara
July 9, 2006

I AM Sanat Kumara, having come to you again.

From this day forth until the end of the current cycle of Dictations, every day before reading a Dictation, I want you to invoke the electronic presence of the Master giving the Dictation. This seemingly simple technique will enable you to feel our presence and will present quite a new view of many theses of our Messages because the presence of the Masters during the reading of the Messages will many times magnify the effect you experience while reading them. This is a special dispensation, and it will be active still for some time after the completion of this cycle of Dictations. You will be able to judge by your gut sense whether this dispensation is still operating or not.

So, in order to invoke the presence of the Master giving a Message, you should pronounce either aloud or to yourself:

"In the name of I AM THAT I AM, I invoke the electronic presence of [insert the name of the Master giving the Message]**."**

Try to use this dispensation beginning from today's Dictation. Read this Dictation to the end, and then reread it after having made a call and you will feel the difference. I recommend that you always make such calls before reading the Messages that we give through this Messenger. The operation of the call will be manifested when possible and necessary.

All the Masters can manifest their electronic presence, and the extent of this presence will be directly proportional to your ability to perceive our vibrations and to the readiness of your Higher bodies to distinguish our vibrations.

You know that sometimes we give our Messages at a higher level and sometimes we give them at a slightly lower level. And this is not always predicated upon the quality of conductibility of the bodies of our Messenger. It is just because there are different levels of development of consciousness in the individuals embodied now. And different individuals are capable of perceiving different information and different energetic components of the Messages.

We thoroughly verify the information given. And when your external consciousness starts analyzing the information, it is not always useful. That is because any critical perception of information cuts short the flow of energy, and the reading of our Messages becomes useless for you. A Message itself energizes within you a focus on the energies of the Masters, and you will perceive our energies at the moment of reading the Messages. There are keys that energize your higher conductors, and you become able to perceive not only the informational component of the Messages but also their energetic component. This explains the fact that our Messages are impossible to retell. A retelling does not carry in itself the keys hidden within the body of the Message. You take in our Messages as a text written with the help of symbols of this or that language; however, it is not exactly so. A Message carries within itself hidden keys. And when you translate our Messages into different languages, these keys can be lost. Everything depends on the internality of the translator. If the translator is attuned to us, the translation carries our vibrations. If not, the translation carries only the informational component. This explains the fact that even though you speak another language, you still receive the energetic component of the Messages when listening to the Dictations being read by our Messenger and not understanding the words. You feel the energies and vibrations of the Masters.

If you read our Messages translated into your native language, you can lose this energetic component. Accordingly, I recommend that those who translate our Dictations into other languages in the future, before starting the translation, invoke the electronic presence of the Master whose Dictation you are going to realize and translate. I also advise you to start the translation in a balanced state after a good meditation or a prayer practice.

Any imperfections you have are imposed on the text of the translation. And if you happen to distort the text of the Dictation at the process of the translation, the karmic responsibility for the distortion of the Words of the Masters falls on you. Yet, this karmic responsibility of yours can be neutralized by good karma which you acquire at the moment of translating the Dictations into other languages and distributing them. But you should bear in mind that good karma is acquired by you only if your motive is pure and you really do translations in order to spread our Teaching, but not in order to earn money.

The question of interrelation with money is very complicated and difficult. In fact, money does not come to you when you perform some work for the Brotherhood. But when doing some work for the Brotherhood, you receive opportunities that enable the energy of money to pay back the energetic consumption you incurred while being involved in the work for the Brotherhood.

Everything in this world is based on the exchange of energy, and any stagnation of energy leads to the shortage of monetary energy. When you have money you should think about where you need to spend it. Any accumulation of monetary energy is not useful and represents a sign of karma of incorrect attitude toward money. Think about how you should dispose of the money you have. And if you spend this money on pleasure, next time you will not receive the payback of the monetary energy.

On the contrary, if you spend your store of money on good causes, the flow of monetary energy will be intensified, regardless of how much effort you apply to earn the money. You will get a windfall or somebody will give you money under any pretense. Do manage monetary energy correctly. The more you give selflessly, the more you receive.

But you should always remember that you are responsible for how much and to whom you give your money, because in the case that the money you give is not used on good deeds, the karma of the misuse of monetary energy will fall upon you.

In contrast, if you contribute money for good deeds, then good karma of correct use of your money will give you a chance to dispose of this good karma at your sole discretion. Therein lays the principal of the church tithe. It is, essentially, a very right and exact principle, but only if the church or any other religious organization spends your tithe on good deeds — not on multiplying their own property.

The principle of the reasonable and right use of the Divine Energy is manifested in everything, and monetary energy is in no way different from any other kind of energy. One kind of energy turns smoothly into another kind of energy. And your tithe, if you manage it correctly, provides you with the manifestation of opportunities in the physical plane. These opportunities can pour upon you in the form of financial abundance, a joyful future for your children, your own health, and the health of your nearest and dearest.

Good karma can also be used for your own personal purpose. For this you are given a chance to write letters to the Karmic Board.[14]

---

[14] More information about getting help from the Karmic Board is found in the following Dictations: "Let your consciousness go beyond the limits of your family, your city, and your country, and take the whole Earth as your native home," Lord Maitreya, June 5, 2006, and "The expansion of the understanding of the Law of Karma," Beloved Kuthumi, July 6, 2006. Refer to *Words of Wisdom Volume 2*.

Today I have given you a Teaching on the karmic responsibility for your actions in the sphere of translating the texts of the Dictations and in the sphere of managing cash funds. And this vital Teaching requires an immediate use in your lives.

Now, let me leave you and say goodbye until we meet again!

I AM Sanat Kumara. Om

A Teaching about Happiness

Gautama Buddha
July 10, 2006

I AM Gautama Buddha, having come again. And as usual, I have come in order to give you my guidance and to give that Message to the world, which the world needs now.

Today, I would like to draw your attention to those circumstances of your lives that exist and do not allow you to acquire inner balance, peace, harmony, and happiness.

This is not exactly the happiness that people mean when living in the thick of their lives. My understanding of happiness differs from your understanding of happiness. Do you know why? This is because you consider happiness in terms of the one life of yours that you are living now. I consider happiness not only in terms of the current life but also in terms of all my incarnations, and in terms of the incarnations of all living beings that are currently incarnated on planet Earth or waiting for their coming incarnation.

That is why we have a different understanding of happiness. But we will be able to bring our views of happiness closer if you let yourself go beyond the limits of your views of the reality around you. Make the latitude of your perception of the world a bit wider. Go beyond the limits of what is surrounding you in your life, your daily concerns, and the routine because sooner or later, what you admit in your consciousness manifests in your lives. If you are always focused on your current problems, then you will get nothing but these problems in the future.

Happiness is just the state of your mind. Even when it seems to your external mind that there is no end to the problems and concerns of your life, if you manage to raise your consciousness a little bit higher, you will realize that, in fact, you are the happiest being in this Universe.

It seems to you that I am playing a joke on you. However, from my point of view as an ascended being, I envy you who are incarnated now. Believe me; it is all in your consciousness and in the way that you perceive everything that is taking place around you. Most of your problems, 99 percent of your problems, you create yourself simply because you cannot set your consciousness free and let it go beyond the limits of the reality around you. Happiness is just the state of your mind. In fact, the Teaching that we are giving is the Teaching that will bring you happiness.

Your consciousness is learning to perceive everything around you in terms of the other, Higher reality. And you acquire the knowledge of the Law of Karma. This knowledge and your skills allow you to manage your life situation. You must understand that it is you yourself who separates you from your state of happiness. In other words, you do not allow yourself to be happy.

Let us find an example to illustrate this situation. For example, you are concerned about your neighbors or some other people who possess more things than you. You become envious and wish evil to those people, and in this way you become more and more miserable. You are literally boxed in, and your consciousness cannot go through the nets of envy and anger.

Now let's see how a wise man behaves. He can feel joy when other people are happy. He can also be happy with the fact that another person can buy something or do something, though he cannot. This man acquires the merits in his heart that allow him to elevate his consciousness over the commonplace and feel joy and happiness in his consciousness.

When you learn to feel joy seeing other people's achievements, in this way you will find an opportunity for you yourself to be successful. Even if according to your karma of this incarnation you are not allowed to possess much or live comfortably, in this way you will create more favorable conditions for yourself in your next incarnation, and your following life will be more successful and will be full of the things that people consider to be the manifestations of happiness. However, if you continue to develop your positive thinking, you will be able to understand that there aren't any signs of happiness accepted in your society that can bring true happiness. True happiness consists in your capability to sacrifice yourself for the wellbeing of other living creatures. You sacrifice yourself, and from the point of view of the people who are now living on Earth you are a failure; however, your state feels like quiet inner happiness and bliss. And you will never exchange this state of yours for any riches of the world.

Oh, this state that I am telling you about is available only for the initiates of the highest level. Many of you who are reading these lines may think that what I am talking about now is not about you, because you are concentrated on your human problems too much. However, it is not a secret. I am telling you that this state that I have described will be accessible for all of you at a certain stage of your development. This is the state of the mind of a Buddha. And later on, all of you will become Buddhas. This is the next stage of human development. No matter how you try to put off this stage, it will come anyway because thousands of beings who have already reached the level of consciousness of a Buddha are standing in a line in order to come into embodiment in your world and to render this world their help by taking the sins of the world upon themselves and suffering for humanity. Thus, they expiate the karma of humanity and give humankind one chance after another so that it can return to the evolutionary path of development instead of being destroyed by another devastating cataclysm.

I am happy to give you this Teaching today, as many of you are not happy only because you are lacking the knowledge of Truth.

Ignorance is a common disease of humanity. Ignorance cloaks you in a narcotic-like fog and puts out your sparkle of reason, which you got from the Masters of Wisdom long ago, and that sparkle is hidden inside of you for the time being. But the moment will come when your sparkle starts burning, and the flame that will kindle within your being will be able to light up the path for many lost souls. You are burned, but you light up the path for others. That is why a torch or a candle is a symbol of enlightenment.

Devotion and service are those qualities that you must aspire to accumulate within yourselves as soon as you start coming out of the fog of ignorance. Your state of happiness directly depends on how successfully you will be able to overcome the ignorance and laziness that is inherent in the majority of humanity at this stage.

I say goodbye to you. It is sad that I cannot share my state of happiness with the greatest number of individuals who are incarnated on Earth now.

**I AM Gautama,
wishing you enlightenment and happiness.**

Do not rush searching for truth that is coming from the human consciousness; strive for the Truth that is coming into your world from the Higher octaves of Light, and then you will manifest a bright future for planet Earth

Beloved Cyclopea
July 11, 2006

I AM Cyclopea, who has come to you on this day.

I have come, and as always I would like to use every opportunity that is given for the communication between the Heavens and earthly plane to benefit the development of your consciousness.

Your purpose is to become advanced cosmic beings. You grow with your consciousness into more and more subtle layers of the mental plane first, and then of the Higher planes as well. My vision of your growth and your purpose, based on my experience, tells me that you will live up to the hopes that have been put in you. I am glad that it is possible to give sprouts of the eternal knowledge after so many years of complete lack of faith and darkness that has been covering Earth for the past centuries. It is not at such a high level yet. It is important to awaken the consciousness of the current generation so that new generations receive the foundation for greater growth of their consciousness and become capable of perceiving greater knowledge about the Divine Truth.

You fill up your consciousness with a multitude of unnecessary things. Now the time has come when you have to treat everything on which you focus your attention consciously. That is because everything to which you draw your attention has a very strong influence on you. Therefore, you need to understand that sometimes one low-quality film that you watch, or one person carrying negative vibrations that you meet is enough to either stop your development or navigate it toward an unnecessary direction.

Therefore, we would like you to develop within yourselves the quality of the Divine vision and foresee the situation.

It is the quality of the Divine vision that I teach mankind at my retreat. I am happy to now come out to such a wide audience that is reading these Messages in many languages. I am happy to get across my Teaching to you — not when you are asleep, but when you are in the awakened state of mind.

The time has come now when your Divine capabilities should awaken, and you should gradually recognize your Divine purpose. Unfortunately, this science is not being taught at your educational institutions. It is even rare to find books on the shelves of your stores and libraries that would truly teach the Divine knowledge. That is because unfortunately, the literature that is common in your world only misleads you from the true Path and deprives you of the Divine mindset, making you rely on the carnal mind and intellectual speculations. This path is not a Divine Path, because it makes you develop not the Divine qualities but purely human qualities. In order to develop Divine qualities in yourselves, you need to give up all attachments to the goods of your world. It is necessary to step on the Path of Initiations and follow it. At different times there have been schools on Earth that taught the Divine science. I foresee the revival of these traditions on Earth in the near future. In order to do that, it is necessary to change the consciousness of people to such an extent that such schools get support and approval at the government level and are included in the federal programs of education and upbringing of children and adults.

It is that task that is vital, and I am declaring to you that the government of the country that recognizes our Messenger at the official level and can fulfill our plans at the official level will receive all our blessings and help. That will be the next very important step in the development of planet Earth. That is because until this time, even if the rulers of various countries were under our influence, our relations were shrouded in mystery and hidden from prying eyes. Now the time has come when we are ready to come out of the veil of secrecy and give our knowledge and our Teaching openly because the situation on the planet is currently favorable to this course of events. To make it more clear to you, I will say that the past Messengers had already tried to establish contacts with the governments of different countries on the federal level, but they did not succeed. We did not leave our attempts, and we declare now through our Messenger that the Great White Brotherhood is open for collaboration at the federal level with all governments of all countries in the world. We have nothing to hide anymore, because the Truth is being proclaimed freely through the Internet, and our Messengers have the opportunity to freely declare the Truth without being persecuted.

Now I would like to dwell on another important subject that concerns the future of mankind of planet Earth. Your future is directly connected with your children. Depending on how well you manage to prepare the future generation, that generation will be able to develop Divine qualities within themselves and fulfill their Divine purpose. Do not forget that by taking care of the next generation, you are practically taking care of yourselves. That is because not so much time will pass by in earthly standards before you incarnate on Earth again. Depending on your efforts that you make now to bring up the growing generation, you will receive incarnation in a more favorable environment that will facilitate your spiritual development. God has thought through everything, and all consequences come out of their causes. Think over what I have told you. Even if the efforts that you direct at bringing up your children do not lead to success in your current life, your momentum of care about the future generation will leave an indelible imprint in your aura, and the attainments of your causal body will be used by you yourselves in the future lives.

The Law of Karma and the Law of Reincarnation are the two most important laws that must be studied in your educational institutions side-by-side with physics, mathematics, and chemistry. Believe me; the benefits of learning these laws will be far greater than the benefits of learning the laws of Newton or Pascal.

Now I would like you to think over carefully in your hearts and create an image in your hearts about what you personally can do so that the new generation that comes to this world, from their very first steps can receive the true knowledge and a true representation of the world into which they have come — knowledge that is not based on old human truths but based on the Truth that has been affirmed for centuries. For no matter how our Messengers were persecuted in the past and are persecuted now, the Truth that they have been teaching lives and will live forever. For everything that is from God will live eternally and everything that is from a human will be forgotten either in this or the next generation.

Do not rush searching for the truth that is coming from the human consciousness; strive for the Truth that is coming into your world from the Higher octaves of Light; then you will manifest a bright future for planet Earth.

**I AM Cyclopea,
foreseeing a bright future for planet Earth.**

A Teaching about the Path of Discipleship

Beloved Lanello
July 12, 2006

I AM Lanello, who has come to you again on this day.

I have come to speak with you about the essential. Our talks become more and more business-like every time because your consciousness becomes capable of embracing more and more of the Divine Truth. That is why the complexity of the Dictations is increasing. It is not even the complexity of how the material is given, but the complexity of the subjects that are being discussed. That is because the scope of subjects touched upon is widening, and you are able to perceive in your consciousness a wider range of subjects and go beyond the concepts that you are familiar with. That is why each time we give the material already known to you in a slightly different manner or we try to include elements of new concepts that you did not come in contact with before.

All topics discussed concern each person living now. However, there is a subject of especially vital importance. That subject concerns your relationship with God and with the Ascended Masters. There are a great number of religious systems and various religious trends. It is becoming more and more difficult to make sense of all these trends. As soon as people experience the need for certain knowledge or as soon as a scientific discovery is made, the opposing forces instantly use all their skills and resources to entrap the consciousness of people into the net of false concepts, false ideas, and false dogmas and rules. It is exactly what you are seeing now in the area of various religious systems and beliefs. Besides the faiths known from the past, numerous new faiths emerge. Many people who have gained some understanding about God and the Ascended Masters, are striving to declare themselves to be new gurus and take control over the flock that hangs on every word of theirs. This is becoming a sad manifestation of your time. People do not realize the whole karmic responsibility when they come under the influence of such gurus. They do not realize that all the imperfect vibrations and manifestations during group meetings and prayer practices flow from the aura of such a master into their own auras. These imperfections add to their own imperfections, and instead of getting free from the load of karma, they acquire all of the imperfections of their gurus into their electronic belt.

It is especially sad when people go from one group to the next, like tumbleweeds blown by gusts of wind. This is becoming the scourge of our time.

All we can do in such a situation is to warn you that this scourge exists, and it is dangerous because all of your choices impose karmic responsibility on you, karma that you have to work off in the future.

Now I would like to give you an idea about how you should behave in the sea of different currents that surround you. You must ask yourself what is driving you when you try to join one or another spiritual group because the purity of your motive determines the level of vibrations of a group or a religious leader that you will be attracted to. Have you ever thought that, in fact, the circumstances surrounding you simply help offer you for your choice exactly that which is lying deeply in your consciousness and subconsciousness? If you are striving to acquire different magic techniques to gain control over the circumstances of your life or the circumstances of the lives of people surrounding you, then you will automatically and inevitably become attracted to the group that is practicing black magic and you will burden yourself not only with the circumstances of that choice, but also share the karma of the leader and the members of that group.

The time has come for you to treat everything that happens in your life and all your choices consciously. That is because sometimes one choice of yours determines your entire future path not only in this life but also in the course of future incarnations. Having once committed yourself to a group that is practicing black magic, you automatically gain all the karma that has been acquired by that group into your electronic belt.

Treat everything with consciousness. First and foremost, treat consciously the analysis of your inner state and your motive that is driving you.

Here are the true motives, which are inherent in our disciples:

- Our disciples strive to give up all their imperfections and all their attachments to the things of this world in order to render all possible help to all living beings of planet Earth who need this help.

- They aspire to purify themselves and all their lower bodies in order to fulfill their service in a more productive way.

- Our disciples aspire to establish the connection with God, residing within; our disciples honor the Hierarchy of Light and consciously stand on the steps of the Hierarchy.

- And no circumstances of the external world can make them lose the Path when they themselves hear the answers of their Higher Self and consult their Higher Self in all difficult life situations.

Now I would also like to draw your attention to the fact that many of our disciples, having acquired a lot of knowledge and skills, still leave the path in order to chase after prestige, fame, and money, which is very sorrowful. That is because for those of our chelas who already stood on the Path and served us with devotion, the withdrawal from the Path is equivalent to the most serious crime — treachery. There is only one way to work off that treachery — to be incarnated in an even more complicated karmic situation, where it is even more difficult to come on to the Path. You can always return to the Path of Initiations, but sometimes several very difficult incarnations are necessary for that, and only then you will be allowed to return to the consciousness service to the Brotherhood.

I am not striving to scare you. I am giving you the Teaching that you need now. This Teaching is very important at this stage. That is because it is too often that we see how our disciples, who get inspired and receive an opportunity to serve us, the Ascended Masters, use some absolutely insignificant excuse to stop their service and step away from the Path to chase after the mirages of the physical world. We regret to admit that the percentage of our disciples who we lose on the Path is too high.

Therefore, if you have found this Teaching and have accepted with all your heart the Dictations coming through our Messenger, please double the surveillance of your motives. Take under control all your thoughts that distract you from the Path. Drive away all insidious whisperers who are instilling doubts in you about your chosen Path and making you go after more and more new intellectual toys.

To find this Path, which you have earned in your past incarnations, is a great honor for you. Therefore, safeguard what you have acquired and strive to multiply it with your Service to the Brotherhood.

During my incarnation in America as Mark Prophet, I had a chance to encounter many cases of treachery and stepping away from the Path. And I recommend that you treat everything that is said in the Dictations, given by us through this Messenger, more consciously. Believe me, not a single word that we say is odd. Everything that we say is meant for you to think over many times in the stillness of your heart.

I was glad to meet with you today. I will be glad if we have a chance to meet with you in the future.

I AM Lanello.

A Teaching on prophets and prophecies

John the Beloved
July 13, 2006

I AM John the Beloved. I am known to you as the author of the Apocalypse. I have come again in order to give a Teaching based on the internal knowledge — the knowledge that was accessible only to prophets and mystics. Such people still exist in this day and age, but they are often mistaken for charlatans who declare themselves prophets, clairvoyants, or psychics, but the threshold of their perception of the Divine World is so low that at times it would be better for their future if they stopped their prophecies and became silent.

What do you think — is there any karma carried by prophets, and what is that karma? I will tell you, since I know very well what kind of karma we are talking about.

There is no difference between prophesying and any other activity that you can be engaged in the physical world. And prophets come in all shapes and sizes. There are prophets making prophecies from the Light, and there are prophets who soothsay from darkness. Each prophet chooses for himself which forces to serve.

Prophecy: the gift of contact with the invisible world. This gift is not acquired during just one embodiment. When this gift is granted to a person prophesying from God, this person usually realizes the full karmic responsibility that rests on his shoulders. Prophecies represent probabilities of the occurrence of events sensed from the Higher plane. Depending on the plane and the level at which the prophecy is sensed, it can be more or less accurate. But, because things that are familiar on the physical plane are missing in the Higher plane, the gift of prophecy involves interpretation of events based on impressions from contact with the Higher plane.

Since the human mind is involved in the process of the representation of impressions, a distortion of information can take place at this stage, and the authenticity of the prophecy is lost. I wrote the Apocalypse with symbols, so I managed to avoid the karma that is laid on the Prophet if the prophecy did not come true. And each expert in forecasting provides his veiled knowledge in the form of verses, parables, and quatrains. This is very fair because it makes it possible to avoid karma if the prophecy is erroneous.

There are other prophets who use human interest in oracles and soothsayers, and give their prophecies in down-to-earth language, based on the knowledge they draw from the lowest levels of the astral plane or while being under the effect of mind-altering drugs.

These prophecies do not contain big truths. And usually they do not come true. The probability of such prophecies coming true is fifty percent. This is the case when people say, "There's many a slip between the cup and the lip."

However, the desire to satisfy human interest in soothsaying puts a great karmic responsibility upon such prophets and clairvoyants. In the case where the prophecy is incorrect, the more people who know about this prophecy, the greater the responsibility is. The fact is that any prophecy programs the consciousness of people who give credit to it. And if there are many people who wish to believe the prophecy, then these people create by their consciousness an opportunity for the realization of such a prophecy. And if a phenomenon predicted by a forecaster does not coincide with the Divine vision, but it is realized and takes place due to the momentum of human consciousness involved in this phenomenon, karma lies upon both the forecaster and the people who contribute to the realization of this phenomenon by their consciousness.

Therefore, any prophecy is a double-edged sword. If a prophecy alters the Divine plane for the better, then the realization of such a prophecy brings good karma to all the people who take part in its realization by their consciousness. If the Divine plane is worsened as a result of the prophecy, then a negative karma is created from the prophecy.

Prophecy is a phenomenon as dual as everything else in your world.

The people who come under the influence of the energy of prophecies of false foretellers create negative karma.

The prophets of Light have always been out of favor because the majority of people did not like the oracles coming through them. People have always treated such prophets cautiously. They would rather have no dealings with them and even tried to physically destroy them. The karma of reprisal for actions against a prophet of Light falls as a heavy burden on the next generation.

In contrast, any veneration of God's prophets brought good karma to the family of the person who showed hospitality to a prophet.

True prophets were always Messengers of God, and their mission was necessary in order to contribute to the proper development of human consciousness. Those who declared themselves as prophets without having been stamped with the seal of God incurred a descending heavy karma on themselves. Therefore, always observe and examine and do not get involved in any activity relating to prophecies if it is not from God, if it is demonic.

Although hundreds of years have passed since my incarnation, I am giving you this Teaching because it has not lost its relevance. On the contrary, it has acquired urgency since many visionaries and clairvoyants have appeared who do far more harm than good. And if you are involved in their activity, hire them, and pay for their services, then you create karma from a wrong action.

I have come to give you this important Teaching on the true and false prophets in order to help you to be able to approach everything you meet on your Path in this sphere with your eyes open in your consciousness.

It is very important where you direct your energy. None of the false prophets would be able to foretell if you did not give them the energy of your attention and your money, thus encouraging them to take up this ungodly business.

False prophets are the children of impure human consciousness, ignorance, and superstition.

Now that the body of the Teaching has been given, I would like to make a prophecy relating to your future. Before my coming to you, the other Ascended Masters and I were pondering whether it was worth giving you this prophecy through this Messenger because we had to consider the purity of the conductors and the degree of distortion of the information that might occur. We have decided to run a risk, and I will proceed.

In this difficult time in which you are living, you constantly think about many things and especially about the future of your planet, whether there is a threat of the next global cataclysm on it. That is why it is very important for you to hear that it is unlikely that any global cataclysm will take place during the lifetime of the generation living now. However, everything can change if you do not endeavor to transform your consciousness daily. The stable equilibrium on the planet that has been achieved so far exists and depends on the fact that many people have raised their consciousness to such a level that they are able to think positively and to direct their efforts to the Common Weal, goodness, and the Light. If the number of such people increases with each year, no global cataclysm will occur during the life of the next generation either because each preceding generation paves the way for the next one. Through your consciousness you are preparing a sustainable development for all life on Earth during the next cosmic cycle.

I wish you to successfully continue keeping your consciousness at the highest level.

**I AM John the Beloved,
with great respect to your lifestreams I AM.**

I wish that an increasing number of people become aware of our Path and enter the steps of the Hierarchy

Beloved Serapis Bey
July 14, 2006

I AM Serapis Bey, who has come to you again!

I have come now to give you guidance. In the same way as six months ago,[15] I wish to give you knowledge and information. However, the situation on the planet has now changed, and I am glad that it has changed for the better. The day when we are able to speak with mankind of Earth on equal terms is not too far away. Now I have come to those who are ready to listen to me because your level of consciousness allows you to do that. Do not think that in this life your accomplishments have allowed you to step on the Path of Initiations. I know many of you since the times of Ancient Egypt, and you received initiations in the pyramids together with me. However, the circumstances pulled us into different directions on the path of Life. Today again I am meeting with you, my old friends and acquaintances. If it is meant for you to recollect the circumstances of that life of yours when we met in the pyramids, you should understand that the initiations both at those times and at our time are given for the same quality — your attachment to everything material, including even your attachment to everything

---

[15] Refer to the Dictation "I have come to warn you that this Dictation can be the last one" Beloved Serapis Bey, December 23, 2005, in *Words of Wisdom Volume 2*

that belongs to more subtle planes, the planes of thoughts and emotions.

Because you retain your attachment to the material world, you continue to come into incarnation. One cannot give up materialism completely without trying all the temptations of your world. First you taste those temptations and then reap the fruits in the form of karma; then you overcome the karma that you have created and gradually untangle the nets that tie you to the material world. You can go through the initiations without leaving your lives, while staying in your life. That is a completely new approach that is characteristic of your time. I will explain that based on examples.

In the past, in order to get into the school for the initiates, one had to pass entrance exams on humility and obedience. Only then would one get admitted to the instruction at the school. Now you have the opportunity to get the knowledge without taking the entrance exams. However, the circumstances of your lives make you overcome within yourselves what is preventing you from acquiring the qualities of humility and obedience. The multiple sufferings and deprivations, illnesses and miseries that you experience are the accelerated descent of karma for you to come to the realization in your consciousness that there is Law, and that Law requires you in full; it requires your full submission to that Law. Moreover, you attain that submission yourselves during the hard work on yourselves, on your consciousness and subconsciousness, on all the accumulations of your past lives that are hidden inside your lower bodies.

You yourselves are capable of taking apart that debris in your consciousness that prevents you from accepting the Law of this universe. For many incarnations you demonstrated non-compliance with the Law and acted as you wished, as your ego dictated to you. Now, out of your own free will, you have to part with your ego and submit yourselves to the Higher Will and the Higher Law that exists in this Universe. As you move along the Path, you should manifest the quality of unity with all of life more and more. When some tensions arise between you, those tensions are conditioned by your imperfection, the energies that have not been worked through. You cannot momentarily get free from your karma, from the negative energies that you have acquired in the past, but you can make the decision to get rid of them and begin the process of liberation from the ego by daily work on yourselves, by daily choices and initiations.

Each of you needs to realize that it is only your consciousness and your internal motive that constrain you and slow down your advancement on the Path. If you develop the qualities of humility, submissiveness, and constancy, you will be guaranteed the ability to move forward successfully. It is impossible to get rid of your karmic load instantly, but it can be done by means of daily efforts, day after day, year after year. There are a very small number of people who are able to become free from karma quickly. As a rule, those people come into the world already with great achievements in order to fulfill a special Divine mission. The rest of the people have to understand that their positions on the path are determined only by past mistakes and wrong choices.

The first commandment I am giving you is that you must realize that nobody is guilty of the condition and position on the path that you have at present. Only you yourselves are responsible for all the circumstances of your lives. As soon as you realize that provision of my Teaching, you will become open to perceive many Truths that had been blocked by your consciousness before.

The veneration of the Hierarchy, of the Masters, is a very important quality on the Path. That is because without veneration to the Master you will not be able to advance on the Path.

When you grant your devotion and Love to the Master with love and sincerity, you receive into your aura the momentum of achievements that your Master already has. It does not matter whether that Master resides on the physical or on the subtle plane.

Many of you need a conduit in the physical plane, beside whom you will be able to acquire the higher energies. Those energies will help you to get rid of many imperfections and problems that prevent you from your advancement on the Path.

Therefore, I recommend that you use the rope that we give you when you begin to climb up the sheer cliffs to the top. That rope for you is our Messenger. Do not neglect her help and do not jerk back your hand when she offers you a helping hand. It is much more difficult to climb the cliffs alone. We are offering you a tested Path that is based on the Guru-chela relationships and on the Path of Initiations when you receive all our help and support by voluntarily entering the steps of the Hierarchy.

That is the Path that has been tested for centuries. That is the Path along which you were led by all great initiated beings of the past. Now the time has come when you should get the understanding of that Path. Use the opportunity that the Heavens give you and strive to get what is given to you. The doors of opportunity are open. A new dispensation is being given. Those of you who managed to enter the steps of the Hierarchy and get under the effect of this dispensation in time, have received an unprecedented acceleration of their development. Many of those who have been reading these Messages from the very beginning and visiting our events that we host with the help of our Messenger feel our blessings and our help.

I wish that an increasing number of people will become aware of our Path and enter the steps of the Hierarchy.

**I AM Serapis,
with wishes for success on your Path.**

My angels and I are ready to come at your first call!

Saint Michael the Archangel
July 15, 2006

I AM Michael, having come!

I have come! I have come in order to manifest my arrival in the physical plane through this Messenger!

I am happy to meet you again, and I hope that our meeting will be beneficial for you because all our contacts and interactions are very important.

You know me as the head of the Army of Lord who fights against any manifestation of negative energy. Yes, I serve to guard the interests of God of this Universe and do my job as my honor directs me.

My angels and I are ready to come at your first call or demand to give you the help that you ask for. Many kinds of evil spirits are staying in the astral plane of planet Earth, and according to my position, I am the one whose duty is to watch that these evil spirits do not impede the evolutionary development on the planet. I keep the order and assist your evolutionary development. I respond to your calls and carefully perform accordingly, but only when they correspond with God's Will.

Now I am ready to serve with redoubled power and energy, as I am glad to notice that a large number of human individuals have come to their senses and try to understand the Law of this Universe and to follow it. It makes us very happy. However, there is an aftertaste of sadness in this good news because there are those who have fallen so low in their consciousness that they cannot follow the evolutionary path any further. We act as grave diggers for those people. After the death of the individuals who have completely deprived themselves of the connection with God, there is a dark energetic cloud left in the subtle plane that cannot evolve further. Our task is to take this cosmic garbage away, to give way to everything that follows evolution an opportunity to progress. It is sad that many humans have attached themselves to the physical plane so tightly that they cannot continue their development. This life of theirs will be the last one because they have had no connection with God for many incarnations and they do not aspire to have this connection — the evolutionary process is over for them. They cannot stay on Earth any longer, and they will have to resume their evolutionary path on other planets in lower forms or get off the path of their individual development completely and return to the heart of the One for repolarization. All of that creates much work for my legions and me, but this work of ours clears the Path for you, those of you who follow the Law of this Universe.

You should not pay much attention to the things that are not related to your evolution. But my legions and I would be grateful to you if you read the prayer calls so that we could do our job in the subtle plane more successfully.

You know that many catastrophes and natural disasters happen in which many people perish. People perish for different reasons, and you cannot judge about those reasons or analyze them. But you can help the souls of those people who make their transition in tragic circumstances. And if you read a prayer call to me and my legions and ask us to take over the control of people's souls who perished in one or another catastrophe, it will make our work easier.

So please, if you are the witness of any catastrophe or you know about it from the news, do read the following call prayer:

"In the name of God the Almighty, in the name of my Higher Self, I ask beloved Archangel Michael and the Guardian Angels to take control over the situation connected with the following incident [indicate the exact place and give a description of the incident, for example, the catastrophe connected with the fall of the aircraft in ...]. **I ask you and your angels to help the souls of the people who perished in the catastrophe and escort them to the level of the Higher plane according to their attainments gained in this and in previous lives. May it be done according to God's Holy Will. Amen."**

It is hard to overestimate your help to those souls because you give these souls a chance to not stray on the lower levels of the astral plane but to rise with our help to the retreats of the etheric octaves where they will be given all necessary help and rehabilitation before their next embodiment.

Never judge whether the people around you are worthy or not in God's view. Human consciousness can neither know the level of achievements of other people nor the degree of their merits before God. It can be seen only from our level and plane who is who and what the merits of everyone are before God and people. Do not burden yourself with the excessive care of saving other people's souls. Do think more about saving your own soul. My angels and I are always ready to come and help you and to protect you from unforeseen situations in which you may find yourself if your karma allows my angels and me to render this help to you. Therefore, please do care about acquiring merits and good karma so that in critical moments of your life you can have enough energy for your prayer call to be fulfilled.

My angels and I always stand guard and are tirelessly on twenty-four hour watch. We serve mankind of Earth. I ask you not to forget about us and to call us for help in your everyday prayers and in the silence of your hearts.

Oh, it is so good to hear the words of gratitude from the people who have been given help. I simply bathe in the rays of your Love when you send me your Love and Gratitude. At those moments I am overwhelmed with so much Divine energy that my efforts directed at helping mankind of Earth increase manifold.

I am happy that there are people among you who are ready to send me their Love without asking me for anything. Your Love helps me to serve those who need my help and protection with redoubled energy.

And now I am ready to give you one more important direction. And that direction is related to your connection with your Higher Self. Many people make attempts to communicate with their Higher Self now. It makes the Ascended Hosts happy and they welcome it. But you should always remember that you are exposed to danger on the way to communicating with your Higher Self, just as you are in any activity having a dual character on planet Earth. When your motive is not pure enough and the purity of your low bodies is not enough, but your desire to have this contact in the subtle plane is strong, you can get the experience of communication — not with your Higher Self but with beings of the astral plane who, at best can play a trick on you, or at worst can enslave you and use you for their benefit. So, approach your contact with your Higher Self under the guidance of an experienced instructor, and before starting your meditation, always address me with a call or request to protect you from any negative impacts in the subtle plane and from the influence of any beings, demons, and non-incarnated spirits.

I strongly advise that you do not miss this call before every meditation of yours and before any attempt to communicate with your Higher Self.

Remember that nobody can forbid you from experimenting on your communication with the subtle world, but you bear the entire karmic responsibility when you start interacting with the forces of the dark, and basically staying and acting in the astral plane. And you always get in touch with the astral plane during your meditation — at least until you learn to rise to the Higher octaves of Light instantly like a high-speed elevator.

I have given you much information for your consideration today, and now I am saying goodbye to you.

**I AM Saint Michael the Archangel,
and I bring you the blue flame of my protection.**

It depends solely on you yourselves whether you will be able to provide your Higher Self with auspicious conditions for a conversation

Beloved Hilarion
July 16, 2006

I AM Master Hilarion, who has come to you with instructions for inner work. That is because the instructions that you receive from us are meant to be thought over in the stillness of your heart. We act through your consciousness; we try to expand your consciousness and get across to it the Truths that have unquestionably testified themselves for centuries. Those Truths you can test inside your heart.

Listen to your heart. Find the moment of stillness when you are calm and everything within you is in a perfect, harmonious state. Such moments are very rare, but those moments happen in the life of every person. God grants you those moments of inner silence so that you can consciously strive to repeat those states when everything within you is at peace and balanced. It is at such moments that it is the easiest for you to hear the voice of your Higher Self, the quiet inner voice in the stillness of your heart. Sometimes you cannot even differentiate that voice from the inner speculations that your mind produces, but you need to try to make the differentiation. That voice is notable for being exceptionally respectful to you; it is very gentle and is characterized by simplicity, unpretentiousness, sincerity, and love. You cannot but feel the difference from your daily monologues that you carry on inside.

You need to listen carefully. That is the voice of your Higher Self. It is not so often that you get to hear that voice. However, if you expect to hear that voice in your external consciousness, you can always make the distinction and differentiate that tender voice from the hundreds and thousands of other voices that belong to the astral plane.

You need to learn how to orient yourselves in your inner space. You need to strive for inner stillness and peace because in the bustle in which you live, you will not be able to hear your Higher Self. It is indispensable for you to hear your Higher Self because you will not find the advice and knowledge that you receive from within in any encyclopedia or book or in any television program.

I will give you an instruction that will help you to listen to your inner voice. That instruction concerns the changing of your lifestyle. You need to seclude yourself in order to hear your Higher Self. It simply cannot come close to you when you are too concerned about everything that surrounds you in the physical world. Imagine a child who has come into your world, who has just been born. Everything is stressful for that infant; everything that surrounds you in your life and that you are used to, is perceived by the infant as daunting and unseen. The noises from cars, the sounds of rough music — any sounds of your world — are unusual for the soul who has just come into your world, and they require certain adaptation.

Your Higher Self is similar to a child who comes into your world through you. The surroundings in which you live are sometimes so awful that your Higher Self instantly leaves your world only to wait decades for a favorable opportunity to come to your inner space again for a conversation.

Therefore, it depends solely on you yourselves whether you will be able to provide your Higher Self with auspicious conditions for the conversation. This physical world is so different from the Divine world that it is either difficult or impossible, not only for your Higher Self but also for all Ascended Beings that reside in more subtle planes, to stay in your world. Therefore, you need to create the conditions in your world so that we can come visit you together with your Higher Self and talk to you.

It is fairly clear that you will not be able to change all circumstances of your life instantly and move to a quiet, secluded place, leaving your established job and family. No, you are not required to do that, but you need to strive for the proper behavior models, for the quiet, charming music, for the gentle rustling of the grass, for the prattling of the birds and gentle babbling of the water. When the proper models of music, films, paintings, and everything that surrounds you fill your consciousness and your closest company, then you will be able to gradually overcome the negative effects of your world and transition into another, more subtle world. Your transition into the subtle world will be assured when you are able to assure the presence of the subtle world in your inner space and in your outer space. Then the angels and elementals will be able to come visit you, and you will be able to see them with your regular human eyes. Everything is in your power, and everything can be achieved through the change of your consciousness gradually, step by step. Yet, all the steps that you take should be made in the right direction. That is what constitutes the difficulty because the majority of you forget on the following day about all your good intentions and plans that you have made in your head while reading the Dictations of the Masters.

Therefore, the constancy of your aspirations must be developed in the first place. Do not allow your carnal mind to distract you, and do not give in to its arguments that you still have enough time ahead of you and that you can allow yourselves small innocent weaknesses that you are so used to.

Feel the border of the subtle world and remove from your consciousness everything that prevents you from crossing that border. Remove from your consciousness all wrong models and manifestations, everything that makes you deepen into materiality and get attached to it.

Proper mindset is essential. Nobody besides you will be able to overcome your imperfections and your attachments. The help of the Heavens will come at once, but you yourselves must realize your imperfections and wish to get rid of them. Sometimes a very small attachment requires many daily efforts in order for you to be able to part with it. In return, if your aspiration is firm, every following attachment of yours will require less and less time and effort to get rid of it.

Retain proper orienting points in your consciousness. When your life knocks you out of the state of peace and balance, you should have tokens of your past achievements, such as photographs, films, or diary notes in which you have recorded your elevated states of consciousness. For each of you there will be your own token or symbol that will remind you of the subtle world, such as a picture or image of the Master who is close to you. Do not neglect anything in order to elevate your vibrations again and return to the state of harmony and unity with the subtle world.

The higher the vibrations of your bodies, the higher the layers of the subtle world you will gain access to in your consciousness. You transition into the subtle world inside your consciousness by changing the vibrations of your body by yourselves. Your task is to gain understanding about the difference in vibrations and strive for the more elevated vibrations. Do everything that allows you to remain in the state of high vibrations as long as possible. For some people it is music; for others prayers; yet for others meditations. Use the whole array of means that are available to you in order to constantly retain yourselves in the high state of consciousness, away from the dark thoughts and feelings. Then you will be able to observe how everything in your life begins to change — your environment, your work. You will have to get used to the fact that everything around you will change together with the change in your vibrations. Your environment and what will not be able to adapt to your vibrations will leave your life, or you yourselves will leave everything that restrains your spiritual growth. You need to be able to differentiate very well between the caprices of your ego and the aspiration toward the more subtle and sublime world that is inherent in you. You need to distinguish very finely all the karmic moments that you still have not overcome and that make you — force you — to stay in the conditions that are uncomfortable for you. Nothing can be done here; everything that we have created ourselves needs to be worked off, even if it is very difficult and unpleasant for us. However, all those subtle moments of differentiation are under the full control of your Higher Self. You will always be able to receive all the necessary consultations from your Higher Self.

I have told you a lot today — all that is essential for you. That is because the further the development of mankind goes, the more and more subtle edges of illusion you encounter. You need to be ready to make your choices under any inner and outer circumstances.

I wish you to make only right choices!

I AM Hilarion.

**I wish you to manifest
only positive qualities in your lives
and to be constantly striving for
the glorious summits of the Divine World!**

Beloved Lanto
July 17, 2006

I AM Lanto, who has come to you.

I have come in order to give you a Message from our level of the etheric octaves, as always. The situation that exists on Earth and the problems that mankind faces but does not recognize due to being inside the problematic situation, becomes obvious from this level. In fact, for you, beloved, our Messages are the source of information that allows you to receive the orientation in your world. That is why we tirelessly come in order to give our Messages, and for that we use the opportunity that the Heavens provide: the communication with mankind of Earth through this Messenger, who is currently incarnated.

The institution of Messengers has always existed. There have always been people who incarnated on Earth with the mission to provide the connection between the worlds, to serve as transmitters of the Divine energies and knowledge to the physical plane. Without that opportunity, mankind of Earth would not be able to develop because it requires constant care and patronage that can only be provided by more highly developed beings that reside on a more subtle plane, in the subtle world, and in the fiery world. That is why we chose it to be our mission to serve mankind of Earth and to lift it to our level of development. It seems to you that everything that I am saying does not concern you directly, but I can disclose one small secret to you. I now have the opportunity to speak with those with whom I had already had conversations before their incarnation on Earth. It seems accidental to you that you have found these Dictations and are reading our Messages. However, you had already known before your incarnation that you had to find this Teaching because this Teaching is inevitably attracting you with its vibrations, and you feel what lies above the text and is written between the lines. It is a special feeling, an intuition, and the program that had been established by you yourselves before your incarnation on Earth.

You would not be able to develop if you did not receive daily guidance in your dreams when you visit our retreats; and you would not be able to develop if your souls did not receive the necessary instructions during the period between your incarnations on Earth. Unfortunately, the vibrations of your dense world deprive you of the opportunity to remember what you receive on the subtle plane as the call to action. Nevertheless, in your lives you constantly fulfill the plans that you set yourselves. You call it intuitive actions or using your intuition. Many people believe that they meet certain people by chance and that the situation unfolds by itself. Well, you can have these or other beliefs, but the process of evolution will go according to the predetermined plan. It is impossible to predict all the nuances and small details, but the general course of the evolution on planet Earth is being carefully monitored, and the millions of beings that reside on the subtle plane facilitate your development. Those include angels, elementals, the Ascended Masters, and many other representatives of various cosmic hierarchies and structures. You should not try to grasp the structure of the cosmic hierarchy too much. The time will come and you will receive all the necessary knowledge and understanding. Now, the most important point for you is to elevate your consciousness to the level where you are able to consciously perceive the subtle world and the goals of the subtle world. Then you will be able to acquire your own communication with the Higher part of you and through it, the communication with us, the Ascended Hosts. When the level of consciousness of mankind allows, that communication will be easily achieved and it will be inherent to the majority of Earth's population, just as the Internet has become widespread at this time. That new communication network will allow mankind to transition to a new level of communication and gain access to the cosmic data bank in the same way that you now receive access to the database contained in the Internet.

That is why we come again and again in order to awaken your consciousness from the long sleep and show you the opportunities and chances that will open up in front of you when you willingly give up your attachments to the physical plane. Remember how difficult it was for you to go on the Internet for the first time and gain an understanding of how it works? Now you are at the threshold of a new opportunity; you are at the threshold of a new cosmic opportunity that will allow you to go on the cosmic Internet. In the same way, there will be people who will be the first to gain that opportunity, and there will be those who will have to stay ignorant for many more incarnations. It is not because the opportunity will not exist for them but because they are too lazy to use the opportunity that is provided to them by God. Therefore, set aside your laziness and your attachments to the physical world, to your human habits, and finally look up to the Heavens! Widen your range of perception of reality! Strive for the Higher worlds and you will receive what you strive for!

It is impossible for you to achieve something if you do not have the understanding of what you need and what you need to strive for. That is why we come and give you the understanding of what you need to aspire to, and we also give you the instruments and approaches that you need to learn.

All the Divine perfection lies within you. You simply need to learn how to gain access to that perfection. In order to do that, you need to clear your conductors from the trash that you have collected on Earth during thousands of incarnations. You need to learn how to part with everything that you do not need in your new life.

Do not be afraid of changes; do not be afraid to part with the old habits and attachments, all that restrains your advancement and prevents you from breaking forth to the new level of consciousness, and gain truly cosmic opportunities.

Your attachment to your world impedes you. You need to understand that in the end, everything is determined by the level of consciousness that you have, and your level of consciousness is determined solely by your ability to break free from what prevents you from following the path of the evolution. You drive yourselves into a corner with your negative thoughts, with your negative perception of the world, with your criticism of everything that surrounds you. You need to learn how to experience a constant feeling of inner joy, even when the external circumstances of your life unfold in the worst way possible, or so it seems to you. That is because the dark period will inevitably be followed by a period of light, the dark night will be followed by the dawn of the new day! It will be this way as long as this material Universe exists. Soon, your feeling of joy will become such a genuine manifestation of your nature that you will not experience any negative feelings or dismay ever again!

I wish you to manifest in your lives only the positive qualities and to be constantly striving for the glorious summits of the Divine World!

**I AM Lanto,
wishing you a happy journey!**

We give you the Living Word, the Living Teaching, and expect you to bear our Word and our Teaching into life through concrete work in the physical plane

Sanat Kumara
July 18, 2006

I AM Sanat Kumara, who has come to you again on this day. I have come with the goal to get across the Divine Truth to you. You dreamt about gaining access to the fullness of the Divine Truth in your hearts. Now the time is coming when the Word of God should be open to you — not because this Word has been incomprehensible to you until now but because your hearts have been closed to the Divine Truth.

You can only hear in your hearts what you are ready for and what you are awaiting. In our turn, we are always ready to give you what you strive for. It is very similar to child upbringing. When the children are growing up, the toys that they used to play with become unexciting, and they turn their gaze toward new toys, which their consciousness has grown up to. Gradually, children become adults and enter the adult life, continuing to play the games that their consciousness is ready for in the adult life. Finally, the moment comes when none of the games of the physical world are able to satisfy a person's consciousness, and that means that this person is ready to transition to a new level of consciousness, into a different world.

In the beginning, the transition into that world goes unnoticeably and faintly visible. That world opens up inside of you. At first you feel that other world — different from your physical world — only a little and then more and more. You come in touch with that world in your sleep, during the moments of your enlightenments in the stillness of your heart. That world gradually begins to grow from your hearts into your physical world. Your physical world begins to change, becomes thinner, and acquires the characteristics of the subtle world. That penetration of the worlds begins inside of you, and you are that frontline troop of volunteers who are growing into the New World with their consciousness, bringing the coming of that World for the entire planet closer.

This process is happening. It began a long time ago. Lately, this process has been accelerating more and more. The transition into the New World, to the new level of development, may happen much sooner than it had been planned if the rate of growth of your consciousness increases with the same rapid speed.

Believe me, your consciousness is the greatest restraining factor that is hindering the course of the evolution on your planet. You still resemble students who had been held back in school due to not being able to learn the lessons given to them. We had to use many artificial maneuvers in order to drive your development from the deadlock where you got stuck. Now the dark Middle Ages of your consciousness are coming to an end. The awakening and the dawn of a new day are coming. I am happy to acknowledge this transition of your consciousness to a new level.

The Heavens are rejoicing that such a great number of individuals have reached the state of awakening of their consciousness!

Do not lower your guard, because the morass of the physical world is able to suck in your consciousness again and bring it to a lower level, typical of an animal-human. Remember and always know that you are Gods, and the next stage of your evolution is to finally become a man of reason and a God-man.

You differ from us only by the level of your consciousness, and many Ascended Masters are ready to sacrifice a part of their causal bodies in order to assure the growth of your consciousness. Indeed, many of the Ascended Masters sacrifice a lot and come into the incarnation partially by penetrating into the individuals who had given permission in the subtle plane for such a co-inhabitation. It allows you to be able to gain a leap in the level of growth of your consciousness. By acquiring such acceleration, you can have an influence on those who are close to you: your relatives, friends and coworkers. Such a leap of your consciousness cannot be hidden from the eyes of the people who have known you for a long time. They will neither be able to explain to themselves what has happened to you nor why they have lost interest and are no longer striving to associate with you. Yet other people, feeling the vibrations in you that they have been striving for over a long period of time, will find areas of common interest with you. You will become able to unite at a new level of consciousness and create a new future, residing at this new level of consciousness. You can have an influence on everything that surrounds you. The ability to unite and perform joint work is an undeniable proof that you have stepped up to the new level of your consciousness. You can tell other people about your merits and accomplishments as long as you wish, but if your inner accomplishments do not manifest themselves in the physical world in the form of concrete work and results, then those accomplishments of yours are worth nothing. Most likely, it is astral jokers who played a practical joke on you and told you about your greatness, which you have not yet achieved because your level of consciousness does not allow you to rise higher than the astral plane.

All of your accomplishments must be manifested in the physical plane. Your main accomplishment is the ability to collaborate and fulfill concrete work on the physical plane. You should not construct mythical projects on the subtle plane, but roll up your sleeves and build a senior home, a kindergarten for children, plant an orchard, and help your neighbor. There is a lot of work in your world, and all that work is done by those who have made certain spiritual accomplishments instead of just thinking that they have accomplished something.

In this way, we will be able to change the world by acting through those who have prepared their temple for our arrival and have expressed their readiness to serve.

The time has changed now. In the past it was necessary to read prayer calls and pray in order to work off your karma; now the time has come to perform concrete work on the physical plane. When you begin your collaboration in order to fulfill the plans of the Masters on the physical plane, your karma is being worked off at a flash-like speed. That is the new dispensation for your time. The working off of the karma will be accelerated for those who take concrete actions on the physical plane directed to fulfilling the plans of the Brotherhood.

Our plans remain unchanged for millions of years. Our plans are to give the Teaching and to follow the Teaching. It is especially good if you apply your efforts in the area of bringing up children and young people. That is because in ten or twenty years your efforts will yield real results when the new generation enters adult life and builds that life based on the Divine principles.

Today I wanted to draw your attention once again to the necessity of your work on your consciousness and your simultaneous collaborative work with each other on the physical plane. There is no time to wait until you become completely perfect. Your aspirations will yield results much faster if you apply all the acquired knowledge in your daily life as soon as you receive it. Whatever does not get reinforced in practice becomes useless, dead knowledge.

We give you the Living Word, the Living Teaching, and expect you to bring our Word and our Teaching into life through concrete work in the physical plane.

**I AM Sanat Kumara,
with Hope in you and Faith in you.**

About the dispensation of the 23rd and other opportunities being given by Heaven

Beloved El Morya
July 19, 2006

I AM El Morya Khan, having come to you in order to give a Message. On this day I must remind you of the dispensation concerning the 23rd day of each month. This dispensation allows you to get a chance to work off the karma of the following month based on your right spirit and behavior during the 23rd day. You know the terms of the dispensation.[16] Today I would like to draw your attention again to the moment concerning working off your personal karma. You can use the given dispensation to help work off planetary karma and the karma of your country. But I would like to remind you and to clarify once again that you can also use that opportunity to work off your personal karma and the karma of your nearest relatives who have karmic connections with you. So, if on the 23rd you perform the praying practice one hour per

---

[16] Messages given by the Masters related to the topic of the Dispensation of 23rd: "About the opportunity to unburden your karma of the next month and about the letters to the Karmic Board," Beloved Surya, June 23, 2005; "About the new Divine Dispensation," Beloved El Morya, June 27, 2005; "I have brought you two pieces of news — one is sad and the other one is joyful," Beloved El Morya, January 7, 2006; "Instructions about your attitude to everything around you in your dense world and in the finer worlds," El Morya, April 20, 2006; "About the forthcoming day of the summer solstice and the Divine favors connected with this day," Lord Maitreya, June 15, 2006. Refer to *Words of Wisdom* Volumes 1 and 2.

day and make the proper call, all the energy will be multiplied by the number of participants taking part in the dispensation of that day. And that energy will, first of all, be directed to transmute the karma that impedes the steady evolutionary development on planet Earth. The rest of the energy will be directed to solve your personal karmic problems, which you will ask for. This is an opportunity for you to lighten the karmic burden. So use it, ask and you will be given according to the efforts that you apply, not only in the form of a prayer but also in everything that you do on that day. Any activity of yours may be devoted to work off the karma of the following month.

Let Divine energy through you and direct it to dissolve your karmic problems, whether they are connected with your husband, wife, children, parents, or your colleagues at work.

This is a very important dispensation that really works now and helps you to break through your karmic problems. Any mechanism that Heavens give should be used by you at full capacity.

Now, when I have reminded you of your opportunities and God's grace concerning the 23rd day of each month, I would like to approach the main point for the sake of which I have come. I have come in order to give you the view of your situation, not the situation of each of you exactly, but the situation that has formed on Earth, the current situation on planet Earth. You have known from the previous Dictations, which we have been giving in this cycle through this Messenger, about the improvement of the situation on the planet. However, you should not relax or stop applying your efforts, because the process has just begun, and any relaxation is inappropriate. Only when you are capable of applying your efforts every day will you be able to maintain steady rates of transformation of planet Earth.

Now your efforts are still not enough, and the reserve of the energy used by us for stabilization is not being filled. Filling the energy becomes possible when more and more collaborators are able to give us the energy of their hearts. We appreciate the Love that you send us. Thus, your Love can fill in the missing amount of energy. We also appreciate your deeds, which you unselfishly do for the Brotherhood. We much appreciate those who in their consciousness are able to reach the level of the awareness of collaboration with the Hierarchy. The Heaven's help, which our collaborators feel at critical moments of their lives, is determined by the measure of the sacrifice that they have been able to make before, serving us. We send you thoughts and wishes, and you feel the energy you need to be able to perform the Brotherhood's affairs on the physical plane. The number of our incarnated collaborators becomes bigger and bigger. I cannot come to each of you and express my acknowledgment and gratitude for the work that you do for the Brotherhood, but I can express my acknowledgment and gratitude through this Messenger. Accept my low bow. I sincerely bend down before the Light of God in you and before those of your Divine qualities that allow you not to lose the way and to act in the interests of the Brotherhood, being on Earth at this difficult time for the planet.

Feel responsibility and keep your aspiration. In fact, the love of constant effort and tireless application of effort distinguish our disciples. You can unmistakably identify our chelas among you. They do not whimper or complain about life, but day after day they continue doing their job for the sake of which they have incarnated. No life troubles or tests can stop them, for their Faith is strong and their connection with their Higher Self doesn't allow them to lose the Way.

Our collaborators do not force anybody to pay attention to them. They do not tell everybody about the big work that has been completed and that is being done. No, they prefer to do their job quietly and tirelessly, without attracting excessive interest from the opposition. Everybody knows his job and does it.

Our collaborators are scattered about different countries and continents. I would like to note the special work of our collaborators in such countries as Russia, Bulgaria, Latvia, Germany, Ukraine, Lithuania, and Armenia.

We are waiting for those to appear on the land of America who will also wake up and restore their lost connection with the Hierarchy. Every new dispensation and every new opportunity that the Heavens give, offers new perspectives for those people and those countries that use the opportunity and participate in it. So, do not be shy about maintaining your relations with the Russian Messenger. There are no national or continental boundaries for our Teaching. We taught mankind of Earth even when there were no signs of the continents that now exist on the planet. And we will continue our training work and education of mankind because we believe that mankind of Earth will stand all the tests, and with dignity they will manifest those Divine qualities that are still lying dormant in most people of the planet.

We hope for collaboration with everyone; and to start your collaboration with the Hierarchy you can use my focus, my image, and address me every day with your requests and problems, your questions and wishes. The divisibility of my consciousness and the opportunity given to me by God allows me to be present in many places simultaneously and to give you my directions and recommendations. I hear all of you who address me. You only have to learn to hear me. I come to you and speak from the silence of your heart. Try to hear me. Move away from the fuss, sit quietly in front of my image, or simply imagine me in your mind. I assure you, that if your aspiration to hear me is strong, you will certainly hear my voice deep in your heart. It won't be a human voice usual to you. It will be the answer to all your questions. You will receive the answer and you will know that I have given it to you.

Have some training. You may not hear me from the very first time. Develop your quality of communication with the fine world.

I am always with you in the silence of your hearts, but I cannot be with you unless you prepare your temples for communication with me, unless you become free of most characteristic human habits. I will list some of them: alcohol, smoking, listening to rock music, negative states of your consciousness — offence, anger, depression, self-pity, etc.; all of these prevent me from getting in touch with you on the Higher plane and prevent you from hearing me.

Don't give way to despair if you have many imperfections. If you have chosen the Path and you tirelessly go along it every day, then very soon everything odd that impedes you will be cast away by you as useless and burdening to you on the way.

Only your Divine, eternal qualities will remain. Literally, in a few years you will look at yourself, at what you are now, and you will be surprised at how much will have been changed in you.

I am leaving you and looking forward to our new meetings in your hearts.

Well, I say goodbye to you!

I AM El Morya, always with you!

Do not miss your chance, and try to stay in the corridor of the evolutionary opportunity

Beloved Zarathustra
July 20, 2006

I AM Zarathustra, who has come again!

I have come, as always, in order to give you instruction in accordance with the needs of the current day.

Your request to receive this Knowledge must be fulfilled to the degree that the Law allows. It may seem to you that you know everything, and that you know how to do everything, and that you have perceived everything in this world. Let me tell you that in this case you are simply driven by common human pride. That is because it is impossible to perceive the Laws of this Universe when you are at your human level in the development of your consciousness. Only when you give up this human pride of yours will true Knowledge be able to enter your temple. Only by using the empty space that has become available in your vessel, can you finally be filled with true Knowledge. Until then, you fill your vessel with everything that is not only worthless but also extremely harmful for you. That is because the all-acceptance that exists on the planet now has never existed before for millions of years. Many manifestations had always been banned, and that ban was implemented at the religious or governmental levels. Now is a different time. You gain the ability to access a lot of things that are not beneficial to you but are no longer banned. Only your consciousness can serve as the censor that can prohibit you from doing and reading certain things.

That is why we come in order to give you an opportunity to understand what is not beneficial for your consciousness and what is necessary for your future development. Yet, you make the choice; you choose by yourselves. The choice that you make these days literally determines your future; it determines the course of your individual development and the course of the evolution that is taking place on Earth.

You do not get any bans, but the moral law that exists inside of you should determine by itself what is and what is not beneficial to you. The gift of distinction that is now taking the center stage is as essential to you as air and food. You need to learn how to make the distinction. This life of yours is the key life in the course of the evolution of your soul. That is because your choices in this life determine the future course of the evolution of your soul. You either go forward at a fast pace, or you will have to tag along at the back of the evolution. I will not be surprised if one of the lives of your upcoming incarnations resembles the life of a savage somewhere in New Guinea, because the preferences that you have made in this life are not any more advanced than the level of development of the Papuans. You will continue your dead-end branch of the evolution sitting by a fire and devouring your portion of meat.

God is so merciful that He will grant your wishes to do nothing but eat, sleep, and copulate. Such degradation has always taken place on the planet. Those tribes of people whom you consider undeveloped made their final choices sometime in the past when the time had come for such a choice. The further evolutionary path has closed for them. They work off the karma of the physical and other lower bodies, and then their evolution is over, and the cosmic garbage collectors remove them from the stage of the evolutionary path of development.

According to all cosmic terms, now you are to make your own choice. Many souls have accumulated on planet Earth, and not all of them are suitable for further evolution. For some, the question of choice is not so acute, and they can still continue to live comfortably and make their efforts to develop their higher consciousness. For others, all the cosmic terms have passed, and this incarnation is the key that will determine the course of further individual evolution of the soul.

I do not want to frighten you, but it seems rational to us that it is better if you are able to treat the choices awaiting you more consciously and understand the future threats if your choices do not fit the within the frames of the available cosmic opportunity.

That is why we are being so honest. I am glad that the time has come when we are able to tell you about our concerns so directly. If you do not think that it is necessary to listen to us, then that is your choice, and you are making it consciously by using the Law of free will that applies to you. That Law has its time frames. While the other Laws are effective until the end of the manifested Universe, the Law of the free will stops its manifestation when your development does not fit the frames of the cosmic opportunity that had been formed by that Law ahead of time. That is why we warn you. There is time, but it is very short, and for many, the period of choice ends with this incarnation.

Do not miss your chance, and try to stay in the corridor of the evolutionary opportunity.

You have to agree that if a person does not want to study at a school or university, after some time the parents stop their efforts to make their child study and leave him or her on their own. In the same way, we, while obliging you to grow and follow the Law, will sooner or later give up our efforts and leave you on your own to reap the fruits of your choices in one of the Papuan tribes.

Treat the choices that you make day after day consciously. As you advance, your choices become less and less univocal and obvious, the illusion around you gets thinner, and you are required to develop the Divine qualities and abilities to see the subtle world in order not to get lost. In order to leave the borders of the illusionary world, you need to rise in your consciousness to a new turn of evolution. We call you and tirelessly come to make an effort again and again to explain to you the basic knowledge of the Laws of this universe. Yet, many of you wave us away and continue to read and reread ecstatically the literature that puts your Divine opportunities to sleep and gives food only for the revelry of the illusion in your four lower bodies.

You are given physical vision, but you are also given spiritual vision. Why are you not using your gift? Until then, will you be falling under the influence of various villains who have become skilled in fogging your brain and forcing you to make one wrong choice after another? The whole distinction, the entire mechanism of distinction, is hidden inside of you, in your hearts. You all are created after the image and likeness of God. Why do you constantly forget about it and search for support in the physical world in order not to fall? You do not need any support in the form of clairvoyants, psychics, or fortunetellers. You simply need to use the mechanism of distinction that exists inside you. Your Higher Self has been waiting for hundreds and thousands of years for you to finally pay attention to it and listen to the advice that it wishes to give you in the stillness of your heart. No, you are constantly occupying your attention with outer fuss, only to avoid being alone with yourself and listening to your heart.

I was harsh today. I wanted to give you the whole eagerness of my heart and all of my flame in order to warm up your hearts and pull them out of the coldness of ignorance and darkness in which many of you continue to reside.

I have fulfilled what I had come for. I feel secure that now you can no longer say that you did not know anything and you have not been warned about anything.

**I AM Zarathustra, with Love to you
because only my Love has prompted me to have this talk.**

The summer cycle of Dictations that we have given in Bulgaria through our Messenger is over

Beloved El Morya
July 21, 2006

I AM El Morya Khan, who has come again. I have come in order to inform you that the summer cycle of the Messages that we have given in Bulgaria through our Messenger is over.

I am glad that we managed to give this cycle of Dictations in Bulgaria because every time we give our Messages, a tremendous amount of Light gets released at the location where the Messages are received. The country and the people who participate in the process of receiving the Messages acquire a considerable portion of Light. Each time it is about how you use the Light that you have received.

When a little over two years ago the mantle of the Messenger of the Brotherhood had been put on Tatyana, no one could guarantee that Russia would have a bright future. Complete chaos and disorder prevailed in the physical plane. However, we came and affirmed in our Messages that a great future was being prepared for that country on the subtle plane. Less than two years passed before what had been prepared on the subtle plane began to come down to the physical plane. Even the skeptics who were grumbling a year ago, saying that Russia was all lost, have now awaken in bewilderment and are scratching their heads.

The same is true for the country of Bulgaria. If it can proficiently utilize the Light that it has received, then big changes related to education and the economy will be waiting for it very soon. Everything is in your hands! All changes happen through the change of your consciousness.

There is always the danger that the Light we spill on Earth may be misused and distorted, but we always hope that your vessel does not turn out to be leaky and that you utilize the received energy in accordance with the Divine plan and the Divine purpose.

I am glad that we have managed to give a considerable bundle of Knowledge in this cycle of Dictations. Always remember that the Knowledge is given to you to think over, for reflection and meditation in the stillness of your heart. Do not strive to put aside the book with the Dictations as soon as possible. Try to completely absorb everything that is contained in each Dictation, in each drop of the life-giving Divine energy, and in each Word of the Divine Truth.

We come to mankind of Earth in order to strengthen our connections, the connections between the physical and the subtle planes. Our goals and objectives depend entirely on how fully you can acquire the information and the energy that is contained in our Messages.

Do not make us remind you again and again that the tremendous responsibility to transform the physical plane of planet Earth lies with you. Remember that you have come into this incarnation in order to take specific actions in the physical plane. In order for your actions to be perfect and comply with the Divine plans, you must first of all take care of your conductors. You should tirelessly purify your subtle bodies with prayer and fasting, walks in nature, and by association with children and animals. Contemplate on beauty, and under the influence of beauty you will change your inner state. Nothing has the same effect on a person as beauty and nature. Preserve and cultivate proper patterns in your lives. Try to have everything that surrounds you fill you with harmony and beauty. Do not be shy about directing other people; remind them that everything that surrounds them has a constant influence on their consciousness and inner world. This also concerns watching television and uncontrollable listening to the radio. Safeguard yourselves from any negative vibrations from which you can protect yourselves. There are many ways to protect yourselves from negative energies, and many of those methods do not require any financial investments.

That is why I have come to remind you that everything is in your power. You can count on the help of the Masters and make the calls, but you will have to act on the physical plane yourselves. All of the wonders that happen have been carefully planned. The miracle of the transformation of the physical plane will inevitably happen, but in order for it to happen, you need to prepare that miracle in your hearts.

I wish you successful self-perfection. Make sure that not a single grain of the Divine energy is directed to something other than its intended purpose. You are given a lot, and now you have to demonstrate your readiness to collaborate with the Heavens.

All your efforts will be multiplied and will undoubtedly germinate.

It seems that the changes that happen on the physical plane are not related to the Dictations that we give. However, believe me that almost all positive changes on the planet have always been related to the fact that people accepted our Messengers and the Word that they carry. If our Messengers were not accepted and honored, the country that allowed such negative actions was dropped into the twilight of consciousness for many years. We could only ask God to forgive them, for they did not know what they were doing.

We sincerely hope that the nightfall of human consciousness has been left in the past. Ahead is the bright dawn of Knowledge that you carry in your hearts.

I have come in order to give the closing Dictation of this cycle and to announce that we will continue the work through our Messenger as long as such an opportunity for our work is manifested in the physical plane.

Do not forget that each of you has the responsibility to take care of our Messenger. That is because Godly people have always lived thanks to the support of kind people.

I am parting with you, but I hope that our separation will not be long, and we will meet again through this Messenger. With those of you who are ready, I will come and meet personally in the stillness of your heart.

I AM El Morya, goodbye for the moment!

Messages from the Ascended Masters between the fourth and fifth cycles of Dictations

The quality of changing consciousness is the most important quality at the present historical period of time

Lord Maitreya
September 13, 2006

I AM Maitreya, having come again!

I have come, as always, to greet mankind of Earth and express to you all my Love and support, which Heavens are ready to offer you at the given moment and continue providing to you always, regardless of your perseverance in affirming some of your flaws and imperfections.

You are children, and like all children going through adolescence, you are experiencing the difficulties of your age. There is nothing to be afraid of; not that much time will pass and you will change and will remember this period of adolescence with awkwardness and embarrassment.

Look, only a few hundred years ago when we came and acted through people of Earth, those people were exposed to persecution, and they were executed and burned in fire. Indeed, times have changed a lot! I'm telling you that time has accelerated to almost the speed limit. And higher acceleration in change of consciousness is difficult to achieve in your physical world. All of this has to do with properties of your world.

I have come to assure you that everybody who continues to aspire along the Path of Initiations and is doing that with enviable perseverance and consistency, despite the encountered difficulties and misfortunes, is seen by me from my level as a flame directed upward. I can distinguish you and give you all the possible help upon your first call. Sometimes the circumstances of your life and horoscope won't allow me to help you quickly, but I always provide help to the extent that Cosmic Law permits me to. This happens because only a few remain dedicated to the Brotherhood. And if millions flare up and aspire, only a few are able to maintain the flame of their hearts burning from year to year during a considerable period of time, and even a smaller number of individuals are able to purposefully and consciously act according to our instructions.

Now I'm ready to give you some more information regarding the relationship with your Higher self. Very recently a new Message was given by the Highest Cosmic Council regarding special Divine mercy toward planet Earth. Now, those of you who express the necessary everyday aspiration will be helped in establishing the connection with your Higher self. For this you need to write a letter to the Karmic Board and ask so that, according to the Cosmic Law, you will receive mercy, and the descent of karma that blocks you from establishing connection with your Higher self will be temporarily stopped.

Do you understand, beloved? This doesn't mean that everybody will have his or her karma descent stopped. No, we are talking about those individuals who have almost reached the level required to achieve the connection with their Higher Self, but some old karma or energy, some quality that hasn't been worked off, is in their way. In this case, you will receive mercy and this part of karma will stop descending so that you can establish connection with your Higher Self. You will feel this connection, and you will be guided by your experience and your senses in the future. And when karma descent is restored, nothing will be able to block you from reconnecting with your Higher Self again and maintaining this connection, and through this connection, establishing connection with all the Ascended Hosts, and probably with me personally. For right now I am the Master who is preparing his arrival on Earth, and I seek to work with everyone who demonstrates required efforts and aspiration.

And right now, I must tell you about important things that have happened lately and have not been covered in our previous Messages.

I have to say that the efforts of those people who are working on spreading our Messages given through this Messenger have not been in vain, and the situation on Earth is developing in the most favorable way. This doesn't mean that there won't be any cataclysms and catastrophes; this only means that the overall course of humankind's evolution has been taken by us under reinforced control, and right now we are able to totally control the situation on planet Earth. I'm happy that your efforts have been so effective. Imagine if our Messages were accessible to the majority of the population of planet Earth. What would happen?

I will tell you what would happen. The change in consciousness of only one per cent of humanity of Earth is able to completely change the course of evolution on the planet. And changing the consciousness of half of Earth's population is capable of transferring the planet into the next evolutionary level with the speed of lightening. And we would have to be slowing down the process of change so that your physical bodies could tolerate such a rapid change. You will have to stay in your physical bodies for some time so that you can completely work off the karma created by you on the physical plane. And then you will leave your bodies and will exist in a thinner world. It will happen, and you should aim for this.

My presence on planet Earth has never been so vast due to my connection with you, due to your aspiration toward me and your ability to change.

The quality of changing consciousness is the most important quality at the present historical period of time. And those of you who have mastered this quality to a greater extent understand that just this particular quality can change the entire world.

However, to master the quality of changing consciousness, you need unconditional Love and Divine patience and tolerance toward everything that is not yet perfect.

I wish you to overcome everything within you that is not from God as soon as possible, and I wish to meet with each of you who courageously overcome all difficulties in your life and shake your hand.

See you soon!

I AM Maitreya!

I have come to affirm the qualities of joy, aspiration, and victory in your consciousness

Lord Maitreya
October 9, 2006

I AM Maitreya, having come through my Messenger again. I have come to give the next Message to the people of Earth. As always, I would like to say many things, but I will have to focus on the most important matters that are urgent and need to be conveyed without waiting for the next cycle of the Dictations. So, I have come in order to tell you some new information so that you can take a new look at the things that have been previously mentioned and to reconsider some of your views and stereotypes. Today's information concerns the changes that continue taking place at an accelerated pace in the consciousness of people. We are glad that the pace of these changes has accelerated so much that, at last, the time has come when we can surely state the fact that the changes taking place on Earth are favorable in terms of evolution. These changes are taking place in all spheres of activity. I must especially emphasize that the process of changing has accelerated within the consciousness of people inhabiting both Russia and those countries that read our Messages which we are giving through our Messenger. I am glad, and the Ascended Hosts are glad that mankind is entering the zone of sustainable development, and no external circumstances can prevent us from executing our plans.

As soon as the worlds became contiguous, the process of interpenetration of the worlds accelerated, and now nothing can get in the way of the changes that are taking place.

I am happy that a sufficient number of people in incarnation have been found who have responded to our appeals and have taken upon yourselves the burden of disinterested serving to mankind of Earth. Your ranks are increasing in number every day. Of course, there are those who have allowed doubts to seize their consciousness and lost much of what has been gained through strenuous efforts. But not everything is lost, as rollbacks and doubts are inevitable in your world. This is because your world has always developed in an undulatory way. Do not allow negative states to seize your consciousness. I understand that with the change of the season and the coming of the dull autumn days when the Sun is a rare guest, it is difficult for you to keep your consciousness at a high level. That is why I have come today to cheer you up and to give you a Message in the form of an affirmation of the attained progress. Your progress is so evident that only skeptical people may keep on pretending that there are no changes at all. I have come to affirm the qualities of joy, aspiration, and victory in your consciousness; victory is unavoidable and is awaiting you in the relatively near future. Keep up!

I am happy that we have succeeded in passing the Divine Truth to such a large number of human individuals incarnated in this difficult far-reaching time. And I am happy that many of you have awakened from your long dormancy, which you have been in for more than one incarnation. The time has surely come, and the cosmic opportunity predicted by the prophets of the past has opened up for Earth. It will not take long for this opportunity to appear in the manifested world. Observe all the circumstances that are changing around you. Do not stop mentioning the changes taking place in your diaries. There have never ever been such miracles, which are becoming more and more evident now. I will not be surprised if soon the governments of many countries of the world base the policies of their countries in accordance with the

Cosmic Law. They simply will not be able to manage in the old way using old governance techniques, because the consciousness of the masses has changed and demands that all authority institutions adjust to the transformed people's consciousness.

The generation that is coming into life now needs special care and protection. It is exactly this generation that is to fulfill the Divine Plan in the near foreseeable future. Do not be afraid of the changes in your lives or in the situation in the world. Nothing can threaten you if you behave in a proper way and keep the Law properly. None of the disasters or cataclysms can threaten those who faithfully serve God, who exists within all of Life and in each particle of Life.

I have been glad to express my own delight in this Message and to give credit for your efforts, which you apply every day.

And now I would like to give one more little piece of information; this information concerns the events of the so-called Transition that many people are waiting for and preparing themselves for. One should never take any prophecy or any upcoming disaster too seriously because many prophecies were uttered but did not come true, whereas other prophecies that were not uttered did come true. I recommend that you tune in to the present and catch every moment of your life as the one having value for centuries. In fact, nothing exists in the Divine world but eternal "now." And this "now" you create by your own consciousness. One should never pay too much attention to what has already happened or to what has not happened yet. Your mood in every moment of your life is the only thing that forms the future that is waiting for you. Therefore, focus on filling each moment of your life with joy, love, warmth, and happiness because you yourselves are the creators of your happiness, and you yourselves are the creators of your future.

We come to give the Teaching, but you and only you can carry out the changes on your planet when you take in this Teaching and become a bearer of this Teaching for millions of those who have not awakened yet.

I am glad that the time of awakening is coming for many people, and I am glad that I can come so easily and share my state and my mood with you. I will be much happier if I manage to pass my state on to as many incarnated people as possible.

I have been happy with our new meeting, and as always, it is a bit of a pity to part.

See you later, dear friends!

I AM Maitreya!

Book 5

Cycle 5: Messages of the Ascended Masters
from December 20, 2006 to January 10, 2007

**All efforts of your will are required
of you not to take the bait
of the energies of the past
but to aspire to the new day!**

Sanat Kumara
December 20, 2006

I AM Sanat Kumara, having come again in order to tell some joyous news to you! We commence a new cycle of Dictations through our Messenger. And, as always, there is a lot to talk about. This process of our communication and our applied efforts is not in vain. Every time we notice more and more new changes in the consciousness of more and more human individuals who are incarnated in this difficult time.

We come in order to reinforce and anchor our focus of Light, our flame, which we have tirelessly carried and given to mankind for millions of years. And now, as never before, we are happy to state that our efforts are so obviously reflected in the minds of people and in the activity that is taking place in the physical plane. We cannot help being surprised by the miracles that have already been manifested and that will be manifested on planet Earth, both with our help and with your help, and with the help of those people who have decided to devote themselves to serving Life and serving mankind of Earth. Each of you, our devotees, must be aware of the fact that at this difficult and life-changing time, one person only may be missing — the one with whom the circuit of the Divine opportunity becomes complete. So, if you are still in the state of indecision and hesitation, I recommend that you stop paying attention to your minor everyday problems as soon as possible and aspire with all your being to us in order to fulfill those tasks that we affirm in your consciousness and to the fulfillment of those tasks which we are calling you to do.

We are never tired of repeating again and again that we need faithful devotees who, at our first call, are ready to rise and go where their efforts and abilities are needed to fulfill the Divine Plan for the sake of which they have now come into incarnation at this hard time for the planet.

I always remind you of your responsibility and your obligations that you have taken upon yourselves before your incarnation because every time you reading our Messages, you experience inner thrill and willingness to fulfill your duty. Yet, some time passes and you forget about your obligations and your aspiration, and you succumb to the fuss of life which swamps you like a mire, making you rush along the wrong path, the path of chasing momentary blessings and pleasures to the detriment of what is eternal.

And now I would like to remind you once again that the darkest and most severe time of the year is approaching. This is New Year's Eve, the new day's eve. It is exactly before the dawn that the night is as dark as never before. That is why the phantoms of the past, the phantoms of your previous blunders and errors in the form of unbalanced energies, will appear around you and arise from your consciousness. These energies will be dragging you away from the Path. All efforts of your will are required of you not to take the bait of these energies of the past but to aspire to the new day!

It is very difficult for you to believe that the thing that I am telling you about is very vital and urgent for you. Believe me. The festive fuss and buzz must not occupy your attention, but rather, tranquil consideration, in the candlelight, of the things you are to do and of the ways to remove the barriers that prevent you from fulfilling your mission. Do not seek these barriers outside yourselves. Analyze your previous course of life and try to understand what is there within you that hinders you and impedes your advancement along the Path.

You know the Path. You have been shown the Path. Those of you who have gotten an idea about this Path and have felt an urge to overcome inner barriers and imperfections will never turn away from this Path of Initiations that we are calling you onto, and that is enough to instantly pull you out of the mire of life, and like a high-speed elevator, raise you to the top of the Divine consciousness. I am glad that many people have aspired. And I am glad that for many people our Messages are the lighthouse that shows the Path in the dark. I am glad that thousands and dozens of thousands of people have awakened but our task is to wake up millions of sleeping souls.

Therefore, we come and tirelessly repeat the Teaching, ancient as the world itself. Many of you begin to recollect your previous incarnations and those feats that you performed for the Good of the whole Life. This is not accidental, because now there are so many souls of light incarnated on the planet that the Heavens have literally become deserted. Each of those who are on the other side of the veil are hoping for you with all heart and soul and endeavors to help the birth of the new thinking, the new consciousness, not based on previous dogmas but on the Knowledge and Wisdom of millenniums. You have forgotten about the Wisdom that you were originally taught in our retreats. Now the time has come to return to Divine Wisdom and leave the labyrinths of the carnal mind. Your carnal mind is trying to persuade you and lead you along the secret passages and subterranean labyrinths of wrong logic. However, your immediate task in the near future is to recollect the only true logic, the logic of the Divine World. It does not matter how different this logic is from everything that you have encountered in your life; you have to accept this logic and study it — not with your external consciousness but with your heart. Only then, when you open your hearts and aspire properly, you will be able to comprehend the Divine Law and Divine Wisdom. Only the one who abandons earthly logic is able to be imbued with the Divine logic. This is the difficulty of your time because you have to take us on trust and to aspire to those cliffs, sometimes without any safety equipment. Then, if your faith is steadfast, you receive at your disposal the tools that enable you to surmount your path as efficiently as possible. One fine day you will discover that your consciousness has changed unrecognizably and there is no turning back to the past. The Divine Reason within you will triumph over the logic of the carnal mind. We repeat the things that seem obvious. However, a very small number of human individuals can fully comprehend and perceive our Teaching.

All of the Divine is very simple. This simplicity frightens off and is doubtful for those who still search for complicated paths and voluntarily drive into the maze of the teachings that lead nowhere but toward the death of the soul. We do not want to scare you, but warn that the cosmic deadlines have approached, and there is no place for the obsolete in the New World. At the turn of the year you must carry out a thorough revision in your minds, in your consciousness, and willfully leave everything that is not Divine and everything that prevents you from your advancement along the Path. You have some time, yet the time is short.

I have been with you today. I am happy with our new meeting.

I AM Sanat Kumara. Om.

Now, at the change of the annual cycle, it is especially beneficial to make the decision and free yourselves from everything that is unnecessary in your consciousness

Beloved Surya
December 21, 2006

I AM Surya, who has come again in order to give a Message to the people of Earth. I have come to you from the Great Central Sun, having traveled a long distance. However, I am the Master who is very close to you because everything concerning Earth and its evolutions is under my authority and under my immediate patronage and because each stage of the evolutionary development on planet Earth is directly attended and supervised by me. I am leading and directing the evolutions of planet Earth. I am the one who is responsible for the course of evolution on the planet. And I am that being who is always beside you, despite the cosmic distance that is separating us. Now I have come to give you an understanding of the course of your development and of the stage where humanity of Earth is now. As always, my words will be very simple, but behind the simplicity of the presentation, the hard work of thousands and millions of beings of Light invisible to your physical eye is hidden; these beings are watching the evolution on your planet and are ready to provide you with all the necessary help 24 hours a day.

You resemble children in a junior group of kindergarteners who require constant care and guardianship. You may not see all those people who care about you, cook food for you, do laundry, and clean the rooms, but those people are always near you, though you do not always see them with your physical eyes. Our presence must also be felt by you based on the outcomes that surround you. Even though the deeds of the people of Earth are not always reasonable, the fact that we manage to maintain the favorable conditions for your development on the planet demonstrates the pinpoint accuracy in the work of all of the Ascended Hosts, whose work is aimed for the good of the evolutions of Earth. It is not always that you can properly assess our work, yet we are always beside you.

The difficulty is that the veil separating our worlds is still very dense, and we cannot prevent many things that could be prevented and secured against, due exactly to the fact that our worlds are too separated and far from each other — not in terms of the distance but in terms of the level of vibrations. That is why we tirelessly repeat to you about the necessity of elevating your consciousness and raising the level of your vibrations. When your vibrations reach a higher level, we will be able to be closer to you and provide you with more help and support. That is why, in order to raise your vibrations, you should use all the means available to you. There are things in your life that lower your vibrations, and there are things in your life that raise your vibrations. It concerns everything: food, clothes, and everything around you. Your homes and your cities are at a very low energy level. Therefore, by taking care of the place where you live and the environment around you, you automatically raise the level of your vibrations and become capable of differentiating between your states of consciousness and become capable of hearing the sounds of the subtle world and discerning our presence.

It would be strange to count on you being able to hear us if you continue living your lifestyle, the lifestyle that is typical of the mass consciousness of mankind. It is necessary for you now to think about everything surrounding you, and that is the next stage of your development: when you will have to pay more attention to everything that surrounds you in your life at home and at work. You will have to take care of your environment because when you do not apply any efforts to separate yourselves from everything that is low-vibration, you will slow down your development and will not be able to enter the passage of the cosmic opportunity, which is approaching and which has already come.

We are speaking about the transition, and this transition must take place in your consciousness. You yourselves must prepare your own transition. For if you are not capable of doing this in a natural evolutionary way, we will have to take tougher measures similar to spanking you or having you stand in the corner — the most widespread punishments for disobedient little children. Do not be stubborn. It is time for you to grow up, and it is time to learn to obey the Law that exists in this Universe. Otherwise, you will not be able to leave kindergarten to continue your development at school and at the university, and you will not be able to perform the work for which your lifestream is meant.

Therefore, do not procrastinate, but start right now analyzing everything that is surrounding you in your life, and get rid of what will not be useful for you at the next stage of the evolutionary development. Stop playing the games of yesterday and aspire to the new day with its joyful sun and fresh wind of changes.

Your consciousness needs airing and drying in the sun. Remove all useless thought-forms and models from your consciousness; remove everything that is not from God, and your life will begin to change as if with a wave of a magic wand. Let yourselves become gods in manifestation. Allow yourselves joyful states of consciousness; allow yourselves to take care of your dearest ones; allow yourselves to BE and to rejoice at your life. Only when you change your approach to everything around you, will all the circumstances of your life change as well.

Now, at the change of the annual cycle, it is especially beneficial to make the decision and free yourselves from everything that is unnecessary in your consciousness. Do not forget about the dispensation of the letters to the Karmic Board. Write the letters. You have that opportunity until the end of this year. Ask the Karmic Board to free you from what you would like to become free. What qualities and bad habits burden you and impede your development? Direct the momentum of your prayer during the next six months at the elimination of your cherished imperfections, and you will not recognize yourselves in six months. The more prayer energy you promise to the Karmic Board to release during the following six months, the sooner you will free yourselves from all your unfortunate attachments and karmic problems.

So, in order for you to take advantage of the dispensation and write letters to the Karmic Board, you must thoroughly analyze what you would like to get rid of first. Address the members of the Karmic Board, list all your requests and wishes. Take on prayer or other obligations that you are ready to perform regularly during the next six months. Write down your requests and obligations on paper; ask Archangel Michael and the angels of protection to accompany your letter directly to its destination, the Karmic Board; and then burn your letter. You may keep a copy of the letter, and in six months, provided that you have fulfilled the obligations taken upon yourself, see what has changed. I am certain that you will get rid of one or several of your main imperfections. Do not forget about gratitude. As soon as you become free from your problems, write a letter of gratitude to the Karmic Board.

It is a pity for me to part with you because I would love to give you all the necessary help and the most important advice, which will help you very much. I hope that I was able to at least partially help you and have given you several very useful pieces of advice.

I am saying goodbye to you, until we meet again!

I AM Surya!

Take our hand and hold it until Faith returns to you and your doubts clear away like an autumn mist

Serapis Bey
December 22, 2006

I AM Serapis Bey, having come again in order to give the next Message that will help you and that you need. Every Message of ours becomes more and more necessary for you. At last you start to master our rules of play. These rules mean regular intake of Divine Energy. As soon as you dedicate yourself to the process of modeling yourself into a new human, you initiate the process of changing yourself in accordance with our Divine patterns. Every time we come, we endeavor to pour a new portion of life-giving balm into your consciousness, and you become capable of changing.

In fact, in this process of changing your consciousness there is nothing that would make the learning process under our guidance different from any other learning process. You make the choice yourself and decide whether to come under our influence or fall under the influence of mass media or other people who do not represent us but consider it their duty to give you their teaching.

The difference between the Teaching through our Messenger and a good many other teachings through those people who consider it their duty to give you their teaching, is in the purity of the source. We begin giving our Teaching through our representative regularly only if we have had a chance to become convinced about the devotion and sincerity of our representative. Every time we come, we have to remind you about the previously given material, and then give a little piece of the new. Since your consciousness is very limited, everything that concerns our Divine world is so unusual to your human consciousness that at times it causes denial and even rejection.

However, we are not in a hurry at all. It is much more important for us that you take in at least little pieces of Truth rather than rush at accelerated pace along unknown and unbeaten tracks, which are offered in abundance — by this I mean many wrong teachings and sects. You may surprisingly note in your consciousness that once again it is said that there is only one right and true Teaching, and all the rest that you come across in your lives should be rejected. I cannot agree with you, because the Truth is scattered in almost all of the teachings and is present in various sources. However, the whole matter is in the ratio of Truth to lies and in the ability to distinguish where the Truth is and where the lies are. We teach you how to distinguish. We do not teach you to take everything on trust. You may analyze the given Teaching with your external consciousness, taste it, compare it with other teachings, and come to certain conclusions. However, sooner or later you will have to make a choice and choose the Path that we are teaching you because this Path is the shortest and has been predestined for you by the very course of your evolutionary development.

We are the Masters of Wisdom who endowed you with our consciousness in ancient times. There is a little part of us within you. No matter whether you wish that or not, you will have to give us back what was lent to you so that you can develop. The time has come for you to cultivate the Divine reason within yourselves in order to give us back those crutches that we gave to you. Now you have recovered, and your consciousness is acquiring Divine purity again so now you can advance further, guided by our Teaching and our principles. However, not all of you have reached the required level of development. That is why we have to come again to give our Teaching, which is aimed at a general audience and is comprehensible for many. We spread our nets wide and strive to help as many souls as possible to find the true Path and to return Home as soon as possible. We do not make you follow our Path; we just tell you and warn you that this Path is the shortest. It is your choice whether to follow this Path or not, and you advance along it by yourself.

Every time, I can't help but wonder at the many people who long for true Teaching and come to our educational classes. Yet every time, thousands and millions of various reasons and excuses appear, which gradually take our disciples away from the Path. When they return to our etheric, educational classes between their incarnations, they are astonished at their blindness and at the fact that they made one wrong choice after another and that they saw not the things actually revealed before their eyes, but the things that they wanted to see themselves. Well, you have the right to be mistaken.

You can make attempts, go, fall, rise, and go again. I just want to put the rope of confidence into your hands. I would like to convey the whole momentum of my Faith and my determination to you and the whole momentum of my achievements. I wish to help you very much. And I would like those of you who experience negative states of consciousness and frequent doubts in the correctness of the chosen Path to appeal to me more often and talk to me. You will find me in my retreat over Luxor. Before falling asleep, visualize a picture of my retreat and try to formulate your questions and the things that cause your doubts. I will work with you during your night sleep, and you will feel relief in the morning because I will find those right words and arguments that will help you on your part of the Path. I will extend my hand to you, and throughout the day you will be recalling how tightly you were holding my hand in yours and did not want to release it.

I will render you all the assistance that can be rendered to you, but do ask for the help. If in your pride you cannot even ask for our help, we cannot help you. Do not hesitate to remove everything from your consciousness that may prevent you from asking for our help and support. You know that the Law of this Universe has granted you free will, and we cannot violate your free will and render assistance to you without your request and without your call. But as soon as the call is uttered, we must respond. We will give you all possible help and support. Do not neglect our help, especially now at the end of the year when the old negative energies are activated and many of you experience heavy depressive and hopeless states.

We extend our helping hand to you. We wish to help you and can help you. Take our hand and hold it until Faith returns to you, and your doubts clear away like an autumn mist.

Now I am ready to give you one more important instruction that will undoubtedly help you. This instruction concerns your devotion and Love. Please, cultivate devotion and Love within yourself. Do not hesitate to thank us in the moments when you experience unconditional good spirits and are ready to love and hug the whole world. Send your Love to us so that when one of your fellows needs our help, we will direct the stream of your Love and gratitude to that heart in need. Thus, you will be able to help each other. In this way, we will be able to multiply Joy and Love in your world.

I am sending you my Love and support.

I AM Serapis!

We come to tell you about the principles on which the Community is established

Babaji
December 23, 2006

I AM Babaji, having come again to transmit the Teaching, which is as ancient as the world. I have come today, and the Sun has announced my arrival.[17]

I am happy about the provided opportunity because every opportunity for our communication still requires considerable efforts and sufficient energetic consumption for its realization. But we are moving toward you, overcoming all temporal and spatial barriers associated with the difference in vibrations between our worlds.

I have come in order to affirm the ancient truths and the wisdom of centuries in your consciousness once again. This truth and this wisdom say that nothing that has separated itself from the world has ever managed to exist for a long time. Many times there were sages and prophets who separated themselves from the world and tried to cognize the entire fullness of Divine Truth in solitude; their path was not easy and was full of various deprivations. Many of them merely died without knowing the Divine Truth and even without coming in touch with it. It is the path of solitary individuals; it is the path of pathfinders. Very few of them, at

---

[17] That morning was overcast, it was snowing. At the moment when Babaji came, a ray of sun appeared in the clouds, and the sun was shining throughout the transmission of the Dictation. Later the sky became gray again, and it started snowing.

the cost of tremendous efforts, managed to touch the Divine Truth concealed deeply in their hearts, and then the world obtained a new philosopher, a new sage, or a prophet who was able to share the acquired Truth with thousands and millions of other people. These two processes — to comprehend the Truth and to deliver the Truth to other people — are the processes that complement each other and cannot exist without each other, because it is impossible to access the countless riches in the Heavens without sharing them with others. When one endeavored to acquire the Divine treasures personally for himself and for his own development, he failed every time. God wishes that the development of mankind takes place in a more or less regular rhythm, and it is impossible to exist in your world if you are too far from everything around you, according to the level of your vibrations.

That is why I come and teach you, and all the Ascended Hosts come to you to give you their Teaching because it is impossible to be isolated in this Universe. Sooner or later, the individual who becomes too isolated will not be able to exist.

I am trying to convey to your consciousness the principles of a Community — the principles enabling us to spread our Teaching in your world on the basis of the Community. Tested by centuries, the principle of the Community is the principle of consolidation of the new Knowledge and of raising the morality of people of Earth to the new level. Each time a Community is established, it aims to affirm, at the new qualitative level, the Knowledge introduced in the physical plane by the Heavens at a particular stage of human development. The Community, as it is, has no practical value. The Community is only valuable if it fulfills its tasks defined by the Heavens. When a Community is considered as people living together in one settlement, it fulfills the principle of a false community. An authentic Community may only be established around those beings who are vested with our power and trust, because if a Community is established on our principles, we pour in the cup of the Community the Divine Energy needed for its development and maintenance.

And now I recommend that you ponder in your heart over everything that you have been told today and everything that you have ever read about communities and its coworkers.

As soon as the person representing our interests in the physical plane leaves the Community, this Community gradually loses its significance and breaks up. There is still no proper mechanism that would enable the Community to exist without the basis, which is the focus of Light that we affirm in the heart of our Messenger. It resembles a house that cannot exist and be inhabited in the conditions of severe winter if there is no fire in its hearth.

We come to tell you about the principles on which the Community is established. The process of establishing a Community is very gradual. First, a matrix in the subtle plane is created. This matrix completely corresponds to the Divine patterns, the Divine principles of Community establishment. Then, within a certain cosmic period of time, one cycle after another, this matrix begins to precipitate in the physical plane and to germinate in the physical world in the form of an area, a building, and purely human rules and principles that form the basis. The Community always has to adapt to the conditions existing in the country that we choose for the Community establishment. The conditions establishing of the Community are always formed by us in the subtle plane and precipitate in space and time. Now the Community and its establishment are completed in the subtle plane, and we expect this Community to begin its precipitation in the physical plane in the near future. This will not be the materialization in the full sense. This requires a great allowance of energy that we are not able to provide so far. But we will be pleased to accept your help and your resources that you are ready to sacrifice for us in order to establish our Community. Of course, it will not be possible for all comers to enter the Community. This Community will open its doors only for those people whose vibrations and aspirations correspond to our plans and hopes.

I would be very happy if within a few years such a Community could be established in the territory of Russia because it is the country in which we are commencing this establishment. Russia is the country to which we provide our sponsorship, and it must soon realize the principles that we would like to adopt in every country of the world.

I am very glad that today I have managed to give several fundamental points needed to affirm the consciousness of the Community in your minds and hearts. I am very glad that it has taken place at an important astrological moment of the changing of the solar cycle. Therefore, the new consciousness and the new thinking will germinate in your consciousness along with the lengthening of the day in the Northern hemisphere. And everything that prevents the establishment of such a Community will be fading away like nightly darkness at sunrise.

I have been talking about the Community, and some of the principles of the Community have been brought to your consciousness by me. I will be glad if what has been sown will be able to germinate, sprout, and harvest in the appropriate seasons.

Later, when you come to reread this Message, newer and newer details will germinate in your consciousness. And you will be able to comprehend the plan that we have and are bearing in our hearts in the land of Mother Russia.

I was happy to give you this important Teaching particularly at this time.

Now I have to say goodbye, and I do not lose hope for our next meetings. Om.

I AM Babaji.

The time is ripe not to speak about God, but to act in your lives in obedience to the Divine Law

Master Lanello
December 24, 2006

I AM Lanello, having come today to give you one more Message. The advantage of our Messages is in their opportunity to influence a mainstream audience. We give moderate information comprehensible for millions of people. And in the near future we sincerely expect millions of people to trust in us, the Ascended Masters, and to start to transform the illusion of the physical plane under our guidance. The time has finally come for the transformation of the physical world to take place in accordance with the Divine plan for the current time. The age, which is triumphing now, requires transformations in all the spheres of human life. The above is true not only of the spiritual sphere but also of politics, the economy, education, and public health. Everything must be transformed under the influence of new energies and new vibrations that are descending into the physical plane now.

If before certain transformations required a centuries-old period in order to take place, at present the realization of the necessary changes will be just a matter of years. Such are both the dictate of the present time and the decision of the Supreme Cosmic Council for planet Earth. So, strive to change yourselves and to give up as soon as possible the traits and imperfections preventing you from advancing on the Path of transformations. Only when you purify yourselves from past energies and get rid of karmic accumulations, will you be able to discern the tasks ahead of you and the things you are required to realize. But as long as you refuse to accept this within yourselves and continue to dig in your heels, tightly holding on to your outdated stereotypes of thinking and old imperfections, you cannot move to the beautiful horizons of the New Day destined for you.

Do dare to meet eye-to-eye with yourself and with your imperfections. If my words annoy you and it seems to you that you are perfection incarnate, and that nobody, including the Ascended Masters, has a right to lecture you, then you are lacking the essential quality on your Path — Divine humility and obedience. It seems to you that it is you who are the architects of your fate and can do with yourselves whatever you like. Yet, you must realize the Divine logic. Your God the Father is a very caring and loving parent. In this respect you are very lucky with your Father in Heaven. And because He loves you greatly, He cannot allow you to continue your actions that have caused harm to your soul harm at that rate. Trust your Father and humbly submit to His Will.

The change of cosmic cycles is an inevitable requirement of the time. Thus, the things that obstruct the Great Transition within you must be overcome by yourselves. Do not persist in opposition because only when you within yourselves make the decision to get rid of everything unnecessary, obsolete, and negative, and ask God to free you from your karmic load, only then are the Ascended Hosts able to rush to rescue you and to help you in overcoming centuries-old layers of negative energy.

But if you resist and defend your imperfections and bad habits, then nobody will be able to help you — neither God nor man.

Penitence and confession have always been the tools that allow a soul to be purged and follow the Divine Path.

It is not always that people who speak much about God follow the Divine Path. Those who spend most part of the day in prayers do not always follow the Divine Path.

The time has come when you, each of you, must follow in your lives the commandments given by the prophets, those tables of the law that were written on stone tablets in the days of Moses.[18]

Analyze this Decalogue and search your behavior. Do many of you truly obey these laws in your lives? Do many of you act in life in obedience to the Divine Law?

The time is ripe not to speak about God, but to act in your lives in obedience to the Divine Law.

For many of you this will be much more difficult than attending church services, praying and keeping a fast. However, such is the dictate of time. Stop playing cat-and-mouse — at least with yourselves. Be on your best behavior when you are alone with yourself, just as you would behave with other people, and behave toward other people just as you would behave if you had God the Father in front of you.

In every minute and every second of your lives, all your actions and all your thoughts are being unceasingly written into the Akashic Chronicles. And when you manage to see these Chronicles, you will rapidly discover why the things happening in your lives take place this way and not another way and why you are pursued by your ill luck and disasters.

---

[18] 1. You shall have no other gods before Me.
2. You shall not make for yourself a carved image, any likeness of anything that is in Heaven above, or that is in Earth beneath, or that is in the water under Earth.
3. You shall not take the name of the LORD your God in vain.
4. Remember the Sabbath day, to keep it holy.
5. Honor your father and your mother.
6. You shall not murder.
7. You shall not commit adultery.
8. You shall not steal.
9. You shall not bear false witness against your neighbor.
10. You shall not covet your neighbor's house; you shall not covet your neighbor's wife, nor his male servant, nor his female servant, nor his ox, nor his donkey, nor anything that is your neighbor's. (Deuteronomy. 5:6-21).

All the disasters and everything that surrounds you in life were created by you in the past. The Law of Karma operates faultlessly.

That is why understanding the fact that in life, you face the consequences of your own past actions and that nobody except you is blameworthy for the things happening to you, will be the utmost achievement in your lives. And none of the events of your lives is comparable in order of importance to this discovery that you will make in your heart.

And when you see the operation of the Great Law, you will understand that God is very gracious to you, and the actions you committed in the past must be punished with much more destitution and many more diseases and misfortunes. And you will be stunned with the mercy of the Father and will experience full humility and obedience before His Will and His Law.

And only when you repent inside your heart will you be able to know the Kingdom of Heaven and follow the Path without taking the wrong turn and shirking the responsibilities you took upon yourselves before coming into embodiment.

And now I am ready to remind you that Christmas Eve is coming.[19] The western part of humanity celebrates this Christmas holiday as one of the most significant in the year. That is why, on the eve of this holiday, you should think about the fact that inside each of you Christ can be born as soon as you give your Higher Self a chance to act through you. Your Higher Self cannot start acting through you as long as you oppose and disobey the Divine Law of this universe. But from the moment when you in your heart decide to obey the Law, your Higher Self becomes able to act through you, and your actions become actions of a Christ-being in manifestation.

---

[19] In western Christianity, Christmas is celebrated on the 25th of December. In Orthodoxy, Christmas is celebrated on the 7th of January.

I wish you a happy Christmas, and I wish that each of you finds a Christ within you!

I AM Lanello, with Love to you.

One more vital point is added to the dispensation[20] on the 23rd of each month

Gautama Buddha
December 25, 2006

I AM Gautama Buddha, having come to you again to give a new Message inspired by the force of Love that I, as well as the other Ascended Masters, feel toward you, people of Earth embodied at present. The time is very stressful, and the turn of the year is a time of special importance and complexity. It is at the turn of the solar cycle that we come and give you our training, since everything we plant on the growing sun will germinate in spring and summer when the next solar cycles come, which are the day of the vernal equinox and the day of summer solstice. The old is nearing its completion and the new is beginning to show, and this new is absolutely gorgeous!

---

[20] You can become acquainted with the dispensation on the 23rd in the following Masters' Messages: "About the opportunity to unburden your karma of the next month and about the letters to the Karmic Board," Beloved Surya, June 23, 2005; "About the new Divine Dispensation," Beloved El Morya, June 27, 2005; "The best sermon will be your personal example," The Goddess of Liberty, April 22, 2005; "I have brought you two pieces of news — one is sad and the other one is joyful," Beloved El Morya, January 7, 2006; "Instructions about your attitude to everything around you in your dense world and in the finer worlds," Beloved El Morya, April 20, 2006; "About the forthcoming day of the summer solstice and the Divine favors connected with this day," Lord Maitreya, June 15, 2006; "About the dispensation of the 23rd and other opportunities being given by Heaven," Beloved El Morya, July 19, 2006. Refer to *Words of Wisdom Volumes 1 and 2*.

I can say that because I am directly relevant to the future that is to come very soon. We are happy that there are a sufficient number of human individuals who wish to serve us, the Ascended Masters, and we are able to materialize our plans together with you.

I stand before you in great excitement because today at the session of the Karmic Board a vital event has occurred, and this event will not be long in influencing the life of every person on Earth. During the session, it was decided that each person who has achieved a certain level of consciousness will be able to spend a part of the energy that is released during prayer or while serving Life to enable the rest of humanity on Earth to achieve the level of consciousness that is necessary at the current stage of the evolutionary development as soon as possible. We timed this important decision to coincide with the dispensation of the 23rd of each month, and now, starting from the 23rd of January of next year, one more fundamental point is being added to the guidelines of this important dispensation, which is still in operation during the entire period of the next year. Each of you, who wish to, can direct your energy onto the transmutation of karma of those who have decelerated their development and are unable to understand many Divine Truths. This can relate to your loved ones, your relatives, and even strangers to whom you feel a special affinity. On the 23rd day of each month of next year, you can make a call and transmute the karma that prevents the person chosen by you from achieving the next level of consciousness. For the time being, each of you can practice this dispensation for one person only — for example: this can be your spouse, your child, one of your parents, or any person whom you want to help.

We hope sincerely that this new Divine opportunity will let both us and you accelerate the pace of raising the level of consciousness of earthly mankind. Just picture that by the end of next year after the completion of the annual cycle and the session of the Karmic Board, the number of people who will have reached the level of consciousness that allows them to serve us consciously will double! In such a way, by the end of the year we will have a chance to double the number of our devotees — the people capable of taking upon themselves a responsibility for both the planet and the evolutionary development of all living creatures on earth.

I am happy to have brought this joyful decision over to you! And now I am ready to give you a small piece of information that will allow you to orient yourselves in the current state of things in the world. What is meant here is the catastrophic increase in the level of negative vibrations at the end of the year. A lot of people are seized with heaviness, and many celebrate their Christmas and New Year holidays at a very low vibration level, drinking alcohol and being engaged in indecent and reproachful actions. All these things create an extra portion of the planetary karma, which can bring irreparable disasters on some continents. That is why I turn to you as always at the end of the year with a request to keep balance within yourselves and to devote as much effort as possible to balancing the planetary karma and the karma of your country. If you feel such an internal need, you can devote every day remaining until the end of the current year to your prayer practice and make double and triple efforts. Do not hesitate even to obtain leave in order to work for the good of planet Earth at home, in privacy, or with a group of like-minded people. You can read Rosaries, read other prayers, practice meditation, send out your Love and gratitude to Earth, and picture Mother Earth as an alive being allowing you to live and to evolve and taking care of you. Send out your Love to Earth and to those elementals that maintain the human evolution on Earth.

At the end of every year we ask you for any extra energy that you are able to give us, and this in its turn enables us to balance the situation on the planet and to avoid many cataclysms.

That is why I come and turn to you with a request as an entity that wields power and keeps the balance on planet Earth.

I AM Buddha, and I am glad that many of you have decided and have darted to the path of serving humanity of Earth, having forgotten about your own problems and your own difficulties and misfortunes.

In reality, only when you are immersed in serving Life will all your petty concerns leave you one after another, and one fine day you will realize that you are free from all these trifling and unnecessary things that burdened you before. That was another life, a life of a person egoistic and absorbed in his or her own problems. But now you represent a being of Light, anxious about happiness and harmony on the planet.

May the world be well!

May all the living creatures inhabiting our dearly loved planet Earth be happy. Om.

I AM Gautama Buddha.

You must constantly analyze the consequences of your actions and stop trying to teach in those places where your teaching will be immediately dragged through the mire

Beloved Kuthumi
December 26, 2006

I AM Kuthumi, having come to you today through our Messenger. I have to give you yet another piece of our Teaching that you have to assimilate because the time for it has come. The present time is such that every manifestation of the Divinity you meet in life becomes a feast-day for your souls because your souls have been aching for the Divine world whence they came and where it is time to return now. That is why I am always happy to forward a Message from the Divine world to you and to give you short precepts.I know that many of you love me and speak with me. And when you are attuned to my wavelength I almost always hear you and to perceive your thoughts, because this is the way that I serve. Hence, I know about many of you. And I am aware of the problems that you are overburdened with. That is why I would like to do my best and to do everything in my power to show you the roots of the problems cropping up before you and to provide you with a spark necessary for you to be able to overcome within you the reasons for your difficulties.

That is why today we will talk about what is vital and topical for many of you. And this is connected with your interrelations with those people around you who do not understand and accept your teaching, your guidance, your pattern of life, and your system of world-view. Unfortunately, all humans are at absolutely different stages of progress. And by the level of your consciousness, many of you still belong to the previous Fourth Root Race. The majority of you belong to different sub-races of the Fifth Root Race, and there is a certain number — a very small number — of individuals who belong to the final sub-races of the Fifth Root Race and an even smaller number of individuals belonging to the Sixth Root Race, whose time has not yet come, but whose first pathfinders, especially impatient ones, have undertaken their pioneer embodiments at present.

The history of the development of the races is a matter for a time-consuming discussion and will not be a subject of this Dictation. All I want is to direct your attention to an indisputable fact that all of you are standing at different stages of your evolutionary development. And that is why the differences in your consciousness are sometimes so great and the spheres of your interests and the levels of your consciousness differ to such an extent that it seems at times that you speak different languages. For that reason, when you yet again have a desire to start giving a teaching or to propagate your views among those who you think need a sermon, remember this Dictation and call to mind the words of Jesus "Do not cast your pearls before swine."[21]

All that is given must be given according to the level of consciousness. And many things that seem to be so obvious to you that you have already stopped paying attention to them could shock the people who are remote from your views. Even worse, it can create in them a whole range of negative emotions and even actions. And who do you think will bear the karma of these negative manifestations? If you have not guessed yet, I will prompt you: The karma will lie on you. It is because a human standing at a higher stage of evolutionary development takes full karmic

---

[21] "Do not give dogs what is holy, and do not throw your pearls before pigs, lest they trample them underfoot and turn to attack you." (Matthew 7:6).

responsibility not only for his or her actions but also for the actions of the people whom he or she provokes to wrong actions.

This does not mean that people whom you provoke are freed from their karma for wrong actions. I only want to say that the greater part of karma will lie on you because it is you who provoked them to perform the wrong actions. Therefore, before you start preaching and giving anybody a piece of advice about how to act in life, think a good many times about whether you should do it.

Your responsibility is directly proportional to the stage of the evolutionary ladder you occupy.

This does not mean that you should shrink into yourself and stop communicating with people and speaking on spiritual topics with them. Simply, you must constantly analyze the consequences of your actions and stop trying to teach in those places where your teaching will be immediately dragged through the mire.

Think about my words. And always remember that your own behavior in life, the way you react to these or those life situations and disturbances serve as the best model. All of your preaching will lie in your actions. And by the fruits of your actions, people will recognize in you that person who is worth heeding and whose advice is worth seeking. So, I am again driving at the fact that the only person in this world with whom it behooves you to occupy yourself seriously is yourself. And you yourselves are the most worthy recipient of all your forces and abilities.

Do not think that somebody acts imperfectly, and do not think about how he should act. Concentrate on yourself and think about why actions and words of other people irritate you. Isn't it because everything that irritates you is present within you as a manifestation of your past wrong actions?

The physical world around you is a mirror reflecting your imperfect consciousness. Thus, it would be natural to assume that if someone regularly meets with ignorance and misunderstanding, then these qualities are present in him or her. And if you are constantly exposed to malicious attacks from other people, then it means that the negative energy making people act that way toward you is present within you.

We have covered today's material many times. And you have certainly heard and read about this many times. However, your thoughts, your own thoughts that you send me, make me repeat this small Teaching to you again and remind you about those Truths that you know well but for some reason do not risk to apply to yourselves.

I am happy with the opportunity given to repeat this Teaching to you. And I will be even happier if some of you are able to put this Teaching into practice. And even if it seems to you that everything I have told about has nothing to do with you, still do not hurry to put this Dictation away and to shelve it. Try to reread this Message at least thrice on different days, at different times of the day, and in different states of your consciousness. And I think that while reading it for the third time you will start to understand that this Dictation is directly relevant to you.

Trust me, I know human psychology very well, and at times it is a great pleasure to me to think out the puzzles composed from those psychological problems that you yourselves have created during thousands and thousands of embodiments on earth. However, I am always glad to help you. And I always answer the requests that you sincerely pronounce in your hearts while looking at my picture or that you risk to write on paper and send me by the irreproachable post where our angels work. Do you know that when you burn the letter and make a call to the angels of protection to deliver the letter to me or to any other Ascended Master, the physical letter burns but its energetic higher substance is immediately delivered to the address you specified?

I have been happy to give you a small Teaching today.

**I AM Kuthumi,
with great Love toward you and with a desire to help.**

Now, before the New Year's Eve, we hasten to bring home to your consciousness the new tasks that need implementing

Beloved El Morya
December 27, 2006

I AM El Morya, having come to you today through my Messenger.

I have come! I have come in order to give the final Message of this year because we will meet with you again only next year. So, let us strike the balance of this year and check if everything that was planned has been accomplished.

I have to state an important fact that, unlike the previous year, this one has been more successful regarding the consciousness development of mankind of Earth. Not everything has gone smoothly, and not everything has occurred the way we expected. Many people on whom we relied wished to follow their free will and deviated from the Path. Well, this is their choice and this is their decision. Therefore, we will not dwell on sad things.

Nevertheless, I must cheerfully state the fact that quite a lot of people whom we were not counting on, who were far from our Path, the Path of Initiations, have awakened and are providing tangible assistance to the proceedings that we are implementing through our Messenger. This is very joyous and makes us have optimistic expectations concerning the next year that we are gradually entering!

I am glad, and all the Ascended Hosts are glad about the fact that the year 2006 has been so successful!

That is why now, right before New Year's Eve, we hasten to bring home to your consciousness the new tasks that need to be implemented. These tasks are directly connected with the fulfillment of the plans of the Brotherhood.

As always, when a new dispensation is activated, a new Divine opportunity opens. This time the Divine opportunity is open for Mother Russia. We have been waiting for this opportunity for long decades, and finally it is opened up. Now it is you, the currently incarnated light-bearers, who are responsible for the way this opportunity will be realized in the physical plane. We need an outpost, a place in the physical plane through which we can carry out our deeds, through which we can convey our plans and discuss with you the succession and the terms of their implementation. I hope that next year will enable us to fulfill our subsequent plans, and finally we will manage to start doing practical deeds in the physical plane.

We need a publishing house that will implement our tasks and will be sponsored completely by the Great White Brotherhood.

We need an educational center where we can give knowledge on the Divine Truth on a regular basis, an educational center that will serve as a beacon in the sea of chaos that is lavishly foaming up in the life around you.

We need a Community, several communities, and as many communities as you can establish, the communities implementing the spirit of the Great White Brotherhood in the physical octave. With the help of our Communities, we will be able to introduce correct patterns and correct moral guidelines in the society.

We need people with experience in various fields in order to initiate rearrangement of all spheres of activity on the basis of Divine principles. These principles will come from the Divine world as insights and revelations. You will manage to transform life very quickly in accordance with the Divine patterns if you keep your devotion and purity of your motives and aspirations.

The more your consciousness is filled with Divine patterns and Divine vision, the less room there is for the manifestation of all that is not from God and all that wishes to resist the evolutionary path of human development and leads to the maze of pseudo-culture, pseudo-divinity, pseudo-beauty, and pseudo-love.

We leave all these non-divine manifestations to the will of God, and I think you will never waste your Divine energy to sustain and feed any negative manifestations of your world. Always remember that all the energy in this Universe is concentrated in the hands of God. When you improperly use the Divine energy given to you by God, you multiply the evil in this world.

The time has come to do Good. The time has come for you to consciously choose the Good in your consciousness and follow it in your lives because this is the call of the time. You have been vegetating in the illusion for too long, and you have been allowed to explore your free will for too long. Now you must start the transformation of your physical world at an accelerated pace. I hope that we will work in cooperation with you and manage to do everything within the timeline, in cosmic terms because there is no more time left. All time reserves given for returning to the evolutionary path are exhausted.

Now we are entering the narrow strip of corridor of a new cosmic opportunity, and this strip is very short. That is why all your efforts and all your energy will be required of you in order to be on time and to complete the transformation of planet Earth by the deadline that has been mentioned and affirmed.

I will not tell you the exact date when the transformations are to be completed. But I will tell you that everything will take place within the memory of one or two generations. At least the main transformations will take place very quickly.

There are dangers on the path. There are lots of pitfalls, and as always, all dangers and all pitfalls arise where there is strong human ignorance. That is why you need knowledge, Divine knowledge to guide you, and you will be able to change your life and set the example for others.

All transformations will take place very quickly. Hence, I am telling you about your responsibility again and again. Every treachery of yours that you allow postpones the term of manifestation of the Divine plan. If you have not yet considered your life from the viewpoint of the general course of evolution, then the time has come to think it over because you do not exist in this Universe on your own. You are the cells of the one organism of this Universe. That is why the success of the whole matter and the terms of its implementation depend on your proper work in accordance with the Divine plan.

Stop considering yourselves as something separated from God. Feel your oneness with all life — at least for a short while. Imagine that on the other side of the globe people may die because of one negative thought of yours or because of a wrong choice you make.

There is always a Divine opportunity for the course of events, and there is always a worst case that becomes manifested due to the negligence of people.

Therefore, do constantly care — but not about yourselves — do care about the world. And bring into correlation everything you do with the cosmic expedience and the granted Divine opportunity.

I AM El Morya.

We make your consciousness ready for The New Age

I AM THAT I AM
December 28, 2006

I AM THAT I AM. I am speaking from within you. As always, I will give you a short Message that will help you keep to the right direction and the guidelines of evolutionary development because the time has come and it is pressing now. The time has come to think about returning to the spiritual world. It is time to think about Father's Home, the Father's Home from which the whole Creation began and where everything returns.

How often do you think about some eternal things? How often are you aimed at realizing who you really are — not the person who you are according to your professional experience or your relationships with other people? How often do you think about your spiritual relations, about your Heavenly Parents, about where you are going and where your source is?

I come to give you some comments on these important matters of Being because if you do not start thinking about your Higher reality, that reality will not be able to manifest in your lives.

That is the Law of The Universe: Interosculation, or intermixing, of worlds is difficult until some certain stage of development. This allows the worlds and the worlds within worlds to develop and keep their laws. However, when the time of the great cycle change comes, the worlds begin folding up. The vibrations of the worlds get closer and the worlds start penetrating into each other.

However, it cannot happen before your consciousness is ready for the junction and the interosculation of the worlds. This process takes millions of years. And now you are at the lowest point of your way. If we compare it with mountaineering, then you are at the bottom now. No matter how fast you try to reach the summit, there are natural limitations of space and time that interfere with your advancement in reaching the peak of Divine consciousness.

The cycle of submerging into materiality, the immersion in materiality, is completed. And the return to Father's Home has started. That is why no matter how long you resist, you have to start thinking about the world where your souls came from. At the time you were descending, you were callow, immature, and inexperienced. You didn't have all those radiant garments, which you can gain in the near future. The garments of your lower bodies that you wear now are to be cleaned. You have to devote yourself to purification of your four lower bodies and take it seriously. You know that you have a physical body. And you have heard that you have the other energy bodies, which your aura is composed of, that are invisible to physical sight. They are your astral body, or the body of desire; your mental body, or the body of thoughts; and your etheric body, or the body of memory. They are in a sad state now. You have soiled them wandering about in the physical world. Now it is time for serious purification of your bodies.

Start with your physical body. Think about what you eat and what you drink. The structure of your food and water becomes the structure of your body. Think of comparing the food you eat and the water you drink with the standards needed for your rational Divine nourishment. Do you think that those monsters of the food industry that exist in your world are concerned about the health of your physical body? Nobody but you can start purifying your physical body.

The method of cleaning is very simple: You should get rid of everything that is useless and fill your body with good and useful matter and substances of natural products, products that are not genetically modified, products grown without chemicals. Think about the system of your meals and the structure of your food. As soon as you get a thought about the right food you will get the needed literature from above. Now, because there is the cycle change, your physical body will not be able to bear the experiments. Your physical body will not be able to exist under the new energy conditions unless you take care of it.

This also concerns your other bodies. Unless your emotions to your relatives, other people, your country, and your planet are free of negativity you will not be able to exist under the new energy conditions and vibration. Lower vibrations of envy, anger, greed, and hatred cannot exist in the New Age, so you have to get rid of them.

The same is true for the sphere of your thoughts. If you concentrate your mind on negative situations constantly, then there is always a grey cloud of dark thoughts around you, and this makes you incompatible with the new vibrations. You have to make up your mind and to choose to set your mind free of the negative state of consciousness. Unless you do it yourself, you will face more and more difficulties and find it hard to exist in conditions of the New World.

Unless you clear your ether body of negative records and conditions of the past, you will not be compatible with the energies that have already come and keep coming to planet Earth.

As you can see, you actually have no choice.

If you persist in maintaining your old addictions and habits, then it could lead you to falling out of the current space and time. I do not want to dwell on what might happen, because I believe that my words will make you think about your life style and change it as soon as possible. Everything that has recently been prestigious or considered as a sign of scientific and technological progress is completely of no importance now. Living in large cities and engaging in mass entertainment (such as television and holiday feasts with drinking and gluttony) are things of the past which mankind has to leave behind in the nearest future.

You will not be able to live in your cities, and you will rush to be in nature. You won't be able to listen to your music but rather to the sounds of nature. You won't be able to eat your food; instead you will have to look for and find other high vibration food and turn to the Sun's energy and to the vibrations of Divine Love in the end.

Everything that seems fantastic and unacceptable in my words will soon be your life style. Believe me and the experience of the other systems of worlds.

No matter how much time you fiddle away persisting in your habits and old flames, everything that is old and useless will be swept away with the fresh wind of Change and the parching energy of the Fiery World.

We make your consciousness ready for The New Age.

I AM THAT I AM.

I came to remind you of your Divine origin and the necessity to overcome your unreal part

Cosmic Being Powerful Victory
December 29, 2006

I AM Victory, coming to you this day.

I AM Cosmic Being Powerful Victory!

As I am Victory, I am triumphant!

The whole evolution of the Universe is destined to Victory. The quality of being triumphant or victorious is what you need to develop in yourself. That quality is extremely necessary for you because that is the quality that you have been lacking during the whole period of musty human history.

Maybe what you understand by Victory is not the quality that I mean because in your dual world there is an antipode of every Divine quality. For the quality of Divine Victory, there is a non-divine quality of triumph over somebody. But I came to teach you to firmly establish Victory. At the time when you reject any human imperfection and faulty condition to overcome the unreal manifestation, you establish Victory in yourself.

I came to remind you of your Divine origin and the necessity to overcome your unreal part. You have gotten used to your unreal part from the millions of years of wandering about your world.

However, nobody can make you overcome the unreal part of you. You have to make that decision in your heart by yourself.

You have to turn to Divinity and leave your unreality, or the further evolutionary development of this Universe is impossible. We used to come and talk to you about the old man and the other true man in you, but now the time for talk is over, and you have to start undertaking certain actions to set yourself free from the duality of illusion, and turn yourself to the oneness of the Divine World. Believe me, the illusionary manifestation is concentrated only in your mind, and you must overcome your illusionary consciousness. There is no other way. And the way for you to overcome your illusionary manifestation makes up the major part of the Teaching given through our Messenger.

You have to make it your everyday rule and begin by analyzing the manifestation of unreality in yourself that comes up on your way to the Victory. Try to abstract your mind from the world around you and imagine that you are in the Divine World. There are no usual forms in that world. There is nothing that has to be made with the hands. You don't have to take care of the body. That is the Fiery World, the world where fiery thoughts rule, the world created by the power of thoughts, which lives because of the Divine Love that fills all the space of the Fiery World. Thanks to that Love, that World exists.

Now think of the things of your world that may be necessary in the Divine World?

Will you need the things around you such as money, luxuries, food, or clothes?

No, none of the listed things will be needed in our world. So, what is left then?

What can be left with you in our world?

I will tell you. In our world only your Divine qualities may stay with you: unselfishness, devotion, faithfulness, love, compassion,

Divine mercy and charity, and purity. There are so many qualities in the Divine World that you may keep with you. But in order for you to have these qualities, you have to develop them in your physical manifested world.

Otherwise, when it is time to return to your Father's House, you will appear there without your radiant garments of virtue. It is worthless to wander about the Divine World naked. You will always feel compassionate looks from the inhabitants of the Divine World, but you will feel embarrassed for wasting time during your earthly lives. That is why you have to find the strength and courage to leave your human qualities and try to acquire the Divine qualities and perfection based on the description of the Divine World that you get from our Messages.

Everything that seems good in your world is not good in the Divine World. But there is room for manifestation of the Divine qualities. These are the states when you experience the feelings of self-sacrifice, Divine compassion, and unconditional Love. Each of you was able to experience these states of consciousness at least once. You only have to remember these moments and extend them in your life for as long a period of time as possible so that all your life consists of high, Divine states of consciousness.

I come to remind you of your Divinity because in your everyday fuss you lose contact with that reality. It is time to remember your true Home and your Divine life purpose. Do not be afraid to look funny in the opinion of people around you. We will see who laughs when you get to the Divine reality. If I say that the cycles shorten and time accelerates, I mean that not so much time is left for experimenting in the physical world. Hurry up, because what you can easily get during your physical life is impossible to reach when being in the Divine World. Due to the density of the manifested world, every action in this world has almost a flash-like result. And to reach the same result in the Fiery World you will need millions of years.

Our worlds are complementary, and what is possible in your world is impossible in our world. Unfortunately, you have to take that on trust because to reach my world you need millions of millions of earth years.

I hope that there are individuals for whom every word of today's Message brings such an important energetic and informational component that your lives will change so quickly you could not even expect it in your most daring dreams.

I wish for you to develop the quality of Victory and to aspire to your Divine Victory with all your might.

I AM Victory!

Let us focus on implementing our tasks together

Lord Lanto
December 30, 2006

I AM Lanto, having come to you today through our Messenger in order to affirm the points of our Teaching, which you need in your consciousness once again.

As always, I have come with joy and with the feeling of deep Love that I feel toward the people of Earth who are in incarnation now. You, like no one in former times, are being revealed many secrets because your consciousness is able to comprehend much that could not be given earlier. And do you know why? It is because you are incredibly lucky. Your development has accelerated almost to the maximum speed, and the changes of your consciousness amaze even those evolved beings who have no direct relations with the evolutions of Earth.

Planet Earth is the focus of cosmic attention now. If you translate this into your earthly language, regular reports are being sent from Earth, and angels deliver on their wings all of the joyous news regarding planet Earth to the most distant places in the Universe. It may seem to you that I have come especially to cheer you up because I am saying such things. However, there are no special gestures or any stock phrases in this case. Every time has its own laws, and the laws of your time enable all the necessary changes to be performed within the tightest schedule and in the most efficient way.

It may seem to you that the situation remains just as it was before, and everything surrounding you is not changing or is changing rather slowly. You are thinking in terms of the present day, but if you go back 10 to 20 years in your consciousness, you would be surprised. It would seem to you that everything is dormant around you and moving at a decelerated pace. No, the acceleration is amazing and the development of human consciousness is attracting rapt attention from various world systems. This takes us, the Masters of Earth, a lot of extra work because we have taken the responsibility for the coordination of the activities of various missions to help those who have rushed to Earth now. Therefore, all our efforts are gathered in this one impulse — to help mankind overcome the crucial point of its development as easily as possible.

You know that if a car runs at an excessive speed, those situations that are not normally dangerous on the road may become an increased risk, and any stone lying on the road may lead to a disastrous result. That is why we are concentrated on the road, and we focus all our efforts on preventing any unfavorable situations and manifestations.

How can you help us in this situation?

You really can help, and we will accept your help with pleasure because it will be timely indeed.

So, what do you have to do in order to ease the situation and prevent the unfavorable development of events? The recommendations at this point are exactly the same as the recommendations for driving a vehicle at an excessive speed in unfavorable weather conditions. It requires attention, concentration, and imperturbability. You should not allow your attention to be distracted by anything that is not directly connected with the goal, with your driving. You must be utterly focused on the road and what is happening on the road. Closely monitor everything and do not let your mind distract you because your mind is very mobile, and sometimes it takes you into such a maze that you may even forget about everything, even the fact that you are moving along a dangerous road at an excessive speed.

Therefore, keep your focus on your movement and on everything that is associated with your travel.

Do not let anyone distract you. Adjust all the circumstances of your life to keeping up the chosen speed of your advancement. You may slow down your development, but think over how far you will fall behind the evolutionary opportunity. Moreover, the evolutionary opportunity may pass by, and you will not even notice it.

Thus, you should focus all your efforts on keeping the set pace of changing your consciousness. Your concentration on the path will contribute to your advancement.

To give our favorite analogy about mountaineering, imagine that you are on a cliff and you simultaneously try to listen to a concert of a popular singer or chatter on the phone with your friends. Of course, you may continue doing all your favorite things in your daily life, but any gust of wind without your timely effort to stay on the rope may lead to very disastrous results.

Therefore, let us focus on implementing our tasks together. You can help us if you try not to be distracted and not to stare at the sides; and in turn, we will monitor the pace of the changes and coordinate your development.

I hope that we will succeed because it just cannot be any other way.

Every time I get a chance to say a few words to you, I wish to dwell on the most important points that will be especially useful for you and will give you maximum help on your Path. Therefore, today I decided to give you another important piece of advice concerning the changes in your consciousness and related difficulties. Try to take everything that is happening around you as a natural course of events. No matter how amazing many things that you face in your life may appear, try not to be nervous when seeing these events. Do not react emotionally too much, because any emotional outburst may prevent you from keeping the pace of your progress. I draw special attention to the stability of your emotions because your vulnerability means that your emotional body is not always properly purified, so it may lead to unpredictable reactions.

Try to balance your emotions. And no matter what is going on around you in your life, consider everything — not in terms of the present day, but in terms of eternity. Then everything that previously caused your inner violent reactions will be perceived by you as if from a bird's-eye view.

The succession of changes in the scenery of your life will just accelerate. You will be required to demonstrate the quality of adaptation to the rapidly changing circumstances of your life. Those initiations that were given earlier in the closed schools of mysteries and required years of training by their disciples will take place naturally within several months or even days in the new conditions of your life.

The initiations have accelerated and have become possible in ordinary life. This is a new dispensation and a new chance that is being brought to you along with the change of the cosmic cycle of time.

Rejoice, because what was previously possible for you within several lives, you can now go through with confidence in one lifetime. To many of you, it will seem that you live many lives within this one life of yours, and you will not have to come into embodiment again. The program of one life comes to an end, and the program of the next life can begin almost immediately.

The miracles in your life have just begun. Get used to the miracles.

**I AM Lanto,
with great Love to you.**

The sooner you change your behavior and yesterday's habits, the sooner the whole world will enter into the New Age

Beloved Zarathustra
December 31, 2006

I AM Zarathustra, having come to you today at the change of the annual cycle according to your chronological system. In my time, when I was embodied on Earth, there was a different way of enumerating days and years. However, this does not prevent you from celebrating your holidays and associating them with certain dates.

Everything is relative in your world, and now many things have changed and become different from what they were a few thousand years ago. It would be absolutely outstanding if human nature changed as quickly as everything in your world. However, what is exactly associated with human consciousness and perception of the world around you changes in the slowest way. And, in my time, people also envied, hated, argued, praised God, and then immediately forgot about God.

Therefore, we sincerely hope that human nature can be changed in your time and that it is possible to raise human consciousness to a fundamentally different level: the level of consciousness of man of reason — not animal-like man, which is still inherent in the majority of mankind. No matter how deplorable it is for you to hear this at the end of the year, I still take a risk to remind you about it: Your efforts to uphold your traditions of celebrating your holidays and your persistence in upholding these traditions deserve much better application. Well, you still have some time to persist in displaying your habits. However, it would be much better if you managed to find strength within you and sweep away old stereotypes and try to listen to us, the Ascended Hosts.

Plenty of traditions you devoutly follow are to be revised. It is very important because the new generation unconsciously, at the subconscious level, absorbs your way of behavior and your traditions of celebrating significant dates. Then you are surprised, expecting your children to be smarter than you, more elevated, and more subtle. However, during your daily activities the stereotypes of your behavior and the way you live are imprinted on the consciousness of your children, and sometimes they cannot get rid of that until the end of their lives.

Just think, wouldn't it be easier for you to start getting rid of your imperfections rather than continue replicating them in your children, adding your own imperfections to those karmic problems that your children bring with them when they come into embodiment? If you really care about your children and wish them all the best, then make it a rule to control your behavior at home, at work, and outdoors. Make it a rule to control not only your actions but also your thoughts and feelings because when your behavior gains Divine traits, your children will truly learn a lot from you, and then they will render you a hundredfold at a time when you will not be able to take care of them anymore, but rather, you will need their care and custody.

You imprint all the right and wrong behavioral patterns in your children from their very birth and even before their birth when one fine day you surprisingly find out that you are going to have a baby.

Today is the very day that gives you a chance to give up the old and proceed to the new behavior. Try and wish to change yourselves in the new year to such an extent that you correspond in your behavior to the best Divine patterns which your consciousness is able to reach.

Try to start the new life, and you will see how difficult it will be for you, not just to make the decision, but to fulfill it in your life — at least for several days of the new year.

I might have made you too tired with the thoughts concerning your self-improvement. However, the sooner you think about what you can change in yourself and in your behavior, the sooner you will be able to change your relatives and everyone with whom you communicate. Do not try to change your neighbors; try to change yourself, and your neighbors will have to adjust to the newly accepted stereotype of behavior.

Someday, someone has to start. Gradually it will go out of fashion to watch TV, to spend evenings with a bottle of beer and a cigarette. The wrong patterns will vanish, and the new behavioral patterns will replace them. You yourselves establish rules in your lives. It is necessary to start changing your lives in accordance with the call of the time.

Have a try, and you will see that you will feel better because your behavior corresponds to the call of the time and to the new vibrations that have come to Earth. The cycles have changed, and time continues to accelerate. That is why the sooner you change your behavior and your habits of the past, the sooner the whole world will enter the New Age.

You do not need to blame anyone or tell anyone how he or she should behave. You just need to change your own stereotypes of behavior and show others how to do it by your example.

It is time to make a revolution in your consciousness. The changes in the stereotypes of behavior that will take place in the near future will stop surprising people within just several years because new rules of doing things will come into force in the new time, in the new rules of conducting family relations, and in the whole family life.

The new family will be based on the Divine principles, not on the principles of devotional vigils and perpetual self-torture. The new time will be different due to the implementation of the Divine principles in the behavior of each member of the family. And you will surprisingly find out that your relationships with other people will have a very little difference from those relationships that are accepted in your family because all of you are relatives and belong to one large human family, having the whole globe as home. It is exactly like you divide human society into families and then surprisingly find yourselves in a larger family; similarly, you will surprisingly find out that there are no contradictions between various nationalities and nations inhabiting various countries. The difference between various nations is no greater than the difference between you and your distant relatives living thousands of kilometers away from you.

I agree that there is a time for everything, and everything that we have talked about today will not take place next year. But this is very likely to happen in some year during the next millennium.

At least I am keeping this positive pattern in my consciousness and I insistently recommend that you keep in your consciousness as many positive patterns as possible, especially during the mass holidays. Someone must keep the balance while many people have not yet assimilated the elementary norms of Divine behavior in their consciousness.

**I AM Zarathustra,
wishing you success in the New Year!**

A Message at the beginning of the year

Gautama Buddha
January 1, 2007

I AM Gautama Buddha, having come to you again today at the beginning of a new yearly cycle.

Every time a new annual cycle begins, we come to give you instructions related to the new cycle of time. And I have come today to give such an instruction.

You know that a yearly cycle is subject to the operation of the Law of Karma in such a way that karma descends not in one lump but is spun out throughout the whole yearly period. Every month you receive the return of a certain amount of karma. This way you have an opportunity to work off your past karma gradually, year after year and month after month. If you had a chance to immediately work off the entire amount of your karma (your negative energy, the energy you distorted in your previous lives), you would not be able to endure it. Your bodies would be torn to shreds momentarily. That is why the action of the Law is such that every moment of your life you are given a chance to come to grips with the exact amount of negative energy of your past that you can cope with at that moment. You are never given more than you can endure. Therefore, you are simply required to be reconciled to the Law of this universe and to wait humbly for the return of the karmic energy that you created yourselves and that is given to you in cycles in order to be worked off.

A new year is considered by convention to be the beginning of the working off of a new layer of the energies of the past. By completing year after year successfully, you work off your past karma and charge toward a new level of consciousness. And if it were not for the new karma that you are tirelessly creating, just a few years would be enough for you to get free from the lion's share of your past karma.

But not all of you can sensibly dispose of your Divine energy and the time of your embodiment. That is why for many of you the amount of negative energy that you work off through suffering, diseases, and misfortunes is immediately replenished with new karma that you are untiringly creating by wrong actions and wrong choices in your lives.

If it were not for the Divine mercy, you would be completely deprived of an opportunity to progress onward because many of you are creating such huge karma in your lives. However, owing to the Divine mercy, this karma does not return to you at once, but is waiting for a favorable opportunity when you are able to meet with the negative energy of the past and not only withstand your karmic burden but also think over the reason why so many misfortunes rain thick upon you all at once. In such a way many of you will be able to comprehend the existence of the Supreme Law and will wish to aspire with all your being to obey this Law.

Many have reached such a level of consciousness that they appeal to the Karmic Board with requests to speed up the return of karma so as to have a chance to work off the maximum amount of karma during the current embodiment and to acquire an opportunity to serve at a new level of consciousness free from karma.

The only thing I would like to warn you about is the following: After you have written such letters and the return of your karma accelerates, do not forget what you yourselves have asked about and do not repine at your unhappy lot. The fact is that the process of karma descending, when being sped up by your request, can be suspended exactly the same way and returned to its natural flow. Do not forget about your requests, and if you have been too hasty and overrated your strength, write another letter to the Karmic Board and ask them not to speed up the process of the descending of your karma in the future.

Many of you do not realize the obligations that you took upon yourselves while being in your higher body, at the level of your soul. Thus, when you face difficulties in your life and these difficulties exhaust you too much, do debate this matter in your mind. Talk to your Higher Self, and seek its advice. In any case, owing to the great mercy of Heaven, the process of karma descending can be regulated by you. It is especially important if you have good karma created by helping living creatures and the Masters because your good karma can be always used in order to mitigate the heaviness of your karmic burden.

As soon as you have realized the action of the Law of Karma and you aspire to act in your life in harmony with this Law, you meet one of the predominant constituents of your further progress, and the mercy of Heaven will not fail to come to your help at your first call.

Pitiful are those individuals who disregard the Law of Karma and go on living by the principle: "After me — the deluge." You should think about this expression of yours. It might be that in your next embodiment you will get into the deluge that you drew upon yourselves.

Think about how many misfortunes and problems people could avoid if every minute of their lives they thought not only about the consequences of their actions but also about the consequences of their thoughts and feelings.

One of the objects of our Messages is exactly to teach you to be aware of your every action, every thought and feeling because there are no secrets for God and for the cosmic Law, and all your thoughts as well as your actions and deeds are recorded in the Akashic Records. You can play cat-and-mouse with one another and hide your true motives and your negative thoughts. God sees everything, and it is impossible for you to hide even the slightest secret workings of your heart from Him.

It would not be amiss for you to make it a rule to constantly feel the presence of an invisible witness near you who keeps watch over your actions and even over the workings of your heart. Then you will be able to approach all your actions and choices in life in a more responsible manner.

I wish to give you one more important piece of advice; if you are guided by it, you will be able to increase the percentage of worked off karma very quickly: Every time you face a choice about how to act in your life, try to understand the motive you are driven by while making this choice. And if you strive to do something for your personal benefit, it is a wrong motive and the result of your choice will increase your karmic burden.

If you are guided in your choices by the motive to do good for other people and other living creatures, then even if it seems to you that your choice can cause damage to you and is unprofitable according to all the human laws and from the viewpoint of elementary human logic, never say die. From the viewpoint of the Divine logic, you will make a correct choice, and this choice will inevitably lead to the easing of your karmic burden. You lose in the small things, but you win in the great.

For example, you are driving along a mountainous road and a person who needs your help appears on the road in front of you. You expend time in helping him and lose this time. The sun sets and you are delayed on the way. But if you do not yield to the feeling of annoyance, tomorrow a new gateway will open for you that you were not aware of before, and this gateway will speed up your movement a lot, and you will get to the right place much earlier than you planned. This is how the Law of Karma operates.

Never think about the profit you will get if you perform good actions. May your karmic debts and merits be counted by those heavenly beings that must act by virtue of their positions. Simply perform good actions and do not think about a reward.

I am glad to have reminded you at the beginning of the year about the Great Law existing in this universe, and I hope that I have done it, as always, just in time.

I AM Gautama Buddha.

A talk about God

Lord Shiva
January 2, 2007

I AM Shiva, having come again in order to give you the next Message!

Shiva I AM!

I have come to pay my visit exactly at the beginning of the year when many of you are concentrated on future plans and are surprised watching how your lives and everything around you are changing. I have come to give you direction for your inner work and for your outer work again.

Your inner work of self-perfection always means only the realization of yourself as the Divine manifestation and giving up everything within you which is not of the Divine.

Every time you try to find within you something that is unreal and put this quality on a pedestal instead of the Divinity, it is called going astray from the Path. And you should thoroughly watch all such moments.

In your life you will encounter the worshipping of your relatives, your spouses, your children, people whom you love. In your life you will encounter the worshipping of things, such as luxuries and money. You will encounter the worshipping of power and force. You will put much on the pedestal and worship this fetish like God.

However, much time will pass, and you will start realizing that there is nothing that can take the place of the true Divinity in your heart.

Some of you have already started realizing this simple truth. And as too many deities were thrown down from their pedestals by you or by life circumstances, you are afraid of losing your attachment to something once again. Therefore, many of you approach with suspicion the true God residing in your hearts and trying to establish contact with you.

Do not be afraid. The time has come at last when you are supposed to meet the real manifestation of Divinity. You are supposed to meet God within you. And this takes place only when you throw down from the pedestal one false idol after another.

Do not be afraid. There is always a criterion that will help you to distinguish the true God from many false gods and goddesses.

And you yourself always know when you face the true manifestation of Divinity in your life.

When you are calm, peaceful and filled with Divine tranquility in your heart, nobody in the world will be able to convince you that you have not found the true God.

It is impossible to take this for anything else. However, many of you still seek for and find false gods and graven images.

How can you find one true God in your heart without losing your way?

The truth is that you cannot find true God until you reject false gods and any attachments to your world. If you try to find God in order to realize some desire or quality of yours, you will not be able to find true God. You will not be able to find true God until you aspire to Him with all your heart, until you give up every human aspiration, including the aspiration to worship God.

It is difficult for you to believe and understand this, but many people replace the true faith in God with blind worship of a deity.

The external worship of God has nothing in common with the inner worship of Divinity. And the external worship of God is just the first, the very first step on the way to true Divinity, being on the throne in your heart.

Each of you must come to God. Each of you will inevitably come to your God, being on the throne of your heart. However, each of you will look for many gods living in temples and churches, pagodas and mosques.

You will be looking for your God for a long time. And you will find Him one nice day when it seems to you that life is meaningless for you, when you are not attached to anything in your world any more. You will be back where you started your life, being at a loose end with your family or your job or anything else that was important for you and that has gone. And at that moment when there is nothing in your world to which you feel an attachment, at that moment you will turn your eyes toward the sky in your last hope, and you will say in your heart:

"Lord, help me, Lord. I know that you exist. I know that you hear me. I believe in Your Might and Your Mercy. I love You, Lord, and I believe that all you have done to me was necessary only for me to come to You. Lord, forgive me everything that I did through my foolishness. I thank you, Lord, for your Teaching and for letting me go through all tests and coming out of them with credit. Lord, help me to find You and never part with You ever in my life."

At that moment, it will seem to you that the Heavens have opened. You will feel what you have never felt in your life. You will understand that everything you have aspired to, you already have and you always had. And all of this is within you, in your heart, but you did not want to see it and hear it up to this moment of your life, when your ears started hearing and your eyes opened.

I BELIEVE and I HOPE that each of you either had or will have such an experience. And I hope that this experience will leave such an indelible mark on your soul that you will always stay in consonance with God until the end of this life of yours. And whatever difficult life situations you get into, you will not blame God and accuse Him of your misfortunes and troubles. You will understand and accept that you are the only one to blame for your misfortunes and troubles because you were full of pride and ignorance. And ignorance covered your eyes.

I am glad that our talk today has taken place. And I am glad that I could bring home to your consciousness that state which will enable you to overcome yourselves and rise to God.

**I AM Shiva,
the destroyer of the unreal in you.**

A piece of news from the session of the Karmic Board

The Great Divine Director
January 3, 2007

I AM The Great Divine Director, having come to you today in order to give another Message associated with this day, the beginning of the annual cycle of time enumeration.

There is one more thing that is important: The annual winter Karmic Board meeting is over, and I am ready to share some of the decisions with you.

I am looking forward to the moment when you will be reading this Message of mine with bated breath, for this Message brings you a lot of unexpected surprises. I am like your festive Father Christmas who has come with a sack of gifts and is waiting on the doorstep.

Let us look into my sack and see what I have brought to you. This time we have many more joyous pieces of news than sad ones. We would like to bring to your consciousness last year's results. These results, as you all probably suspect, are much more encouraging than the results of the previous couple of years. The whole point is that many of you have awakened and started in your awakened consciousness to take actions leading to the awakening of other people. You know that everything is interconnected in your world. All of you are much more united in the subtle plane than in the physical plane. The things that have become accessible for one person's spiritual achievements can be assimilated by many.

That is the law. That is why we are nursing those of you who are on the threshold of opening the new consciousness. Literally, we resemble babysitters who are ready to take care of you and complete everything you have started doing but cannot complete due to your laziness and neglect. Every one of you who can reach a certain level of consciousness serves as a catalyst or a transmitter of information in the subtle plane for thousands of souls with whom you have karmic bonds or the same human genealogy.

That is why we would like our Teaching to be translated into as many languages as possible and spread as widely as possible all over the world. We are ready to render all possible assistance to each of you who acts in this direction. Do not be shy about asking the Karmic Board for help. Write the letters to me personally. If you face any problems that impede your service in spreading our Messages and your karmic situation allows it, your requests will be considered and all measures will be taken in order to help you and remove the barrier within you and change the karmic circumstances.

This is so, because each of you involved in spreading our Messages works for thousands of people. And the souls of those people are able to wake up in the subtle plane and to receive through you, in the subtle plane, all the necessary information.

You cannot imagine how fast everything spreads in your time. This is not only due to the Internet and other rapid communications but also because the time itself gives you tremendous opportunities. And we, the Ascended Hosts, are ready to give you another opportunity. Therefore, it happens that during our meetings we seek out all available reserves to render assistance to you. Literally, we seek every free erg of energy in order to help you cope with the problem that obstructs your path of service. So, do not hesitate to appeal to us if you have requests and problems. As soon as we get an opportunity, we will fulfill your request and help you.

The service of those who unselfishly send us the energy of their prayers is especially vital. In this case, we have an opportunity to create a reserve of energy that is used to help those of you whose work and service are directly related to changing people's consciousness.

I am glad that this year, for the first time in many years, I have a chance to tell you: "Stay on this course!"

Your efforts were not in vain, and the cooperation between you who are in embodiment, and us, the Ascended Hosts, becomes more and more successful!

Each time before we start a new meeting at the end of the year I am thrilled — for the picture is not always obvious, and sometimes the trend toward a favorable course of events is hardly notable.

This time before starting a new meeting, none of us doubted that it was the first time in many years that we had reached a tangible trend toward the favorable course of events on planet Earth. Of course, there are certain countries and entire regions where the state of affairs is very serious and where our and your unselfish help is needed. However, we are glad that on the largest continent, which is Eurasia, the state of things is beginning to improve.

The Western hemisphere lags behind in its development of the level of consciousness. It saddens us. And we feel deeper sadness when we turn our eyes to the land of America. Unfortunately, the tremendous potential of that country is still not directed toward evolutionary development. We are applying our efforts to find an approach to reach the consciousness of those few representatives of that nation who are able to accept the new methods in our Teaching, the new approaches in the sphere of spiritual development. I sincerely hope that our efforts will yield the fruits in the new year. The difficulty is in the very character of that nation because the Americans cannot admit that their country has failed our hopes. Now it has to retune itself, find the strength and the desire within, in order to sit at the desk once again and begin to learn, to learn new thinking and new consciousness, regardless of the country from where this new thinking and new consciousness comes.

To change stereotypes and to change your consciousness — this is what you all will have to learn in the near future, regardless of the country and the continent you are living in.

The development of human consciousness has neither state frontiers nor religious boundaries. The development of human consciousness is unlimited and infinite.

It is impossible to limit God. And it is impossible from your human level of consciousness to dictate to God what He is to do.

We hope to consolidate the success in the year 2007, which has already come and begun its walk on the planet.

What kind of year will it be? Unfortunately, even we, the Ascended Hosts and the members of the Karmic Board, can only speak about a probabilistic course of events. The future remains unpredictable. And it would not be interesting to live if the results were predictable and known beforehand.

We are ready to overcome the difficulties!

Are you also ready?

**I AM The Great Divine Director,
with faith in our mutual success!**

A talk about the healing of the soul and the body

Beloved Hilarion
January 4, 2007

I AM Lord Hilarion, having come to you today.

As always, I have come to give you instructions necessary for the internal work each of you performs when communing with yourself in the innermost recesses of your heart. How rare are such minutes when you are on your own. All your concerns pale into insignificance and you suddenly find yourself alone with your thoughts.

Think of how good it would be if you communed with yourself not just from time to time but every day, devoting just a few minutes to this communication with your heart.

I, Lord Hilarion, remember the minutes when, being in incarnation and leading a solitary life in the backwoods, I had a chance to observe myself as if from outside all day long. I understood that I was flesh and blood in incarnation with all the functions of my body. But at the same time I began to realize that within me there was another man who was not connected directly with the functions of my physical body. It was a strange feeling of double personality. I was on earth in incarnation, and at the same time I understood that I was immortal. I was eternal. I was thrown upon my own resources in that incarnation, and I tried to understand the reason for my being, but at the same time I was much more than my physical body. In fact, my physical body was just like a suit of armor enabling my Higher Self to dwell within me.

During those moments of clear understanding of who I was in reality, my consciousness rose to inconceivable heights from where I clearly saw the unity of the entire biosphere existing on earth.

I clearly saw the unity of all the kingdoms of nature, angels, and elementals. During those joyful minutes of tranquil commune with my heart, I felt around me thousands of beings — invisible to the human eye but nevertheless living — who were speaking to me and trying to get in touch with me. In those moments I experienced unity with every bug, with all the birds and animals.

How beautiful it was! And this was possible only when I was alone with myself. There was nobody around me except animals, birds, angels, and elementals.

Then people came to me. Those people were seeking healing from me. They aspired to come to me in order to get hold of a grain of my quiet happiness and serenity. But as soon as those people with their concerns and problems arrived in my world, the dwellers of my world hid because the vibrations of those people were unfamiliar and hostile to the vibrations of these dwellers as well as to my vibrations, which they had become accustomed to during the period of our quiet communication.

I rendered help to many people. I healed their souls. I prepared remedies from herbs, and I gave them those arcana. But it was not herbs that healed their damaged and feeble bodies. It was the people who cured themselves once their consciousness rose to a level where they began to realize what harm they had done to their souls and physical bodies by committing wrong actions and tolerating wrong feelings.

When non-divine feelings take possession of you, it is much like a whirlwind devastating your higher bodies. And if hatred, sorrow, sadness, envy, jealousy, and other negative feelings do often possess you, then every time hurricane after hurricane dashes through your higher bodies until finally your higher bodies come to a very ragged condition and can no longer serve you as conductors of the Divine energy. And you start suffering from those diseases that force you to seek healing from many herbalists and healers.

You will be incredibly lucky if you happen to meet on your path a healer who will cure not your body but your soul.

This is because it is your higher bodies that need healing — your emotional body, your memory or etheric body, and your mental body. It is these bodies that represent a more mutable part of you and that are destroyed by being constantly affected by negative thoughts and feelings.

The destruction and the diseases of the physical body are just the results of the damage and diseases of the higher bodies. That is why it is your soul that needs to be healed first. It is necessary to bring you to the understanding that you yourselves with your wrong actions, thoughts, and feelings throw your physical bodies into a disease.

Many of you go on keeping aggression in your hearts, blaming doctors, relatives, your jobs, and your bosses for your poor states of health. But this is a wrong concept. The first step toward your healing should be your understanding that no one is guilty for your diseases but you. And you yourselves provoked all your diseases when you raged, did harm to other people, used foul language, performed evil deeds, and ate and drank products polluting your organism.

You yourselves are the reason for your illnesses. And when you come to the understanding of this simple truth, you make the first and the main move toward your healing.

The next step is to make a decision never to perform such actions that led you to the disease. For some people this means getting rid of negative thoughts; for others, negative feelings; and for some, negative deeds.

You should desire to get rid of everything that was the reason for the ailments of your body and soul. Only after that, you are ready for the next step — the step when you sincerely call to God in your broken heart and ask for the healing of your soul and physical body from ailments.

Many of you are in such a sorry plight that it already does not seem possible to cure the physical body in the current life. However, when you understand the causes of your illnesses and set the correct patterns of behavior and mindset, this will bring peace to your souls. And in your next life you will be able to realize the reason for your diseases much faster, and from your youth you will take care not only of your physical bodies but also have the right attitude in your thoughts and feelings.

It is a rare case when a person starts to understand by himself the direct interconnection between his ailments and the deeds he performed in youth and in his mature years. And if we could show many of you the obscene deeds you committed, many would be surprised because it is impossible to tolerate things like that in your enlightened time.

Yet, sorry to say, your civilization is oriented to ruin your souls. And many of the so-called feature movies have a devastating effect on your higher bodies, destroying them like a tsunami. Guard yourselves from viewing such "works" and especially carefully guard your children. The higher bodies of children do not possess adequate protection yet, and the whole nightmare that they see on your television screens simply programs them for diseases and death.

We are warning you and trying to explain to you the reasons for your ailments.

At any moment you yourselves can break the vicious circle of the problems of your civilization. The only thing required of you is just to make a decision and to act in your lives in harmony with the Divine principles.

Now I would like to touch upon one more important thing. Whenever you call upon the angels, God, and the Masters to help you, always try to get into a humble state and ask for help from the point of reverence for Life and the Creator.

This is because all mercy emanates from God, and it is only the impervious crust of egoism sticking all over your hearts that prevents you from receiving this mercy.

**I AM Hilarion,
with Love toward you.**

A Teaching on the substitution of fear with Divine Love

Saint Michael, the Archangel
January 5, 2007

I AM Saint Michael, the Archangel who has come to you today!

I have come. I AM coming to announce that the New Day has come! The New Day is the day into which your planet is entering. And the New Day is coming in your consciousness. The twilight is over, and your consciousness is clearing from all those night fears in which it has been staying for thousands of years.

You have produced masses of fear by your imperfect consciousness, and now these masses roam about the astral and mental worlds independently. And when you face these fruits of your own consciousness, you feel fear and horror that seem to have no limit or control.

I have come to put an end to your fears! I have come to herald that with the beginning of the New Day, all your fears are fading away and they don't have any power. You and your consciousness are the source of fear and its power. That is why as soon as you clear your fears away from your consciousness they will no longer exist in the outward things, because they will lose the energy that you have been feeding them.

A large number of people feel fear. Fears are actually a scourge of your time. Fear exists where there is lack of Divine Love.

And there is lack of Love everywhere in your world. You cannot fight with your fears. The energy you will direct to that fight will only strengthen your fears. But you can dissolve your fears with a universal solvent, which is the Love of your hearts. Therefore, all that you need to do in the nearest future is to open your hearts to Love, Divine Love. And as your world is filled up with Divine Love, your fears will vanish like the mist clears away with the beginning of a new day.

Your state is determined by your ability to let Divine Energy in, and when you are short of Divine Energy you experience different negative conditions including fears.

The fear of death is dominating your world. You are afraid of something that does not exist in nature. You are afraid of something you created by your imperfect consciousness. You are afraid of death, but death does not exist. Death exists only in your consciousness. There is only eternal life and eternal bliss in the Divine World. Death is, in fact, only the transition of your soul from one life form to another.

Your painful perception of states concerned with death is caused by your fear of death. And when you manage and overcome your fear, death will no longer bother you. Moreover, birth and transition will not be so painful and frightful as they seem now in your world. Change your consciousness and many problems of your world will become less critical and vanish like darkness at noon. Although the shadows of the past will stay, they will not be able to take up much of your attention.

I have come to tell you that death does not exist, and I have come to tell you that all your fears are generated by your consciousness. When you let Love in your consciousness, it will dissolve all your fears including the fear of death.

How can you let Love in your heart? It is actually very easy. You have to let all the burdensome things like anxiety, hatred, anger, and envy go away from your heart. Hatred is particularly interfering. Hatred is the sister of ignorance. Hatred supersedes Divine Love in your hearts and precludes the manifestation of Divine Love. So, now when you know your enemies who try to conquer your heart, you can gradually get rid of them step by step.

I will give you a universal method that will help you to clear away from your heart all features that are in your way and that are not Divine.

So, when you have a minute of free time, imagine yourself taking a clean piece of cloth and dipping it in sparkling, absolutely clean water splashing at your feet. Bend over to take some water in your hands. Dip the cloth in the water and imagine you are holding your heart in your hands. Your heart is like a crystal vessel. But it became muddy and cannot let Divine Light in. Take your vessel, your heart, and imagine you are washing all negative qualities and feelings away layer by layer: hatred, hostility, fear, anger, ignorance, laziness, and envy. Each of you has several qualities to get rid of. Wash all these coatings of negative qualities and manifestations.

Repeat that procedure every day. Do not think that you can do the job all at once and clean up your heart from the centuries-old coating of negative energies.

Strive constantly to keep in your mind the image of releasing your negative qualities. Imagine how your heart passes more and more Divine Energy through it every time.

Sometime later your heart will be completely cleared from all accumulations of the past. And you will be able to assimilate in full measure the vibration of Divine Love running through the whole world and Creation. You cannot perceive these vibrations due to your own imperfection and your unwillingness to get rid of it.

I am sure that each of you will think about it and decide to change your approach and the style of your life and will stop frowning, happily exposing your smiling face to the New Day.

Imagine yourself sitting on a river-bank or near a lake or a spring while the sun is shining brightly in your face. The gentle touch of the rays of the sun is so pleasant! The sun penetrates deeper and deeper inside you every day. And one day you yourself become the Sun, giving your Light and Love to all those who need Light and Love.

The time will come when the sun of your Divine consciousness will be able to shine through you and give its warmth to many people who haven't set themselves free of things that do not allow them to force their way to the sun of Divine Presence in them.

You are sun-like. You just need to clear centuries-old coatings of dirt off your vessel so that it can become clean and transparent. You will fill your vessel with Divine Energy, and you will give everyone who is thirsty a chance to take from your vessel.

Divine Energy never comes to an end. Only the human consciousness limits the flow of Divine Energy in your world.

The New Day is coming when there are no limitations but Divine Freedom and Divine Love.

**I AM Saint Michael the Archangel,
with eternal Love to you.**

A Teaching on your soul

Beloved Kuthumi
January 6, 2007

I AM Kuthumi, having come to you again.

As always, I have come to give you an exhortation that you need and that your soul needs, yearning for the real Divine world.

We come time after time to take care of your soul and give it the nourishment that it needs. And today I have also come to give a small Teaching about your soul and for your soul.

Let us think together for a minute about what your soul is. Does your soul represent your entire manifested self?

What is meant by "soul"?

Actually, you are a very complex entity. You have your Divine part located in the Divine world that has never left the Divine world. You also have a soul, the part of you that has been specially created by the builders of forms for your journey through manifested worlds. And your physical body represents a vessel for your soul for the period of earthly incarnations.

You have a very complicated structure. If it were not for the call of the time, I would not come to give you this important Teaching on your soul.

The point is that many of you are confused by what the term "soul" means.

Your soul is closely and inseparably connected with your physical body, but the connection of your soul with your more subtle Divine bodies was lost at some point during your soul's development. This was caused by the turning point when you wished to leave the Divine world and to descend into matter. You wished to gain human experience; it was necessary for the evolution of your soul because your soul could not evolve without the experience of human evolution. It is impossible to develop if you do not constantly gain deeper experience. You descend into a more and more dense manifestation of the physical world, and it looks like your soul and your Higher Self descend to the bottom of the physical ocean in a bathyscaphe. In this case, your physical body serves as a bathyscaphe, and your soul inseparably connected with it, represents your subtle bodies: your astral body, your mental body, and your etheric body. Your subtle bodies are inseparably connected with your physical body and evolve thanks to your physical body.

If we come back to the analogy with a bathyscaphe, your subtle bodies represent the electronic systems and life support systems of your bathyscaphe.

But the bathyscaphe can perform certain tasks at the bottom of the ocean only if it is operated by a human.

Many of you are in such a state of your consciousness when the bathyscaphe gets out of control. Your subtle Divine bodies lose the connection with the bathyscaphe, and the bathyscaphe moves on its own.

Another example that can be used is the image of a sailboat that lost control in a storm. You live your merely physical life and do not think about who you are, where you came from, and where you are going. This restricts your goals and tasks to the physical world only and prevents you from further development.

There was a stage when you had to gain the experience of descending into matter, the experience of your embodiments.

Your subtle bodies and your soul have managed to evolve and to become more perfect during your journey through matter. Your structure became more and more sophisticated. But at a certain point you lost the oneness with your soul. You ceased to perceive the Higher worlds and lost the connection with your soul. Your soul became separated from you as well as your subtle bodies. This caused your soul to suffer. You lost many parts of your soul during your numerous incarnations. Your soul suffered very much when you allowed inharmonious behavior and explicit ungodly actions, and those sufferings made it partially leave you. That is why your subtle bodies bear imperfections of your previous embodiments from your very birth.

You must understand that there is a finer part of you. This is your soul, which is like a little child. Many manifestations of your world hurt your soul badly. It shrinks and may even leave your physical body. But without your soul you lose the ability to manifest Divine feelings. You lose the connection with the Divine world even more because it is through your soul that your Higher Self can manifest itself.

You need to return to a harmonious development of your soul, your physical body, and your Higher Self. All your bodies are to be balanced and harmonized.

You need to gather all the lost fragments of your soul in order to be able to move to the next step of your evolution. You need to restore your integrity, inner harmony, and peace.

This can be achieved by special practices and methods. Every period of time revealed new practices and new methods that could adjust your subtle bodies. Each method was appropriate for that particular time.

Now, as new energies and vibrations have come to Earth, the best thing for your soul is to spend time in the quiet of nature. There are still corners on the globe where nature has not been exposed to the devastating effects of civilization. These very places must serve as refuges and clinics for you. Staying there, you will be able to restore the integrity of your soul, body, and your Divine part.

You will not be able to achieve this in big cities.

You will need some time to restore your energies.

If you manage to practice your meditations in the wild for as long as possible, then gradually you will be able to attract all the fragments of your soul from space. Then, as soon as your soul feels your love and care, it will be attracted to you from space and will never leave you on your path.

I am trying to give you a very important Teaching. I am trying to bring home to your consciousness the fact that your further evolution is impossible unless you manage to restore the integrity of your soul and the harmony between all your bodies.

In the wild it will happen naturally. Then, as soon as you manage to heal your soul and cure its centuries-old wounds, you will be able to serve as an example for those people who are tired of living in the hell of your technocratic civilization. In a natural way your civilization will be able to return to the path that was originally planned for it: the path of spiritual evolution and development of Divine faculties and potentials.

No matter how you try to assure yourself that you have integrity and you are harmonious, I must tell you that the harmony you achieve with the help of self-hypnosis has nothing to do with the natural harmony, which all of you will certainly attain.

I have given you an important Teaching, a Teaching on your soul.

I AM Kuthumi.

The time for choice

Sanat Kumara
January 7, 2007

I AM Sanat Kumara, having come to you through my Messenger again. I have come quickly in order to transmit an urgent Message to you concerning your planet, which is going through a difficult time. Do you hear me?

I AM Sanat Kumara, the one who you know as The Ancient of Days, the one who came to your planet in its darkest hour and has not left it even until the present day.

I AM the one who is the most caring father for you. And, being your father, I have come to give you a Message concerning the time you are living through.

All of you are in the state of transition of your consciousness to a higher level. All of you must perform the transition in your consciousness. However, there are those among you who do not wish to follow the evolutionary path of development. You decelerate the process of evolution, and that is why the time that we have warned about is coming for you.

Any changes on the planet are possible only if they are authorized by the supreme guiding and coordinating body of this Universe. And so I have come in order to give you the explanation that has just been received which concerns planet Earth and its evolutions.

At the end of this year, those of you who will not manage to overcome the qualities within themselves that prevent you from your advancement on the Path will be especially and forcefully pushed forward in their development.

Unfortunately, those of you who need to receive this Message of mine in the first instance hardly read our Dictations that we transmit through our Messenger. However, in the subtle plane you will receive this warning through the consciousness of those who read our Messages.

Our warning has been uttered in your physical world; hence, everyone in your physical world is able to and must hear it, no matter if you perceive our words with your external consciousness or not. On the inner plane you will receive our Message. And you will face the choice whether to follow the evolution or to continue stroking your ego and having fun in the illusion.

There are those people among you for whom the term "cosmic opportunity" has not come yet. And you still have some time, so you may continue your development. However, there are those who have missed all the given deadlines, for them I am giving this Message today.

You know it within yourselves to whom this Message refers. You are missing one cosmic opportunity after another. You think that there will be no limit for you to shirk from the path of development that is predestined for you. Well, the time has come for you to be very forcefully pushed forward to make your final decision and choose either your further development or give up for lost your further development.

God is very merciful. He just leaves those who do not wish to comply with the Law established in this Universe on their own. Those dead end branches of evolutionary development, which you can see on some islands in the oceans where they continue to sit by the fire and devour their chunks of meat, have also previously made their choice — the choice which you are now facing.

In accordance with the new dispensation, you will make this choice consciously. You will know in your external consciousness the final choice that you will make. And we will leave you alone. Evolution will stop existing for you, and you will roll down the stairs backwards for many millennia.

Already by the end of this life you will be watching the fruits of your own choice.

All of you belong to different stages of evolutionary development.

There are representatives of the Third, the Fourth, the Fifth, and already the Sixth Root Races among you. Now the time for choice has come for those who must transit on to the next stage but cannot do it because of their laziness and neglect. I am speaking of those representatives of the Fifth Root Race who are not eager to follow the upward stairs and continue living as if nothing is going on in the world, as if the time has not changed and all processes have not accelerated.

It behooves you to look into yourselves before the end of this year in order to realize how you intend to exist further.

Your time has come, not because you have fallen behind in your development. Your intellect is all right, but you have fallen behind in the results for the development of your soul. The choices that you make push you farther and farther from the evolutionary path of development and make you slip into the evil path, the path of development of the carnal mind. In this case your intellect does not serve you in the best way. You try to solve sophisticated Divine tasks in the terms of your mind. But Divine solutions come only if you reject earthly human logic and dedicate your entire self, your whole being, to serving the Supreme Law.

So, I have come today with one piece of news that is not very joyous. In order to equalize the balance of energies in your consciousness, I wish to give another, more joyous piece of information.

For those of you who have chosen the path of evolutionary development and who are following this path despite all difficulties that they face in life, I have brought a piece of news concerning a new opportunity and a new dispensation. The opportunity of an accelerated development of your consciousness is opening up for you. Already by the end of this year many of you will notice how quickly your consciousness will change, and these changes of your consciousness will draw to you the people who are going in the same direction with you. You may recognize each other by the burning flame in your eyes, by the beat of your hearts, or by the wonderful and generous giving of yourselves to serving all Life.

You will be able to unite on the new principles and to arrange life on the basis of the Laws that exist in Heaven.

For you we are preparing the projects of our Communities in the subtle plane. Uniting in the physical plane, you will be able to represent the prototypes of new settlements, new communities, and new towns.

I am glad to finish today's Message on this joyous note!

Always, in all times, there existed an opportunity of making a choice. Some people chose one path; others preferred another choice.

This is the very process that is described in the Bible as the process of separating the wheat from the chaff.[22]

The time has simply changed, and this process, which formerly took many lifetimes, you can now watch within your one current lifetime.

I wish you to make only the right choices in your lives and to follow the evolutionary path of development.

With God's blessing!

I AM Sanat Kumara.

---

[22] Matthew 13:25-30, 36-43.

A Teaching on genuine Faith

Beloved Jesus
January 8, 2007

I AM Jesus, having come to you today.

To make the purpose of my visit clear to you, I would like to dwell upon some well-known things that are accepted in your society at the current stage of its evolution. So, you live in your world and rarely come across the things that you should think about in the first place. You are concerned with everything that surrounds you in your life. You think about how to support your family, what to wear, or what to eat. There is much fuss in your life. It seems to you that you live quite reasonably, like everyone around you.

However, if you think about what you do in your lives and how reasonable it is from the viewpoint of the Teaching that I gave you 2000 years ago, nothing has changed. I may come into embodiment once again to tell you about the same things that I told you then.

Do you remember that I told you not to worry about daily bread, that the lilies of the field look much better than you do? The birds do not plow or sow, but they are fed. The Lord can take care of you in the same way.[23]

---

[23] Matthew 6:25-33:
25. "Therefore I say to you, do not worry about your life, what you will eat or drink; or about your body, what you will wear. Is not life more than food, and the body more than clothing?

Being at the top of the evolutionary ladder of earthly evolutions, why are you paying so much attention to your most trivial needs? You literally make a cult of clothes, food, and prestigious things.

Nothing has changed since I came into embodiment 2000 years ago. You have mastered the usage of many modern things. You have advanced appliances, cars, and computers, but your consciousness is still on the same level as it was 2000 years ago. It is regrettable.

Do you understand where I am going with this? You are concerned about lots of unnecessary things that exist in your world, and you are busy with such things 99 percent of your time. Think about how you can come to your Heavenly Father if you are constantly busy with earthly problems.

Even when it seems to you that you dedicate yourselves to God, go to church, pray, and follow the rules of the church, even then you do not think about God as much as you are concerned with what other people think of you, how you look when you are in the church, and how other people look, those who are around you there. When I have a chance to be present in the church during a service — and I cannot be present at every service — I am

---

26. Look at the birds of the air; they do not sow or reap or store away in barns, and yet your Heavenly Father feeds them. Are you not more valuable than they?
27. Can any one of you by worrying add a single cubit to your height?
28. "So why do you worry about clothing? Consider the lilies of the field. They do not labor or spin.
29. Yet I tell you that not even Solomon in all his splendor was dressed like one of these.
30. If that is how God clothes the grass of the field, which is here today and tomorrow is thrown into the fire, will He not much more clothe you—you of little faith?
31. Therefore, do not worry, saying, 'What shall we eat?' or 'What shall we drink?' or 'What shall we wear?'
32. For the pagans run after all these things, and your Heavenly Father knows that you need all these things.
33. But seek first the kingdom of God and His righteousness, and all these things will be given to you."

surprised by your thoughts that I listen to and by your feelings that I sense. You know, it is very rare that you can find people who have truly Divine feelings. As a rule, you come to a temple to solve your earthly problems, to improve your life, and to ask that you and your relatives stay healthy. And sometimes, on the contrary, you even wish evil to other people that you know.

You continue solving your mundane affairs there in the church. You do not think about God. If you come up to my image, it is only in order to ask for something that you lack in your earthly life.

Think about my words. It can seem to you that I speak in riddles, and it is unclear what I am driving at.

I am talking about exactly the same things that I was talking about 2000 years ago. I am trying to make you understand that it is necessary to think about your soul, about your relationship with God, and about God within yourselves. I taught that you should be alone with God during your praying, and I condemned hypocrisy.[24] I revolted against the letter of the law; I made you think about the spirit. Now I am talking about the same things. Nothing but your relationship with God should interest you. And then, when you are searching for God in order to gain the meaning of life and begin to teach this meaning to others, you do not come to God, but you are only distancing yourself from Him.

Only when you find complete satisfaction in communication with God within you, and you do not need to share your quiet joy with anybody, because you are fully satisfied and happy, only then will you find true God. I am touched watching you, and you start feeling my presence.

---

[24] Matthew 6:5-6:

5. "And when you pray, do not be like the hypocrites, for they love to pray standing in the synagogues and on the street corners to be seen by others. Truly I say to you, they have received their reward.

6. But when you pray, go into your room, close the door and pray to your Father, who is unseen. Then your Father, who sees what is done in secret, will reward you."

I am always close to you. But your state of consciousness and your concern about earthly problems separate us from each other.

I am so keen to communicate with you! How rare are the moments when I manage to initiate direct conversation with some of you. I am so happy about these moments. I am very much aware that every person who has had this experience of direct contact with me will no longer be able to live like all the rest. Such a person will seek solitude and inner communion with me. And then he will not be able to imagine himself and his life without this communion.

This quiet joy and serenity that such a person emanates in his life is better than any sermon or homily. He is a living example of a union with me and with God within him.

The best and most devoted Christians reached this inner union in the quiet of their hearts. However, there were others who tried to playact serenity, love, and grace. But one short glance cast at them was enough to determine the degree of their hypocrisy and to keep away.

I would like you to find the gift of recognition in your heart to identify all of the wolves in sheepskin, no matter what beautiful words they use in order to camouflage, no matter what they do. It seems that many people do the right things, talk about God, go to church; but in their hearts they are much farther away from me than many of those who do not parade their faith but fulfill the Father's commandments in their hearts.

I have come to you today to remind you about the Teaching that I gave 2000 years ago, and it has not lost its relevance. I would like to remind you that I was crucified for the Teaching that I had brought. And if I came today and started giving my Teaching, I would be subjected to the same persecution from scribes and Pharisees who occupy churches.

There are genuine servants, but there are even more false servants. That is why I want you to make a distinction in your consciousness not to condemn indiscriminately this or that church, this or that teaching.

The right Teaching may be incorrectly interpreted by unpurified human hearts, but it does not mean that the Teaching is wrong. First of all, seek God within yourself, in your heart. When you achieve inner harmony with God, you will not fear any wolves in sheepskin or any false pastors.

I was glad to come to you today to remind you about my Teaching that I gave earlier and that I bring again through this Messenger.

I AM Jesus.

An admonition for those on the Path

Lord Maitreya
January 9, 2007

I AM Maitreya, having come to you through my Messenger!

I have come to forward a Message about some urgent matters with which you ought to be familiarized.

You know that we come to you and that we have an opportunity to come due to a special dispensation. This dispensation allows us to communicate with you and give our Messages through specially prepared individuals who serve us and hold posts as our Messengers or bearers of news. And now we have a chance to speak through one of our Messengers.

We are glad that the Teaching we give has received fairly wide publicity and that your hearts are opening to it. But unfortunately not all is as good as we expected it to be. And many of you, after having found our Teaching given through our Messenger, are set ablaze at the start, but after some time, retreat. The consciousness of such a person withers little by little and starts to be interested in the things — different trinkets of your world — that seduce him or her away from the right way.

You should learn to make a distinction between the true Teaching and the surrogates overabounding in your world.

We have already told you, and I will repeat this one more time: Ninety percent of the shelves in your bookshops groan with teachings that contain no more than ten percent of the Truth. And you make your choice in favor of these surrogates and turn away from the pleasures of our table kindly offered to you.

Why is it so? It is because in those numerous teachings that exist in your world, one does not need to make a choice. One has neither to observe the discipline of a follower nor to have any obligations. Nothing is required of you except for your energy, your Divine energy, which you use without control, giving your attention to surrogates. And the whole illusory world of pseudo-teachings exists only because you power it with your energy.

I will one more time repeat a guideline of the Teaching given to you earlier: You are responsible for every erg of the Divine energy you spend. It seems to you that you do nothing out of the ordinary. You simply attend seminars or go through training that seems useful for you. You spend your money, but — what is worst of all — you spend the Divine energy granted to you by God. You make your choice, and this choice makes you create karma.

Yes, beloved, you create karma by supporting false teachings. The point is that you are at different stages of development. And some of you are so innocent that you take for precious gems those imitations kindly offered to you that glitter on the surface but have no internal value.

But those of you who had an opportunity to taste the Truth, who read our Teachings and then suddenly felt a need to look for something else somewhere else, bear the karma of the wrong choice and of the misuse of the Divine energy. And as a rule, in this case you are guided by your ego. You feel dissatisfaction only because you do not want to part with that part of you which tells you, "There are many paths. It is not worth locking into only one thing. All the paths lead to God."

However, this is a common mistake of your days because there are paths that lead to God and there are paths that draw away from God.

I will give you a reliable guideline as to how not to err from your Path.

You should realize what it is that drives you when you wish to seek some new fashionable teaching. What is your motive? As a rule, your ego whispers to you that you should not focus on only one thing and that there is nothing new in the Dictations given by the Masters through their Messenger.

And sure enough, there is really nothing new in our Messages. We have been giving this Teaching through many of our Messengers during many thousands of years. And if you had mastered at least ten percent of this Teaching, you would never barter this Teaching away for the baubles offered to you under the guise of our Teachings.

Look for the reason why you are leaving the Path inside of you. Only you yourselves make decisions and make choices. Unfortunately, we cannot make you follow the Path shown by us. You have freedom of choice, and you have a right to be guided with your free will while making choices in the physical plane.

However, your chances to make choices are given a timeframe. If you learn nothing and if from embodiment to embodiment you keep going under the thumb of your ego instead of parting with it, you receive a stern warning about your wrong choice. But if you stick to your guns and go on following your own path, taking the bit between your teeth and closing your eyes, you are left alone.

Then only the actions of your intercessors in the Heavens, with whom you spend not just one embodiment together, can help you. But more often you are simply left alone, and you have to vegetate in the illusion during many embodiments until evolution gives up your life-stream as hopeless and you are recognized as needless ballast. God gets rid of the dead and ill cells. If a healthy body does not free itself from malignant cells that think only about themselves, the whole organism can fall ill.

That is why we come to you and with indefatigable pertinacity warn you over and over to think out all the steps you make in life.

Those people who have never heard of our Teaching and have never attended our classrooms bear one burden of a wrong choice of the path.

But those who have once decided to consecrate their embodiments to the service of the Brotherhood and have not applied the undertakings, are considered to be traitors, and their karma is much greater than the karma of criminals and assassins.

I have come with this Message today. Perhaps I have put some of you out of humor. But I had to give you this chance to think about everything, and after having conquered your ego, to make a considered decision posited on the standpoint of the Divine reason in you.

I will be glad to give a helping hand to those of you who ask for my help and who appeal to me at the minute of heavy contemplations over your destiny.

I AM Maitreya.

A Teaching on Devotion

Beloved El Morya
January 10, 2007

I AM El Morya, who has come to you on this day!

I have come in order to announce the end of the current cycle of Messages that we have given through our Messenger.

The cycle is over. We truly hope that our efforts and our energy that we used for transmitting our Messages and that we embedded in the actual text of the Messages, will not be wasted. We hope that you will be rereading our Messages, and whatever you do not grasp after the first time, you will be able to comprehend after you read the Messages for the second, third, or fourth time.

There are many obvious Truths that do not even catch your eye because you think that you have heard them many times and know them well. Believe me; if you look at them from a different angle, then they begin to carry a new meaning after some time because you have lived through these moments of Truth in your life. Yes, there is a big difference between how you perceive the Truths when you read them and when you live them through your lives. The difference is that when you open a Divine Truth to yourself with your heart, instead of just briefly scanning through it in a text, then that Truth will never leave you. You will become the bearer of that Truth. That Truth will become inherent to you, like an integral part of your being. This is the state of your consciousness that we are trying to have you acquire. You should not be retelling old Truths but become the bearers of Truth, the bearers of our Word and those who bring our Teaching to life.

Unfortunately, there are few people like that. Only a few of you can completely devote your lives to fulfilling our covenants, serving selflessly, having transformed your entire lives into service.

We know about you. We know each of you who are capable of fulfilling our tasks and doing our work on the physical plane.

Each of you is under our strict control and supervision. Many of you, having received all our trust and our credential letters, still do not find the strength to continue the work that they have started and step away from the Path.

Every time you come in contact with us and receive our trust, do not think that it is a coincidence. For many incarnations, you have been earning the right to even just come in contact with us and fulfill the duties that you had taken on before the incarnation.

The most pitiful situation is when you win our trust and receive the credential letters, but then you slack off in fulfilling your duties. Your mind will always gladly provide you with many logical proofs that you are right. Yet, your heart will never lie to you. Until the end of this incarnation you will always feel heaviness in your heart, the heaviness from an unfulfilled duty.

I would not want to be in your place. For there is nothing more painful in your world, not a single deed that you could commit that would be as severe as the betrayal of your sacred work in the name of Life on Earth.

I have also come to you today to remind you of the duties that you have accepted. If, before the end of this year, you change your decision and return to the fulfillment of the obligations — your duty that you have accepted — we will defend you before the Karmic Board and try to alleviate the karmic consequences of your wrong choices in the past.

There are very few true servants who are currently incarnated. It is unbearable to watch how, one after another, they refuse to fulfill their duty and chase after the illusions of your world.

Believe me, there is nothing in your world that could even roughly be compared to the joy of service, the satisfaction that one receives from fulfilling his duty, from completing his work. When you leave the physical plane and return to the etheric octaves of Light, millions of beings of Light from the entire universe rush to show you their respect and thank you for your dedicated work during your incarnation on Earth.

Do not take for a model those who are prominent. Many of our devoted servants are waiting all their lives to play their small roles. Those seemingly small roles can at times change the situation in the whole country, and sometimes, even in the entire world.

Therefore, listen to your heart closely. Has the time come already to manifest your service to the Life?

We will gladly provide you with all necessary assistance. We will find a way to get across to your outer consciousness the task that should now be fulfilled. However, when the time comes for you to act, do not whine or say how difficult it is for you, and that your old wounds are sore, and that you do not have enough food reserved.

There is nothing in your world that could stop true collaborators from fulfilling their task of life.

Therefore, try to always maintain your devotion and readiness. Train yourselves constantly. Train those internal muscles that will allow you to act when you feel like there is no more energy or capacity.

There is always room for heroism in your life. Your heroism will not be appreciated by the external consciousness of people, but your heroism will be appreciated in Heaven. For only here do they know the value of the heroic acts that you perform in the incarnation when you retain your devotion in, at times, unbearable conditions that surround you in the physical plane.

I was glad to give you this short Teaching on devotion. I am glad even more that I was able to give this Teaching in the last Dictation of this cycle that we completed through our Messenger.

I will be glad if in the future, the opportunities will be in our favor, and we will be able to continue to give our Teaching through our Messenger.

I would like to thank Tatyana for her service.

**I AM El Morya,
with Faith and Hope in you and Love to you.**

Message from the Ascended Masters between the fifth and sixth cycles of Dictations

About the current situation on Earth

Gautama Buddha
March 7, 2007

I AM Gautama Buddha, who has come to you today hastily in order to give an important Message regarding the current situation on planet Earth.

As always, those of you who read our Messages are the people who are ready the most for concrete actions. That is why I come to you on this day in order to clarify the situation and ask you for help. Your home planet needs your help right now. Not the help that you render in your daily prayers but the help in which all of you need to participate. That is because the situation is very fraught, and a series of earthquakes can be the cause of major destructions and lead to a great number of human losses. That is why I come as a Master who is responsible for the conditions on Earth and for the energy balance on Earth. No other Master can address you in this situation.

I am asking you for help that can be rendered by all of you who are reading this Message of mine.

The moment you read my call for help in this Message, without any delay, pronounce the following call in your heart, or aloud:

"O Earth, I know that it is a hard time for you, I know that you need my help today. I am asking my Higher Self, in the name of I AM THAT I AM, to give the Divine Energy that comes into my body-temple today, for the stabilization of the situation on Earth."

Gautama Buddha

Thousands of you who are ready for such sacrifice will be able to change the situation on planet Earth in an instant.

I recommend you to make this call during any cataclysms or natural disasters that happen to planet Earth.

Now, I would like to use the opportunity to provide some information regarding the solar eclipse that will be happening on March 19, 2007. The sun symbolizes Divine reason, and any solar eclipse that occurs puts extra pressure on your subtle bodies. During the time of the solar eclipse, including several days before and several days after the eclipse, I recommend that you pay close attention to yourselves and to your daily routines. I recommend that you have more rest and more sleep, and of course, maintain your harmony.

Your imperfect energies contained in your lower bodies will become activated, and you may experience somewhat discomforting states. For some it will be unexplained irritability and disharmony while others may fall into depression or perform uncontrolled actions. Solar eclipses are especially dangerous for mentally unbalanced people and people with mental disorders. Therefore, make sure that your close relatives have peace of mind. Try to protect them from experiencing any negative states of mind.

It will be very useful to perform meditations and prayers devoted to Harmony, Peace, and Love.

I have come to warn you about an unfavorable flow of energies on the surface of Earth. I have come to reassure you that everything is in your power and that you are capable of harmonizing the situation on the planet with your own efforts, even without seeking help from the Ascended Hosts.

You need only to imagine that the energy granted by God can be directed by your will toward harmonizing the situation on the planet and preventing any natural disasters.

Nature is not blind. And Nature comes out of her state of balance under the influence of your thoughts and feelings if they are not harmonious. In the same way, Nature can return to the balanced state if you apply efforts toward harmonizing yourselves and the people around you.

Pay attention to keeping your thoughts and feelings in a calm, balanced state — not only today but at a minimum until the end of this month.

We are closely watching the situation on the planet and rendering all necessary help. However, today I have come to ask you for help so that you can feel us beside you and so that we can rely on you in the situations when a cataclysm is impending on the planet.

I was glad that our meeting today occurred and that I was able to bring to your outer consciousness such important and essential information.

**I AM Gautama Buddha,
with Love and hope in you.**

Book 6

Cycle 6: Messages of the Ascended Masters
from June 20 to July 10, 2007

Joyous News

**Sanat Kumara
June 20, 2007**

I am Sanat Kumara, having come again through my Messenger. I have come to you on this day to announce the beginning of the new cycle of Dictations, which we intend to give through our Messenger. I come on this day, and the tears appeared on my cheeks against my will. Oh, you cannot even imagine how happy the Heavens are on this day!

It seems to you that everything is still the same around you, and nothing is predicting any changes. The sun is still shining like before, birds are singing, and your daily concerns inevitably appear before you. However, I daresay a lot of things have changed since the last transmission of the Dictations through our Messenger. Less than a half-year has elapsed. You may ask, "What could have changed?"

What was supposed to happen really did happen. And we are happy that the condition that we have communicated through our Messenger in March this year has been practically fulfilled.[25] We needed to see a sign in the physical plane that showed us that our Messenger was recognized by the people of Russia. We needed to see a sign in the physical plane that would prove that people of Earth could hear us and were ready to cooperate with us.

---

[25] See the Appendix: «Appeal from the Masters to the people of Russia," part of a speech given by Tatyana N. Mickushina in Moscow, March 27, 2007.

We received this sign. It was the beginning of the construction of an Ashram for our Messenger. Now we can bring this joyous news to the Great Central Sun and ask for new dispensations and new Divine favors both for the people of Russia and for the whole population inhabiting planet Earth.

We are glad, and I am glad that the most difficult test, the hardest trial, is over. The sign of the successful passing of this test allows the proceeding of our Dictations that we are giving in accordance with the Divine opportunity through our Messenger.

Now, before starting my Dictation, I have been thinking thoroughly over the content of my talk. Do you want to know what I must tell you? I understood and I realized that the way we had hoped the collaboration with people of Earth would be was not fulfilled. We expected the act of unconditional, unselfish, charitable help would be provided to our Messenger from one person. And this act of unselfish donation could have given us cause to ask for some new favors and new opportunities for planet Earth. It didn't happen. Not a single person could reach such level of consciousness to provide unconditional help to our Messenger.

Yet, you can ask why we are joyous, why we are happy.

Russian people decided to outsmart Divine Law. There appeared hundreds and thousands of people who made their unselfish contributions to the construction of the Ashram for our Messenger. There were people who donated very modest sums. But we could see and read in their hearts. Their contributions were equal to the royal one because they sacrificed this money when their families were not well provided for. There were people who donated significant sums of money, and there were people who gave the energy of their prayers, which we used to help.

We thank everyone who participated in the construction. Your contribution is priceless in the eyes of God because it will allow us to get new Divine favors and opportunities not only for Russia but also for the whole planet.

I am happy to announce that the session of the Karmic Board will start any minute. I sincerely hope that those of you who have participated in the construction or have made the contribution into it, will be able to appeal to the Karmic Board with letters and ask for the favors you would like to receive for yourself and for your relatives.

Don't be shy to ask. If your requests cannot be granted completely, then you will surely get the maximal relief of your karmic burden that is allowed by Divine Law.

Thus, I would like to express my gratitude and my thanks to everyone who participated in the fulfilment of our ultimatum[26] that we had given in March of this year. And I hope that the efforts that you made won't cease. Oh, I will tell you that God is preparing for you tremendous miracles! And the prospects that are about to open for you will exceed all your expectations.

However, it is necessary to take into account that you are at the beginning of your Path. There is a hard and dangerous road ahead of you. And if now you are enthusiastic, full of energy and Divine impulses are coming from within, you will need all your strength to overcome the rest of the Path.

We intend to implement the transformation of planet Earth in a short space of time. This means that the resistance of the forces that do not wish this transformation to take place will be increasing catastrophically. Be alert and cautious on your Path. Do not allow illusion to take over your consciousness so that you forget about God and about the Masters and slide down the slippery and dangerous path into the gorge of horror and sorrow.

We call you up the mountain peaks. Do not allow yourself to look down into the obscure gorges of grief with which Earth is still filled.

---

[26] See the Appendix: "Appeal from the Masters to the people of Russia," part of a speech given by Tatyana N. Mickushina in Moscow, March 27, 2007. Refer to the section: "Explanation of the Appeal from the Masters."

We hope that all the dangers that you will encounter on your Path will be overcome by you in dignity. It will be hard for you. You will feel colossal workloads and resistance to all your strength. When it gets especially hard for you, when you are in despair, when you don't see a single ray of Light ahead, please remember me, remember this Message, remember the fact that you are an immortal being of Light and that nothing threatens you while you keep Faith, Hope, and Love in your heart!

It is enough for you to save just a grain of Faith and use it to send a call to the Heavens, to me personally, to any Ascended Master, or to Archangel Michael. And even when it seems to you that you are completely ruined, a miracle will happen, and all the obstacles in your way will vanish like a fog. Never forget that you are in the illusory world. All the horrors and fears of your illusory world will completely disappear on one beautiful day because this is Divine Law. And those who are trying to hang on to the old, familiar, obsolete, moldy things are at risk of vanishing into nonexistence along with the illusory world.

Therefore, leave your doubts and your bad moods, and aspire toward the fresh breeze of changes, toward great transformations and achievements, toward the heights we are calling you.

I am sure that after reading this Message many of you will look at your life in a new way and will make a choice in favor of changes, no matter how scary they might seem to your human mind.

Nothing can harm you. Do not be afraid to lose your body but to save your soul. It's much worse if you prefer to keep your body and all that you gained in the physical world and lose your soul.

I have come and I am leaving you on this day.

I AM Sanat Kumara.

Recommendations to humankind of Earth

Beloved Surya
June 21, 2007

I AM Surya, having come to you again from the Great Central Sun.

I have come again to humankind of Earth in order to give instructions and to strengthen and develop the connection between the worlds. As usual, I would like to pay attention to the news concerning current events that are revealed now and are taking place in your world and are going to descend into your world in the nearest future because in the finer plane these events are ready to descend into the physical world.

You know that we work with humankind of Earth thanks to the Divine mercy, the dispensation that allows us to correct the course of evolution on the planet. And you know that millions of years ago humanity of Earth deviated from the evolutionary path; and it brought some turmoil to the common course of evolution. Many lifestreams got a deceleration of their development, and on the contrary, many life-streams accelerated their development thanks to Divine mercies and opportunities. Each of you can make his or her own choice whether to follow the Divine Law or to continue living in accordance with the laws that have formed on planet Earth and which at the given moment do not quite conform to the plan for the planet, the plan that exists on the Divine level, which should be realized soon.

Please, do understand that we do not wish to cause you pain and suffering. Millions of beings of Light from all over the cosmos are ready to help you. However, you and only you slow down the evolution of the planet. You allow yourselves to perform such deeds and to have such imperfect states of consciousness that are inadmissible at your stage of evolution. We are forced to resort to such measures when literally before your eyes your imperfect deeds, thoughts, and feelings are materialized into outer conditions like unfavorable weather, cataclysms, and troubles that you face in your lives: diseases, afflictions, and misfortunes.

You yourselves are the cause of what happens with you and around you. We all are closely connected in the etheric plane, and we all belong to the common chain of evolutions in the universe. There is no particular difference between you and me. I stand several hundred steps higher than you. And that is the difference between us. Therefore, you should listen to the advice coming from me or from any other Ascended Master who gives his Messages through our representative on Earth, our Messenger Tatyana.

Now you have this opportunity of almost direct communication. Use this opportunity and try to treat our Dictations not as fairy tales you listened to in your childhood before going to bed, but rather, try to treat our Dictations as the guidance that you should follow in your life. Believe me; the opportunity that you have now gives you a great advantage. In such a way we are intending to pull out of the nets of illusion millions of lifestreams, lost souls who were wandering about in the thicket of illusion from incarnation to incarnation and who face whole swarms of fears, doubts, misfortunes, and diseases.

We throw our nets again to pull out thousands and millions of lost souls from the waters of the astral plane.

We come in order to give you an impulse, that energy impulse that will allow you to wake up and to turn your eyes to the Heavens, to the bright sun of the New Day, the dawn of the Day that has already begun.

I have come to you today in order to give necessary instructions for the future. You are the beings of Light who are lost in the thicket of the matter, and we give you a helping hand. Please, do not refuse our help, do not show arrogance that is more typical of teenagers, and do listen to our advice.

Due to the Law of Free Will acting in the Universe, you have an opportunity to choose your future yourselves. You have an opportunity to listen to my and our advice, and you have an opportunity to refuse the outstretched helping hand.

I must warn you that now you are hanging over an abyss, and if the mist around you hides this from your view and does not allow you to see your lamentable state, it does not mean there is no danger of rolling down into that abyss at any moment.

You may not believe me. You may continue to stubbornly refuse the offered help. That is your right. But there are individuals among you who ask us for help, and we cannot but help them as the call forces us to respond. We cannot save you by force, but our duty is to offer a helping hand to those who need it.

We are with you for your whole long Path from the matter back to the Divine world. We are with you all along your Path. And very soon, if you follow our advice, you will be able to distinguish us and will consciously receive our assistance. But now you need to believe our Messages and the information that we are giving through our Messenger.

There were always the people who declared themselves Messengers of Heavens. And they spoke on behalf of God. There were people who listened to and followed the advice coming from above, and there were people who mocked at it and followed their own way.

It is your choice. It is your free will.

My task and our tasks are just to warn you about the consequences of your choice. And my task and our tasks are to point out for you that the time has accelerated, and the consequences of your wrong choices will be visible to you in just a couple of days after you have made the wrong choice. This is done especially for you to track with your external consciousness the effect of the Great Cosmic Law of this universe, which in former times was stated in the following way: "As you sow, you shall reap."

It is a very rational Law, the Law-Teacher that helps you learn the mistakes you made in the past. This is Law that you should learn in schools. The generation, starting their life now, must know this Law. And if there are problems with the introduction of the subject Laws of the Universe at school, you can always explain the effect of this Law to your children and grandchildren. And the more people are informed about this Law, the better the situation on planet Earth will be, as those people who know this Law will beware of breaking it, not because of fear but because of the wish to avoid unnecessary obstacles on their Path.

Believe me, sometimes it is better to get around an obstacle than to climb up a vertical rock without a safety rope.

We come in order to give you our short guidance. Please inform your children and grandchildren about the safety rules of living on planet Earth.

I sincerely hope for your help and support.

I AM Surya, with all my Love toward you.

Exhortations for the current day

Master Morya
June 22, 2007

I AM El Morya, having come to you again through my Messenger.

I AM and I have come!

As always, I would like to give an exhortation that you need at this stage of your Path.

Every time I come, I wish to bring home to you my state and the tension that I experience because I apply incredible efforts to bring sometimes very important and necessary information to my disciples. I send my thoughts, I give signs, and I send angels. Every time you face my signs on the Path, for some unknown reason your mind pretends that there are no signs at all, or it considers the goings on as some misunderstanding or a coincidence.

Every time I come and every time I teach reading the signs, I cannot communicate with you verbally. The easiest way is to send signs into your world. So you have to keep your consciousness constantly at a high level. However, you lack sensitivity, the perception of the subtle realm, the sense of the subtle realm.

You easily perceive the astral plane, and you are ready to collaborate with it. But the Higher planes of existence escape your attention, and external circumstances of your life shield you from the Divine levels and make the connection with our world more difficult.

I teach sensitivity and reading signs. Every time I come, I give exact instructions. Every time you listen to me, you practically forget within a few minutes or hours what you have been told. Your consciousness switches over to the affairs of your world and your surroundings, and with the greatest consistency you escape from your own decisions that you made under the impulse of devotion and Faith, and you rush for the immediate amusements and enjoyments of your world. It is necessary for you to learn how to keep the image of our world constantly in your consciousness. You must constantly feel that our worlds are interconnected. Every time you allow yourselves to get distracted from the reality surrounding you, cast your glance at the Heavens and the Heavens get closer to you. Every time you concentrate too much on the illusory problems of your world, the Heavens move away from you.

Believe me, the vibrations of your world are not the same throughout the day. There are hours, especially early in the morning or late at night when the hubbub of your world calms down, and our world gets closer. During these wonderful moments many of you can view angels and elementals even with ordinary human eyes. On the contrary, in such minutes of closeness to our world, many people whose vibrations have not acquired enough harmony and purity feel inexplicable apathy, depression, and lack of meaning of life.

Therefore, I would like to ask you to observe all situations of this kind in your life. Not so much earthly time will pass, and there will be splitting or differentiation in the population of Earth. People with higher vibrations will perform the exodus from Sodom and Gomorrah of modern cities, from the cloacae of mass consciousness, and from low vibrations.

They will choose pure places, which still exist on the globe, for their settlements. Those people whose vibrations are attuned with modern cities will stay in them. Therefore, in the natural way, there will be an exodus of the people of a new race to the Promised Land. Angels will have an opportunity to painlessly perform their work of removing from the planet all the cosmic waste incapable of further evolution.

This prophecy was given through many prophets. Every time people hear the prophecy, they continue performing their everyday activities and do not hear it in their inner consciousness. Only a small number of people who are able to hear, appeal to the Heavens and get the signs on their Path. They aspire to the Promised Land, and this enables them to continue their evolution.

I am not frightening you, I am giving an exhortation because right now it is the time for a sincere talk with those of you who can hear and who are ready for making concrete steps in the physical plane. I am not forcing you to give up everything immediately and rush to remote places. No, the direction of your aspiration will gradually draw Divine opportunities to you. And one day you will feel an imperceptible desire for changes, and you will change your life in accordance with the flow of Divine evolution. You are required to submit to the Higher Law and to wish to follow the Path of evolutionary development. For this you need to reconsider your life and your attitude toward life.

The reason for withdrawal from the evolutionary path is your concentration on your own self — your excessive self-esteem and egoism. Therefore, what is necessary for you to develop in yourselves in the near future is the ability of self-sacrifice, of compassion, and of helping the people around you. When you are able to perform the deeds that are unreasonable from the viewpoint of the majority of mankind but unselfish and filled with devotion to the Brotherhood, then you are standing firmly on the Path, and we take a tight hold of your hand. You are required to reveal a little bit of unselfishness, aspiration, and devotion, and these qualities will attract to you Divine opportunities that will take you out of modern "Sodoms" and "Gomorrahs" to the path of Light and Joy.

Just think how much you win when following the Path, which we are showing you, and how little you are to sacrifice — only your ego and your desire to receive something for yourself.

It is necessary to raise your level of consciousness to the point that you understand that by doing something for your neighbor, you actually take care of yourself. You either work off your karmic debt this way or stock up your good karma, which will allow you to escape a dangerous situation instantly, just by uttering a call.

We give instructions hoping that many of you are able to perceive our words and not just to perceive our words but also to start acting in accordance with the given Teaching.

It is the practical use of the knowledge that is of most importance. When you know the Law but do not implement it in your life, your karma does not decrease — it increases. You multiply your karma because there is such a type of karma as the karma of inactivity.[27] You have gotten this Teaching, and it means that you are able to comprehend it and to act according to it. If you do not act in accordance with the received Teaching, you evade the Path in this way. You evade the Path even when you do nothing. And your dual world is to blame for that, the world that was created by you with those energies that you chose to spend — not on displaying Divine patterns but on getting something for yourself.

It is time for the transformation of your world now. The first thing you have to do is to begin acting in your life in accordance with the Teaching being given by us.

I was very abrupt and inflexible because the time has changed. There is no possibility to wait any longer.

I AM El Morya Khan.

---

[27] Refer to the Dictation "A Teaching on the karma of inactivity," Beloved Kuthumi, June 24, 2005, in *Words of Wisdom Volume 1*.

A Teaching on the Initiation of the Crucifixion

Beloved Zarathustra
June 23, 2007

I AM Zarathustura, who has come to you again!

I have come on this day and I am happy that the opportunity, a Divine opportunity for our association with you through this Messenger, has continued. You probably do not know that in order for our work to continue, there needed to be proof in the physical plane that people are ready for further work. On the one hand, such proof was made by the people of Russia, the country that hosted our Messenger. People passed this test. We cannot say that everything went smoothly, but we see that our Teaching has found support in the hearts of many people in Russia. Many hearts got ignited with fire, and we, the Ascended Hosts, see this fire. That is because the Flame, the fire of your hearts, is visible to us at our level. We see each Flame in the heart of every person, regardless of where he or she is located. It is by this Flame, by these Flames, that we judge your preparedness and make the decision about future work.

On the other hand, our Messenger was simultaneously going through a very difficult test, which we call the Crucifixion. Everyone who achieves a certain level of consciousness goes through this test. This test is an inherent part of the Path. I would like to tell you a little bit about this test because each of you will be going through it, if not in this life, then in one of your future lives.

This is an inherent part of the Path. Everyone who has reached this point will be left alone with the tests and trials that beloved Jesus went through when He carried his cross to Golgotha and then underwent his Crucifixion on the cross. I would like to tell you about this trial. Every time you reach this point of the Path, you are left alone with this test. You have to move forward in such conditions where nobody understands you. People under the influence of the mass consciousness are simply unable to understand what is happening.

The following happens. The vibration of the person who has reached the Initiation of the Crucifixion rises to such an extent that the opposing forces begin to act through everyone who surrounds this person. It may seem like the entire world has become hardened in its heart, or is insane. Of course, in the time of Jesus, this trial was performed in the physical plane. All torture, abuse, and hardships appeared in the physical plane. Now, in your enlightened era, all tests have moved to the psychological plane. Of course, people perform actions that worsen the conditions for the test, but the main test is performed in the subtle plane. It creates an impression of a true Crucifixion on the cross of matter.

It is difficult for you to imagine, but this test is the most difficult one. You are not given a chance to relax for even a minute during the day or at night. Every possible and impossible situation comes to you in the physical plane as well as in the mental and astral planes.

You are constantly under the pressure of the forces that protect the illusion. The forces that supported you from our level of consciousness become isolated. We cannot render help. We can neither clean the wounds that are made to your subtle bodies nor protect you. All bodies of the subject are wounded and bleeding with Light, the Divine energy that attracts various beings of the astral plane who come to torture and receive their portion of Light.

The same is true for people. They come and take the Light that is uncontrollably leaking from the wounded aura. Only a few are able to realize what is happening. The rest do not see the meaning of what is happening at all. If the subject does not bear this test, whether by coming into opposition or becoming desperate and losing Faith and Love, then he or she is considered to have failed the Initiation of the Crucifixion.

Remember Jesus and His words: "Father, forgive them for they do not know what they are doing." It is genuinely true because people are unable to comprehend the meaning of what is happening with their outer consciousness. Each of them fulfills their role — some say the words of slander, some hammer nails into the subject's hands and feet, some commit treachery, and others help to carry the cross.

A grand theatrical performance is being played out in the material plane. None of the Ascended Hosts have the right to interfere. The subject is left alone with the circumstances of the outer world and with the Higher part of himself or herself. There is no chance to restore the strength or to get the nectar of goodness from the Higher world. During the most difficult moments of the test, the subject's connection with his or her Higher Self is also distorted. It is similar to a terrifying, dark night of the Spirit.

It is a horrid test. However, this test is unavoidable on the Path because it is impossible to continue on the Path without completely parting with the remnants of the ego and attachments to the physical world.

Only a few people on Earth are ready to go through this test and manage to pass it. One of these people is our Messenger.

However, I am not telling you this for you to start vain gossip or scholasticism. I am telling you this for you to also be ready to go through your own Crucifixion in the matter and completely give up all attachments.

We do not mean to scare you by the severity of the tests. We only warn you that it is an inherent part of the Path. Each of you who follow the Path shown by the Ascended Masters will sooner or later undergo your own Crucifixion in the matter and then ascend to the Top of the Spirit.

Before God trusts the most important work to you, He needs to be certain that you are ready for this work and that nothing, none of the attachments of the physical world, will become barriers in completing your work for God.

Do not try to imagine yourselves going through this test now. Remember what I have said: Only a few people on Earth are now ready to go through this test. For the rest of the people, challenges are usually associated with the return of their own karma. The Test of the Crucifixion is related to carrying the cross of planetary karma. For you to be trusted to carry this cross, you need to work a lot more on yourselves and your imperfections, material attachments, and habits.

It is typical for people to overestimate their achievements on the spiritual Path. However, as soon as you have an opportunity, you instantly forget about our Messages and your imaginary achievements and dive into the waters of illusion and debris of mass consciousness with joy and vigor.

That is why, before trying on Christ's robes, you should be honest with yourselves and carefully analyze your lifestyle, your attachments, and your habits. I am not saying that you should give up all your imperfections and habits at once. It will probably be impossible for you. Yet, to choose the right direction and to try to adhere to it in your lives is possible for many of you who are reading our Messages.

I would like to remind you that our Messages are like a rescue line from the waters of illusion for you at this time. Accept this gift of Heaven with all the solicitude and trembling that you are capable of showing.

For now, I am parting with you. I was glad to be able to deliver to you another hidden part of our Teaching — the Teaching of the Crucifixion.

I AM Zarathustra.

Instructions for the current time

Beloved Serapis Bey
June 24, 2007

I AM Serapis Bey, having come to you again.

I have come today to give another Message containing the Teaching as ancient as this world.

We come time after time, not to give a new Truth but to enable you to recollect that Ancient Truth that you knew long ago but forgot because you have plunged into materiality too much. And now the time has come to remember your Source and to return to it.

We are glad that despite many factors distracting you in the matter, a sufficient number of individuals still show their interest in our Teaching. There are many other, as they seem to you, fashionable teachings that offer you many things for consideration and examination. However, if you unbiasedly consider the Truth we are offering and compare it with those teachings which are offered in abundance on the spiritual market, then you will understand the only thing: This is the Truth that has always been with you. This is the Truth that you learned in ancient Lemuria and Atlantis, in all Schools of Mysteries of the past and the present that ever existed on Earth.

There is nothing new in the Teaching offered to you except one thing: This Teaching is aimed to return you to the Higher reality. Through this Teaching you must begin the ascending cycle, the ascending spiral that will raise you from the matter and will enable you to return to that world from which you have formerly descended into the matter. You must remember your Source and your mission. You must comprehend the simple truth that there is nothing in your world that can be the meaning of your life because your world has been created for a while, for that period of time during which you must learn your lessons and mature.

This period of time allowed for your maturation is elapsing. It is very sad that too many souls are still in the state of a deep sleep and cannot be awakened despite all the efforts we undertake. We are ringing the bells of Liberty, we are calling you to your Freedom, to the liberation from the fetters of the matter. And we consider it our duty to inform you of the fact that the time of being in the state of a deep sleep is elapsing. Many of you will be rudely awakened, for it is impossible to wait any longer. You do not heed our admonitions; you continue wandering in the illusion and do not pay attention to our call.

The Heavens are appealing to you. We need your help. Those of you who are ready to accept our Teaching and those of you who do not only read our Messages but also are ready to really do something for the Brotherhood, must respond first of all. We are calling you not only to prayer but also to be ready to do practical deeds in the physical plane. It does not mean that you must leave everything and aspire to the place we show you. You must bring the Divine consciousness and Divine patterns to the place on the globe where you live, to your family, and to your workplace. You and only you are able to bring the new consciousness into the world. And I foresee that it will not be easy for you to do. You will be required to perform a feat, many feats, because everything surrounding you will resist. You will face one difficulty after another, one obstacle after another. It is very difficult to act in the world surrounding you, and it is very difficult to introduce the new consciousness and the new thinking into the world.

Everything must be changed. And everything must be changed in accordance with the Divine patterns, in accordance with the Law that was commanded by the prophets and was reflected in many Holy Scriptures of the past.

Now the time has come when the Divine patterns and the Divine Law must precipitate in the physical plane. Do not expect it to be easy for you. Do not expect that everyone around you will welcome the new with open arms. No, every step in the right direction will be taken with incredible effort. And doubts will come to you about whether or not the direction you have chosen for advancement on the Path is correct. You will be whispered to in the ear and it will be pointed out to you that a Divine deed cannot cause such difficulties and encounter such resistance. However, I would like to remind you that your world has gone so far from the Divine patterns that the return to the Divine patterns is seen by too many people as an encroachment upon the fundamentals. Indeed, over many millennia mankind has developed so much on their own, different from the Divine, which must be demolished, that parting with these obsolete things causes resistance in many people.

Remember how difficult it is for you sometimes to make yourself change something in your life, even simply to give up some bad habit. And now imagine that the way of life for millions of people has to be changed on a tight schedule. What attitude, do you think, will unprepared individuals have toward the new behavioral patterns that you introduce? Of course, each step will be taken with great effort. And every step you take in the right direction will naturally cause resistance from the side of those forces that defend their way of life, from their understanding of the Divine Law.

Over many millennia of human civilization, people managed to introduce distortions into all spheres of life, including the sphere of religion. And many religious dogmas and rules will make people stand up for the established system of religious world outlook. Therefore, do not expect that it will be easy for you. You must realize the whole greatness of the work you are to do. You must consciously stand up for the Divine patterns in everything: in morality, in ethics, in the sphere of education, in religion and in health service. Every sphere of human activity needs changes. It will be a revolution in consciousness. That is why those people who are not ready for the changes will resist and stand up for their way of living and their comprehension of God.

You are to stand up for the Divine behavioral patterns without being involved in a struggle. You are to stand up for the Divine Law. And you will have to demonstrate this Law in your lives. In the past many people were standing up for the new patterns and the new way of living so firmly that they slipped into intolerance and religious extremism. I warn you that you will rather sacrifice your life than allow any manifestation of intolerance or fanaticism.

You are required to repeat the feat of Christ when He chose to go through His crucifixion instead of standing up for the Law with a weapon in His arms.

Every one of you must be ready to sacrifice yourself but not to break any of the Divine Commandments[28] recorded by Moses on the tablets. Now the time has come when you must not only observe these Ten Commandments but also you must fulfill the main commandment: to sacrifice your body but to save in the Spirit the principles that we are teaching you.

---

[28] 1. You shall have no other gods before Me.
2. You shall not make for yourself a carved image, any likeness of anything that is in Heaven above, or that is in Earth beneath, or that is in the water under Earth.
3. You shall not take the name of the LORD your God in vain.
4. Remember the Sabbath day, to keep it holy.
5. Honor your father and your mother.
6. You shall not murder.
7. You shall not commit adultery.
8. You shall not steal.
9. You shall not bear false witness against your neighbor.
10. You shall not covet your neighbor's house; you shall not covet your neighbor's wife, nor his male servant, nor his female servant, nor his ox, nor his donkey, nor anything that is your neighbor's. (Deuteronomy. 5:6-21).

Be ready to lose your body but save your souls.

We will not all sleep, but we will all be changed.[29]

I was glad to give you my help and my instructions today.

I AM Serapis.

---

[29] "Listen, I tell you a mystery: We will not all sleep, but we will all be changed." (1 Corinthians 15:51).

About the spiritual mission of Russia

Beloved Mother Mary
June 25, 2007

I AM Mother Mary, who has come to you on this day. I am so glad that the Divine opportunity for our association with you has continued. I am so glad to come to you again for the talk.

Oh, if you could only know how much I would like to tell you. If you do not object, I will begin with the most important topic. I will begin with the new Divine mercy that has been granted during these very days at the Karmic Board session that is taking place now.

I cannot wait to bring joyous news to you! You know that I am the patron of Russia, and you also know that the people of this country have been giving their attention to me in their prayers since the old times. I help to heal. My icons have wonderworking power; they protect and heal those who need to be protected and healed.

I put my presence in many of my icons. You can always obtain answers to the questions that are troubling you by looking at my facial expression and into my eyes on the icon. I strive to associate with you and I help you as much as I can, my beloved children.

I have just returned from the Karmic Board session. That joyous news that I would like to tell you concerns my beloved Russia. You know that a big mission is awaiting that country — the mission to lead people along the spiritual Path. The path has finally opened up and Russia has come to a point on its path where its future mission is already visible. Russia has reached the point that presupposes the uncovering of the mission.

You know that many prophets of the past spoke about the great role and mission of this country. However, in practice, everything went the opposite way. The image of Russia that has formed in the past few decades in the West is not very attractive.

We carefully observed the development of those individuals whose fates are connected with Russia and who have been incarnating in Russia for many centuries. You know, we made a conclusion that thanks to its best representatives, Russia has earned the right to step on the Path of the spiritual leader of the world. I ask that you do not confuse this role and this mission with the role that — not so long ago — the entire world assigned to Russia, or the Soviet Union, as it was called at that time.

In a way, the current role is a direct opposite of the mission that it had taken on earlier. The difference is that Russia is meant to become a highly spiritual country. It is at this time, despite the seeming lack of spirituality, that the foundation of the future spiritual country is created. It is at this time that the people of Russia who are tired of despair and lack of faith are ready to turn to the source of the Divine goodness, to come down on their knees and say inside their hearts: **"Lord, forgive me, Lord, forgive us, Heavenly Father. We did not know what we were doing. We relied on our flesh, and we created many woes due to our foolishness. Lord, please, answer our prayer. Forgive us, O Lord, for everything that we have done, for all the woes and misfortunes that we have brought to the world. Lord, if it be Your Will, come to our country, enlighten us, and help us follow Your Path."**

After the people of Russia, represented by its best sons and daughters, repent in their hearts, then an unprecedented Divine opportunity will open up for that country.

You will soon face a tremendous explosion of spirituality in Russia. It will not matter to you which temple to visit and at which temple you kneel. That is because in your consciousness, you will rise to the Divine top from which you will no longer see the former contradictions between different faiths and religions. Your hearts will become filled with such Divine goodness that you will stop experiencing any negative reactions toward your neighbors who are different from you. You should unite in the longing of your hearts. You should unite with the motto of spiritual unity of the nation. Only after repentance is the spiritual unity possible. Only after spiritual unity will Russia become capable of settling down to the physical plane the models of spiritual creations of the best representatives of mankind, which are now established in the subtle plane and are ready to come down to the physical plane.

I need to tell you that the future of Russia is not related to the adherence to a certain faith, but to the tolerance of any true manifestation of worship of God. I am not talking about the manifestations of faith intolerance that took place in the past. I am talking about a new level of consciousness of a different quality that will embrace the Divinity and smooth out all the contradictions that the sly human mind has been purposefully exacerbating over the past millennia.

I have come to you on this day to bring to your consciousness the need to understand the mission of Russia. I have not come for you to be proud, but for you to lift your spirits and be able to rise to the new stage of development.

Night, the dark night is over for Russia. Come outside at dawn and watch the sunrise. In the same way, the sun of the Divine consciousness has started to rise in the people of Russia.

Stop looking back at the West. Stop taking the models that are not only useless but also harmful. Your mission is to bring new models. Very soon, the people of the entire world will be surprised to listen to and look at the changes that will be taking place in Russia. The changes in this country will not come from those in power, from politicians or economists. The changes will come from the people's hearts, and those changes will be impossible to miss.

Every time you look into the eyes of the little human beings who have come into incarnation again, try to understand the message that those eyes contain.

Your responsibility is not only to help the new generation to receive everything necessary on the material plane. Your task is also to provide assistance to each of the newly incarnated people to fulfill their Divine purpose.

It is at this time that the individuals who will make Russia the spiritual capital of the world have begun to incarnate. Do not miss your opportunity of world service. Help these children of Earth, the representatives of the new race.

Now I am ready to begin the Blessing. I have come on this day to give you a part of my heart, to give Heavenly goodness to those of you who are reading my Message. I have come to give you the entire momentum of my Love, Faith, and Hope.

I am asking you to do one thing: Never forget your Divine origin and your Divine purpose in the midst of your everyday matters.

I love you with all my heart, and I am ready to come at your first call to help those who are in need.

**I AM Mother Mary,
who was with you on this day.**

Guidance for every day

Beloved Kuthumi
June 26, 2007

I AM Kuthumi, who has come to you on this day.

The purpose of my visit today is to give you certain understanding of the future plans of the Brotherhood for the current moment.

Again and again we come, clarify, and give the understanding of many things that are known to you already. Yet, the facets that open up for you allow you to enjoy the new shine of the precious stones of the good old knowledge.

We come and you become filled with our energy and our Love again. That is because it is impossible to give the Teaching and not to Love at the same time. All knowledge and understanding come with the feeling of deep unconditional Love. We give our knowledge based on Love, and you are able to comprehend the information that we provide only when you are able to feel deep unconditional Love for me, for other Masters, and for our Messenger.

Only based on the feelings of Divine Love are you able to comprehend the Truth. This is the law that works unalterably when the energy is being exchanged between the octaves. When you experience fear, doubt, and other imperfect feelings, you will be unable to comprehend the whole perfection of the Divine Truth. On the other hand, if you are able to cultivate this feeling of the unconditional Divine Love, you will be able to see tremendous Truth even in one single phrase. This phrase will mean nothing to the majority of mankind, but for you it will open up the whole fullness of the Divine Truth because you have received the key to open it, namely: the Divine Love in your heart. Therefore, do not strive to cultivate the pursuit of knowledge within yourselves; strive to cultivate the pursuit of the Divine Love. Your perfection in God is not possible if you cannot develop this quality of Divine Love within yourselves.

You cannot imagine how quickly and clearly mankind will begin to advance on the Divine Path if you are able to understand the importance of the all-encompassing feeling of Love. Many, if not almost all tests on your Path can be overcome only with the feeling of Love. When the Divine Love leaves you, it can be compared to a severe illness. Nobody will help you with that illness if you do not desire to return to the elevated state of consciousness and to the feeling of all-encompassing Love. The feeling of unconditional Love is what you lack; it is what will be the best remedy for you on the spiritual Path.

It is impossible to feel Love if you are driven by other imperfect feelings — for example, the feeling of fear occurs due to the shortage of Love. You are afraid to lose something or you are afraid that someone will harm you, but the reason why you have these fears is that you do not have Love in your heart. Therefore, the best remedy for fear is Love, the Love that is Divine in its essence. If you have Love that is not Divine, then that imperfect feeling can make you attached to the object of your affection. You should feel unconditional Love, which is not related to a particular person but a more general Love. You should love every being in your world and every being in the Divine world.

When you see too many imperfections in other people it also means that you experience the shortage of Love. You cannot notice imperfections and feel Love at the same time. These are incompatible qualities.

In the beginning it will be difficult for you to experience the feeling of unconditional Love. That is because your understanding of love is too much related to human sentiments. Therefore, do not be ashamed if, in the beginning, your love is not perfect.

The strength of your Love is also important. That is because Love is the quality that allows you to act in your world. Strength without Love turns into craftiness and resentment. Therefore, you need to start and do everything in your lives only with the feeling of Love. If you have any personal motive, it makes all your actions imperfect. When you try to do a good deed only with your mind, without hearing the sound of the Divine feeling of Love within you, your deed may lead to a bad result instead of a good outcome.

Remember what Jesus taught you: "By their fruit you will recognize them."[30]

Your actions may be absolutely correct, you may be praying, doing community service, helping others, but no matter what you do, it will lead to poor results. This happens because at the moment when you decided to do something, your intention was not colored with Love. Therefore, the fruit, the result of your actions, turned out to be rotten. Therefore, if I were you, I would rather not do anything instead of starting something without the feeling of Love. That is because karma, as the result of your actions, will be negative in this case.

Do you understand how the Law of karma works? Do you understand that more and more subtle aspects of this Law open up for you as you advance on your Path? That is why we give our Teaching. For those who began reading our Messages very recently and who did not read all Dictations from the beginning but instead began reading the last cycle of the Messages, many things that we discuss will be unclear.

---

[30] "By their fruit you will recognize them." (Mathew 7:16).

Once again, I have to make the analogy of an educational institution. When you go to school, first you go to the first grade, then you transfer to the second and third grades. Only very arrogant people can come straight to the ninth grade and demand to study there. The knowledge cannot fill the vessel if the vessel is not prepared properly. We are responsible for ensuring that you understand the Teaching that we give. That is why we teach you very complex Truths in very simple words; many people become confused by that. It seems to them that everything that we discuss is old truths.

Allow me to note that in this case you are driven by your ego, and the lack of Divine Love will play an evil trick on you someday. That is why we give our Messages based on the feeling of deep, unconditional Love, but you also need to accept the nectar of our Teaching when you are attuned to the Divine tone and filled with Love. I do not recommend that you begin reading our Messages until you reach a balanced state of consciousness. Think about what I said, and try to find the mechanisms in your life that will help you to come into a balanced state of consciousness.

I would recommend that you pay attention to every small detail that surrounds you in your lives. You should maintain tidiness in your house and at your workplace. You should carefully select the food you eat and maintain the cleanliness of your body. Note to yourselves that in addition to the physical dirt, you also collect a lot of astral and mental dirt throughout the day. The best way of cleaning yourselves from that dirt will be bathing in a pure natural reservoir or at least taking a shower or a full bath twice daily, in the morning and in the evening.

I was with you on this day to provide guidance regarding everyday life. Do not think that what has been said does not concern each of you individually.

I AM Kuthumi.

A warning about the danger of contacts with the subtle world

Lord Maitreya
June 27, 2007

I AM Maitreya, who has come to you again through my Messenger.

I AM having come, and as always, I am ready to give you new information regarding your stage on the Path. You may not trust what is being given, but it is wiser to take it into consideration and think about it carefully. For it is not very often that we have the opportunity to speak with you. And admit that it is not often that you are given information from Heaven.

I have come to you today in order to give another Message directly concerning your relationships with us, the Ascended Hosts. You know that many people have recently declared that they receive our Messages. Yet, something within you makes you treat such messages and messengers with caution.

Why is it so? That is because the mere process of communication between us and non-ascended mankind is still quite difficult. The majority of people, if not almost all of those who think that they are receiving our Messages, are most likely under the influence of the astral plane and the spirits from that plane. Not all beings of the astral plane are hostile toward people. Many of those beings are stuck between Heaven and Earth. They cannot take on a new incarnation because they have achieved a relatively high level of development, but there is certain karma that they still have not worked off. They can work off this karma only through the people who are incarnated now. These beings have to search and find conductors among people in order to give mankind certain information and knowledge. In that way, in cooperation with people, they are able to work off their remaining karmic debts.

There are also other inhabitants of the subtle world who have deliberately separated themselves from God and do not wish to incarnate. Many of them call themselves ascended masters and even use our names.

There are also our astral doubles, created by the human egregore. They are not completely conscious beings, but they can give quite coherent messages that contain commonly known statements and truths.

You can always differentiate these beings by the level of vibrations and by the content of their messages. Typically, such beings transmit at a certain vibrational level and their messages are not very diverse.

I give you such detailed information about the inhabitants of the astral plane because we have to face too many problems when certain individuals who think that they communicate with the Ascended Hosts, but in reality they get under the influence of the spirits of the astral plane. When they finally realize, or the people around them realize all the dangers of such a connection, it can be very difficult to break free from such influence. Your psychiatrists usually call this state schizophrenia and religious people call it spirit possession. It may be very difficult to get rid of these beings because you yourselves allowed them to come into your body-temples and desired to cooperate with them with your free will.

If you are dealing with the beings who have not broken their relationship with God and who are working off their karma through you, you are helping those beings and are not creating your own karma. This cooperation is caused by your karmic connections that originated a long time ago. However, if you choose to cooperate with those representatives of the astral plane who have separated themselves from God, then, by receiving their messages, you are creating karma. The more efforts you put into spreading their messages, the greater karma you create.

That is why we have to use the help of specially trained Messengers, who wear our mantles and who have come into your world with a special mission: to restore the Path, along which we are leading mankind of Earth.

Therefore, you are given complete information and complete freedom to choose who to listen to and whom to follow.

I have come today with a concrete goal to give you the knowledge and information regarding your contacts with the subtle world and its inhabitants.

Our Messengers carry the vibrations of Higher octaves. Based on the level of vibrations, you can always differentiate our Messengers from any imposters or deluded individuals.

There is another criterion that I will give you and that you can use to differentiate. Any achievement on the subtle plane about which you are told should have its proof on the physical plane.

Therefore, if you are being told that you are Jesus, or Lord Maitreya, or another Master, please take a look at yourself and at your surroundings, and carefully analyze your relationships with people, with your loved ones. It is not always obvious, but if you do not follow in your lives the Teaching given by Jesus, by Moses, and by the prophets and Messengers of the past, then it is very unlikely that you are those who you are being told that you are.

In your civilized age, people are still too ignorant in matters about faith and about relationships with the subtle world. That is why various villains try to take advantage of your ignorance. Therefore, we send our Messengers to teach you how to differentiate and to give you the true Teaching.

You have the choice. You have the opportunity to choose whether to follow your misconceptions or to return to the Path that we have been teaching you throughout the entire development of mankind.

I was very frank today because the time has come to stop beating about the bush and to finally give you the information that will allow you to avoid delusions.

We have not given any clearer Messages about the dangers of connections with the subtle plane. However, the moment has come, and we can no longer tolerate your calls for help when you get trapped by evil spirits. Believe me; it is much easier to prevent a danger than to call all Heavenly Hosts to deliver you from the danger.

So that you are not scared too much, I need to also say that it is mostly the people who had karma with God in the past that come in contact with the beings of the astral plane who have separated themselves from God. This karma causes these people come into such contacts. The spirit possession that they receive is the result of their karma with God. It is impossible to avoid the return of karma, but it is possible to realize your past mistakes in your consciousness, to repent and to ask the angels of protection to shield you from the influence of the astral plane. God does not want you to suffer. God wants you to learn the lessons of your past mistakes and not to repeat them.

You are given a mechanism to work with your karma by writing letters to the Karmic Board on the 23rd of each month to work with karma of the following month. Why do you not use these opportunities granted to you in their fullest?

If you do not use the graces granted to you, the Divine opportunity may weaken or even disappear completely.

I remind you that now, up until July 1st,[31] you have the opportunity to write letters to the Karmic Board, and those letters may contain your requests to lighten your karmic burden. However, you will need to take on certain responsibilities over the next six months until the next session of the Karmic Board — responsibilities that will allow you to earn good karma to ease your karmic burden.

You can ask for help for your loved ones, and then your good karma will be used for helping them.

I specifically emphasize that karma with God is reflected on the physical plane as a mental disease or spirit possession. As any other type of karma, it can be softened or worked off. You need to realize your past misbehaviors and desire not to repeat them.

As you can see, not everything is simple about your contacts with the subtle world. You need to always be aware of the full karmic responsibility when you come in contact with the subtle plane, receive messages from the subtle plane, and distribute them.

**I AM Maitreya,
sincerely loving you and caring for you.**

---

[31] According to the Teachings of the Ascended Masters, the Karmic Board meets twice a year for two weeks during the winter and summer solstice, around December 20-22 through January 1 and June 20-22 through July 1. During these dates, letters with requests can be addressed to the Karmic Board. The rules of writing letters to the Karmic Board are described in the Dictation "Now, at the change of the annual cycle, it is especially beneficial to make the decision and free yourselves from everything that is unnecessary in your consciousness," Beloved Surya, December 21, 2006. Refer to *Words of Wisdom Volume 2*.

On protection against the lowest levels of the subtle plane

Saint Michael the Archangel
June 28, 2007

I AM Saint Michael the Archangel and have come to you today.

I have come with my legions of the blue flame of protection. I have come to tell you that despite the whole complexity and unpredictability of the situation formed on Earth, we carry on our service and bear the responsibility for guarding everyone who turns to us for help and protection.

I have to tell you that your time is different from past times. There were also moments in the past when the subtle plane, and especially the lowest levels of the astral plane, approached Earth, but now the closeness of the worlds is caused by the very course of evolutionary development.

The Higher planes have cleared the unusual penetrations, and all of those who are unfriendly toward Earth's evolution and do not want to cooperate with us, the Ascended Masters, are pressed close to Earth's physical plane. Therefore, the influence of not the best layers of the subtle world on the inhabitants of Earth is increasing at this time.

This stage of evolution is natural, and you will have to learn to live under conditions when the astral plane and the lowest layers of the mental plane are approaching. Not the best achievements of humankind are concentrated in those layers. Many human generations created low-quality images and thoughts, and now you are forced to face your own creations. It is similar to a battle where you encounter not only your unreal part but also the unreal part of the collective unconsciousness of humankind, which was created by many generations of people.

The worlds have come close to each other, and karma can be worked out only by you. The existing clusters of negative energy have to be worked out by you now. There are individuals who have cleared their auras and chakras to such an extent that they are capable of letting a lot of light into the dense, physical world, and when that Light passes into your world, it can serve to dissolve the darkness that has accumulated on the subtle planes close to Earth.

When the vibrations of your bodies become much higher than the average vibrations of the majority of humankind, you become capable of feeling the astral plane and its inhabitants. Those people who have not achieved considerable progress in cleansing their four lower bodies still live in the physical world and do not feel the subtle plane.

At your time there are places where the worlds closely approach each other and penetrate one another. Not all human individuals are able to feel the subtle plane; however, in order to go further along the way of evolutionary development, it is necessary for you to know a particular safety technique for contacts with the lowest layers of the subtle world, the lowest layers of the astral and mental planes.

There are periods of time when creatures of those planes become visible or tangible for the most sensitive human individuals. You may feel unreasonable anxiety or insomnia; you may see moving figures colored in dirty grey with your peripheral vision. You should know that not a single inhabitant of the astral plane and no energy of the astral plane can cause harm to you while you are confident in your own invincibility and protection. Therefore, you need to learn not to feel fear, no matter what situation you are in and no matter what you sense. Only your imperfections can make the astral plane attack you and cause harm to you. While you are keeping your consciousness concentrated on the Divine world and experiencing a sense of invincibility, you have nothing to fear. Most inhabitants of the astral plane tremble at the fieriness of your chakras. You are a source of danger to them, and indeed, those of you who let the fire into your physical world can clear the astral plane with the fire of Kundalini or with the sword of Kundalini. An unconscious ascension of Kundalini energies neutralizes hordes of inhabitants of the astral plane.

You are invincible to the astral plane. However, if you allow imperfect states such as sadness, melancholy, fear, hatred, or hostility to enter your consciousness, then your vibrations get lower and you become vulnerable to the astral plane. Therefore, we come again and again and ask you to pay attention to the hygiene of your consciousness and to cleanse it from everything low-vibrational and everything incompatible with the Divine world.

Each of you is responsible for the state of your own consciousness. There are some people who do not understand the Teaching we are giving. Many feel irritation when reading our Messages. That only demonstrates that their vibrations and level of consciousness are insufficient to accept the Teaching being given by us through our Messenger. You should understand that there are many levels of consciousness development in your world. There are individuals who stubbornly do not want to develop, and they miss one cosmic opportunity after another.

Now the time has come when people with broader consciousness have to unite in order to cultivate new patterns of morality. You remember what the Bible says about Sodom and Gomorrah. There were always people with a higher consciousness and there were always people who did not want to follow the Divine patterns of behavior. From the Bible you very well know how everything ended.[32] That is why what we teach concerns each and every one who lives on Earth now. Those who understand our Teaching and follow it are happy. You have noticed that we intentionally avoid any religiousness, any religious dogmas and rules. Our task is to give you a new model of the moral law, and if you follow it you will be able to complete your exodus to the new reality.

My Angels and I are always at your service, particularly at difficult moments of your life when you lose control over yourself and become vulnerable to the dark forces. You can always turn to us for help. Whole legions of my guardian angels are ready to give you help and protection 24 hours a day. Do not hesitate to ask us for help; it is our duty and obligation to help people. We cannot start fulfilling our duties until you call us; however, your call makes us respond and come to you to help in a difficult situation.

Now I would like to give you a short call, which you can use in any critical situation:

"In the name of God the Almighty, Archangel Michael, come and help me now!!!"

After this call you can describe the situation, which requires interference and help. Do not be afraid to trouble us with your requests and calls, for it is our job to help humankind.

And now before saying goodbye to you, I have to remind you once again that the best protection for you is keeping a high level of vibrations. Follow the advice given to you by the Masters in order to constantly keep your consciousness at a high level.

I AM Saint Michael the Archangel!

---

[32] "Sodom and Gomorrah" are two towns that are mentioned in the Bible in relation to the extreme wickedness of their inhabitants. The destruction of Sodom and Gomorrah happened after Abraham failed to find even ten righteous men in Sodom. According to the Book of Genesis (19:24-28), God poured a rain of "sulphur and fire" over "the towns of the plain."

A Teaching about the actions on the physical plane

Gautama Buddha
June 29, 2007

I AM Gautama Buddha, who has come to you on this day for new guidance.

I have come to give you a Teaching that you have most likely heard before. However, when you take in a world-old Divine Truth, you are able to understand it at a higher level every time.

There are people among you who are not ready and do not want to know any Truth. They are quite satisfied with the world that surrounds them. However, it is not they whom I am addressing. I am addressing those of you, in whose hearts the fire of striving for a better world is burning, who are ready to sacrifice life itself in order to bring new models into the physical plane, regardless of what area of life these models concern and in which area of activity they are manifested. There are too many imperfections in your world that need to be replaced by more perfect models. We work on that in alliance with our devoted disciples, who have been with us for thousands of years and who come to the incarnation one time after another in order to help with the manifestation of the Divine models in the physical world.

There are different levels of comprehension of Truth, and there are different levels of Service. It is quite enough for some people to read prayers, rosaries, decrees, and mantras. There are other people who have brought their bodies in harmony by means of long-term service to Life, and they are ready to perform work for the Brotherhood. They are ready to perform a Service that is manifest in specific work in the physical plane. Many people come into the incarnation to complete a very small task. They need to support our work and make a stand for it at the right moment. This small task, which has been completed at the right moment, is capable of turning the consciousness of millions of people away from hatred, antagonism, and suspicion toward Divine Love, Harmony, and Divine order.

There are no small tasks among those tasks that our devoted disciples fulfill. All tasks in the course of following the Divine evolution are equally honored. The human consciousness cannot evaluate the true importance of each task of the Brotherhood that is being fulfilled.

There are no little things in the Divine Service. Every time when it seems to you that your contribution is negligible and that you do not have any impact, think of this Message of mine and think of my words about the importance of every action performed for the Common Good in the feeling of devotional Service. Remember, always remember, that it is not the work itself that is important, but the impulse, the momentum that you put into your action in the physical plane.

If you put the whole momentum of Love that you have, if you perform a very small task with great Love, this contribution of yours is capable of changing a lot on planet Earth.

You should not forget that you are not only a physical body. For your physical body, it is important what you see with your own eyes and what you can feel; for your more subtle bodies, the state in which you perform actions is important. The subtle world is very responsive to your inner state and your inner attitude. Therefore, even when you complete right actions in the physical plane but do not do it with the best state of your consciousness, you may create such a barrier in the subtle plane that will turn all your efforts upside down at the most unsuitable moment.

Do not forget that all your bodies should be balanced at the time when you perform actions in the physical plane.

I would also like to talk about the practices in which you try to do something with your thoughts, when you concentrate on the completion of a task in the subtle plane. Indeed, if you are an adept of the highest level, then any of your thoughts and any inner messages that you produce can be completed not only on the subtle plane but also on the physical plane. If you do not have the accomplishments of an adept and are trying to create something with your thoughts and feelings in the subtle plane, you produce the same imperfect models that have flooded our world, but only in the subtle plane. Later, after some time, you yourselves will have to clean up the layers of the subtle plane that you stained with your wrong actions.

Is it not easier for you to begin performing actions in the physical plane, but in a proper state of consciousness? In that case, all your right and wrong states of consciousness will be reflected and you will be able to see with your physical senses the imperfections in your creation and correct them.

It is very difficult to create blindly. Therefore, being in the physical plane, it is easiest for you to begin performing actions in the physical plane but in a proper state of consciousness. Then, you will visually see the result of your actions and will be able to correct the mistakes in a timely manner.

You should learn with practice that is targeted at the transformation of your physical world.

When you interfere with your imperfect consciousness and try to transform the subtle world, in 99 percent of cases it does not render any good results. Believe me, in the subtle plane and in the Higher planes of Existence, there are a sufficient number of beings who complete their work in those planes. When your consciousness allows you to leave the earthly world and no longer incarnate in a gross body, a new horizon of work related to another plane of Existence will open up for you.

Yet, now you have come to your world in order to perform specific actions in the physical plane.

The requirement of a prayer before completing a specific task is still valid. It is because when you are in a prayerful state of consciousness, you are capable of harmonizing yourselves and completing the given task in the best way possible.

Now I would like to speak about your manifestation of low-quality thoughts toward somebody else. Believe me, any of your negative thought-forms are capable of attracting other thought-forms with similar vibrations from the surrounding space. Before you notice it, you end up in such a foul-smelling cloud of low-quality human emanations that you stop seeing the Truth and recognizing it. Therefore, it will be best for you to keep your consciousness constantly attuned to the Divine models. Many people who do not follow any teaching or any religious practice but only adhere to the Divine norms and principles in their lives, have achieved much more than many of those who think that they have achieved great results on the Path but in reality have not made a single step toward the Divine Peak.

I am asking you to think over this Message of mine in your spare time. Do not rush to reject and condemn angrily what you have heard. For there is a difference between you and me, and it would be good for you to gain a small portion of humbleness, which I have.

I AM your brother Gautama.

A Teaching about our Path

Babaji
June 30, 2007

I AM Babaji, who has come to you again.

I want to put so much into these minutes when I have an opportunity to speak with you; however, it is not always possible. The energies that come through to your world together with these Dictations, do not allow us to give more information than what has been allocated. Our worlds are still communicating with each other thanks to the special dispensations or the Divine Grace. A certain amount of energy is allotted to support each of these dispensations. This energy is aimed at providing protection to our Messenger from external influences and inner imperfections when receiving a Message.

No matter how hard we try, our capabilities are limited by the work of the dispensation. I will tell you how you can expand our capabilities, how you can bring our world closer to you. We can take action only when there is a person on the physical plane who is a pure conduit capable of transmitting our energies. In order to become such a conduit, each of you must go through your Path and overcome your human attachments and imperfections. As soon as our conduit appears among you, we begin our work on the transformation of the physical plane through him or her, and each person who comes close to our Messenger receives our energy and help. You cannot always comprehend the essence of the processes that take place. I have been called today to explain certain things.

When you come in contact with our Messenger, you receive additional energy into your bodies and auras from the aura of our Messenger, and the more you communicate with the Messenger and with us through him or her, the higher your vibrations rise. Every time when you receive an additional portion of energy into your auras, that energy begins to force out all your imperfections and all the negativity that you have accumulated throughout your many incarnations. Therefore, it may seem to you that the hardships in your life increase when you find this Teaching and when you come in contact with our Messenger. In reality, you are receiving a mere acceleration on your Path, and the negative energies that you yourselves have produced in the past appear before you, and your negative qualities become aggravated.

That is the attribute of our Messenger — to accelerate the return of your karma and to raise your vibrations. Therefore, we tell you and warn you: Before you come in contact with our Messenger, and especially before you take on a commitment of discipleship, evaluate carefully whether you will be able to withstand those additional hardships that will come into your life at the same time you start the Guru-chela relationship with our Messenger. Do not blame anybody for what will be happening because each step on the path Home is attained with difficulty.

You expect wonders and you expect goodness. The wonders happen. Your advancement on the Path accelerates, and what you were supposed to have in the natural return of karma over many dozens of incarnations, comes back to you in several years, over a term that depends on the severity of your karma. However, you cannot count on goodness in the sense of a constant state of bliss — at least until you work off the lion's share of your karma.

Without this explanation of the processes that you are undergoing, you will not understand how the mantles of our Messenger function, and you will experience unpleasant feelings. Everything must be as clear as possible to you. That is why we explain to you in simple terms the mechanism of how the mantles of our Messenger work and the mechanism of how the dispensation works.

You approach and you start certain relationships with the entire Hierarchy of beings of Light, whose representative on Earth is our Messenger. That is your choice and your desire. Without your free will and without expressing your desire to follow the Path, you cannot stand on the steps of our Hierarchy. That is why we explain to you meticulously all of the mechanisms of the Divine opportunity that accelerate your Path. That Path of accelerated growth is called the Path of Initiations. Before, in the good old times, that Path was accessible and easily understood by only a few people, but now the time has come when the Divine opportunity is open to millions of people who desire to quickly overcome the remaining stages of the evolution and move on to the new, unfolding, cosmic opportunity for the evolution of planet Earth.

There are those who are not ready, and there are those who resist the changes with all their might. Well, that is also your right and your free will. However, unlike our followers, you are slowing down the evolutionary development on Earth, and come in direct opposition to the Divine Law.

I would like to remind you that everything in this Universe is God, and by separating yourselves from God, you doom yourselves to burn in the fire, like the garbage that you burn in the spring in your back yard or in your garden.

If the universe does not get rid of the cosmic garbage, it will not be able to develop further. The same processes take place in your body. If you do not take any measures to cleanse yourselves from wastes and toxins, you will become ill and die.

God operates through the Hierarchy of intelligent beings. The representative of our Hierarchy is our Messenger. Therefore, make the decision in your consciousness regarding your further advancement.

The decisions that you make are not always fatal for you. There are many opportunities that God grants. However, in the case with the cosmic deadlines, any extension is very difficult to obtain.

You may not walk your Path to the end, but I would take courage and try it if I were you. Create the conditions on Earth by which we could transmit our energies and give our education. First and foremost, creating the conditions for the work of our Messenger is your duty.

Always remember that depending on your attitude toward our Messenger, the Heavens determine your attitude toward the Hierarchy of cosmic beings, known as the Great White Brotherhood or the Hierarchy of the Forces of Light.

We are with you during the entire course of your Path. That is why you should think and evaluate all of the pros and cons of your decision. You need to make a conscious decision whether to follow the path of Divine evolution or to try to find your own path.

There are many paths that lead to God, but it is impossible to follow all the paths at once.

Sometimes, when you are trying to find your own unique path and follow it, you are driven by common human pride. You must remember that the main quality on the Path is humbleness and submission to the Will of God. As long as you are separating yourselves from God in your consciousness, you are trying to find your own special path. When you realize your unity with every particle of life, you stop arguing, you stop tearing around, and finally, you attain that state of goodness that you have not been able to attain before.

All of you will come to God. We are just showing you the shortest Path that has been tested over thousands of years.

I AM Babaji, with Love to you and care for you.

The time for choice

Master Nicholas Roerich
July 1, 2007

I AM the Ascended Master Nicholas Roerich, who has come to you again through our Messenger.

I have come after a long pause in our communication. That pause was related to the fact that in my previous Dictations[33] I had given certain directions and aspirations for the future of Russia, and I was waiting patiently for the people of Russia to answer my call. Unfortunately, I have to acknowledge that too few Russians who are living now have perceived my call with their hearts. Many people read the Dictations and forgot about them, while others simply felt disapproval. I have come to make another attempt to convey to you the essence of the Teaching, which is related to the great future of Russia. You may not believe me, but God has a plan for this country and whether you want it or not, this plan must be brought to fruition.

We come in order to awaken the current generation of people and to motivate them to fulfill our plans that concern this great country. This does not mean that we preach the exceptional nature of this nation. It only means that there should be a spot

---

[33] Refer to the Dictations "The benighted times are over for Russia!", Nicholas Roerich, April 14, 2005; "The Plan of God for Russia is the creation of the Community of the Holy Spirit," Nicholas Roerich, May 9, 2005; "I believe in the great future of Russia and I would like to endow each of you with a particle of my Faith," Nicholas Roerich, May 30, 2005, in *Words of Wisdom Volume 1*.

on Earth from which new thinking and new ideology will begin to spread. This ideology will become prevalent in the world very soon, by Earth standards. This ideology is not related to politics or fulfilling any plans on the physical plane. This ideology is related to the arrival of Spirit into matter. It is the same ideology that had been taught by the prophets of the past. If people in their consciousness had been ready earlier to perceive and spread the Divine Truth widely, everything would have happened several centuries earlier. It is only due to the opposition of the dark forces that act through ignorant people that the terms have been stretched out.

And now we are saying that the time has come and the messenger is Russia, ready to fulfill the plan. The only thing that is needed is your support. Only the lack of your real help and support holds back the dispensation of our plans.

We will begin as soon as there are hearts that are prepared and ready to withstand the Divine Fire. As soon as we begin in Russia, we will arouse interest in the entire world right away. An example is needed. It is necessary to start.

The new ideology is ready for dispensing already. The labor pains have run over time. The birth and arrival to Earth of the new consciousness will begin.

We are eagerly awaiting this moment.

Your thinking is connected with your physical world, and it cannot encompass all the possibilities that the Heavens are preparing for you. You just need to believe in our existence, believe that all Heavenly Hosts are ready to come and help you. We are waiting for your call and your readiness.

Awaken from your long sleep! Get up and take action!

Enough sleeping and lounging around, turning over from side to side.

Russian people have always been inert until they receive an active impulse to take action. We come to awaken your sleeping intelligence, to give you that impulse for the development of your consciousness and for targeted actions to transform your world, based on the principles of the Divine expediency.

The whole difficulty is in the fact that your consciousness is waiting for an external impulse, an external organization, and an external leader. However, this time the Heavens put their focus on the arrival of a new type of leader. This leader will be your own Higher Self. All you need to do is to listen to the voice of the real part of yourself. Feel the touch of the Higher worlds. Stop pretending that you do not hear anything and do not feel anything. We are waking you up every day! We are giving you signs and ringing bells!

The warning bell is ringing over Russia.

The time has come to take action! No matter how much your outer consciousness is driving away the thought that Divine actions are necessary, you will have to begin them.

All your actions must be made based on a deep inner urge. All your actions must also have as their base an absolutely immaculate motive, a motive that is coming from your heart. Any of your attachments or bad habits will be impeding you. You should separate in your consciousness the physical part, the attachments to the lower levels of the subtle worlds, and the higher consciousness.

This separation should inevitably happen in the hearts of everyone who aspires. The whole battle and the whole victory lie within you. The Armageddon is happening in your hearts. The separation of the wheat from the chaff is happening in your hearts. You are judging yourselves by making the final choice in favor of immortality or in favor of dying together with the cast-offs that surround you and consist of your carnal thoughts and feelings.

We are calling you to the mountain peak of the Divine consciousness. Stop sleeping! Lift in your spirit! It is a battle of life or death, a battle for each person, each soul that is currently incarnated. And you continue to sleep peacefully...

All your actions in the physical plane require checking against the inner compass stored within your hearts. Stop paying attention to the outer circumstances that surround you in your lives. All these circumstances will change soon; God will change all your life and all of the circumstances of your life. As soon as the sailing ship of your being chooses the right heading, we will fill you with fresh wind, and you will be able to move in the right direction with the speed that the prophets and visionaries of the past had never dreamt of. I am telling you, "New opportunities are ahead of you!"

All the Heavens are now waiting only for your choice and ability to take action.

The Divine opportunity is open to Russia, and through it to the rest of the world.

This opportunity is related to the new consciousness that must come to replace the old consciousness.

Everything will change around you as soon as you change the vector of your aspirations and as soon as you make a choice and strive for the Divinity, throwing aside the cast-offs of your former attachments.

I am calling you to get on the Path! I am giving you the direction. I am waiting for you, each of you who are aspiring.

I am ready to extend my helping hand to you, and pick you up at the most dangerous parts of your Path. All the Ascended Masters are ready to do the same — the Masters, who with bated breath are now observing you, your choice, and the direction of your course.

It is a critical point on your Path. Do not miss it and do not give in to the debris of wandering without the Light for the next 100 years.

I have hope in you.

I AM Nicholas Roerich.

A Talk about the Law of Karma

Beloved Lanello
July 2, 2007

I AM Lanello, who has come to you on this day through our Messenger.

As always, I am very glad to meet with you! And as always, our meeting today is taking place under the sign of tremendous Love that I feel toward mankind of Earth, toward you, my brothers and sisters who are incarnated now.

From my current state of ascended consciousness, a lot of what had happened when I was incarnated as Mark Prophet seems to be a pointless waste of time and energy. When the consciousness becomes free from human feelings and attachments, many circumstances and many things look completely different. When you experience negative states of consciousness, please refer to this Dictation of mine and read it again because your consciousness makes a considerable impact on everything that happens to you. Every time you come back to the same events in your life, you evaluate them differently because the state of your consciousness changes. It is this change in the state of your consciousness that you need to trace in your lives. You need to understand how your consciousness, the level of your consciousness, is related to everything that happens in your lives.

Your karma, as the Divine energy that has been misused in the past, inevitably returns to you. But, if you are armed with knowledge and understand that everything that happens to you in your lives happens exactly because there were reasons for it in your past, whether in this or former incarnations, it is much easier for you to accept the circumstances of your life than it is for those people who are not familiar with how the Law of karma works. Those people are like irrational beings who got entangled in the circumstances that they created by themselves and who cannot untangle the nets. Each wrong movement makes the manacles of their low-quality states clasp them more and more tightly. When it seems that there is absolutely no way out of this situation, the anguished ones finally turn their gaze toward Heavens. The heart opens up with last hope. At this moment, enlightenment comes, a premonition of the Higher world. Some more time passes by, and the person begins to reflect on the fact that there is a Highest Law that rules his or her entire life.

Of course, one needs to have a very high self-conceit to think that you do everything in your life by yourselves and manage everything yourselves. You manage your lives exactly to the extent that the Divine Law allows you.

Do not think that you will be eternally using the Divine energy without control for the satisfaction of your caprices and pleasures of your lower bodies. When the cup of your karma becomes full because of many of your negative deeds, you receive with perfect constancy the return of all the energy that you had used improperly. You encounter those problems in your lives that you yourselves had generated in the past. Only when you begin to realize that nothing happens to you besides what you yourselves had created before, when you stop complaining about your destiny and blaming other people for your miseries and misfortunes, when you are able to repent and lighten your heart with repentance, then the clamps of karma open and you are able to look differently at the world, at yourselves, and at your position in the world.

The knowledge of this very simple Law makes your life much easier. That is because you learn by the examples of how this Law operates. You become capable of properly treating everything that happens to you in your lives. When you properly perceive the lessons of life, you pass your tests and your trials, and you work off the negative karma that you had created earlier.

The more consciously you approach all of your life circumstances, the easier it is for you to live. If you know the diagnosis, you can receive appropriate treatment, and that treatment will alleviate your condition.

Believe me, your state of consciousness determines all circumstances in your life. The circumstances of your life inevitably change together with the change of your consciousness. That is why, for those of you who follows the Path that we teach, I would recommend that you learn how to accept the very prompt changes in all of your life circumstances, of everything that surrounds you. If either yesterday, or today, or tomorrow you do not encounter any changes in your life, it means only one thing — your consciousness is not changing. When you step on the Path of discipleship and follow it persistently, everything in your life begins to change with lightning speed. You will only need one quality — treating any changes calmly — and realize that all changes, good or bad, come in the order that they must come, in accordance with the implacable Law of Karma.

Your life circumstance and your life difficulties are directly related to the actions that you yourselves performed in the past. That is why you cannot complain about your spouse, or your children, or your boss, or your friends and acquaintances. That is because you yourselves generated all of the consequences at the time when you were creating karma with your improper deeds.

The understanding of this simple Truth and submission to the Law gives you an opportunity to act in accordance with this Law in the future and to not create any new karma.

You also begin to realize that not only your improper actions create negative karma but also your right actions, acceptable before God, create karma; but that is good karma. The correlation of your good karma and negative karma gives you the opportunity to regulate the process of karmic return and direct it yourselves, using the dispensations and Divine Graces granted to you by the Masters.

Karma changes from the blind weapon of fate to your helper and Teacher.

When this Divine Truth acquires you to the extent that you analyze each of the deeds that you perform from the point of view of the Law of Karma, you realize that you become free from the effect of this Law and you gain true Divine Freedom.

The same analogy exists in your world. If you obey the law of the society, you reside in freedom, but if you want to break the law, then sooner or later you go to prison and have to serve your sentence.

You are all in the prison of matter. Your liberation will inevitably come to you when you acquire the Divine Law and follow it in your lives.

I was happy to give you this short explanation of how the Law of karma works. I truly hope that this talk of mine will be useful for all of you.

I AM Lanello.

A Teaching on the change of epochs

Beloved Jesus
July 3, 2007

I AM Jesus, who has come to you.

Today, I am happy to give you another Teaching that you most likely know, but it is still necessary to remind you.

Human consciousness is so agile and it slips away from all our instructions so easily that we are persistently putting our efforts into returning you to your purpose, to urge you to remember your Source.

You came to this world millions of years ago. You have come to go through the necessary stages of evolution and gain priceless human experiences. When you began your path in the physical world, you were like little children. Now you have grown up. In the same way as little children who come into your world still remember their purpose, and then forget it when they reach maturity, you have also forgotten the purpose for which you came to this world. We come to call you back to the real world from where you have come.

This Truth that we have been teaching for millions of years is very simple, yet you expect something very complicated from us. Your mind is tirelessly seeking more and more of the new unresolvable tasks in your world. Your feelings are trying to find an equivalent in your world, to the most wonderful experiences that are typical in association with the Divine world.

You are seeking and continue to seek Truth in your world. However, I have come and I am telling you, "There is no Truth in your world." Your world has been created as a giant stage so that you can gain experiences and then leave this world of yours.

When you come to kindergarten, you take toys from the shelves and play with those toys. Later, when you grow up and leave the kindergarten, you no longer have interest in the toys with which you had played when you were children.

Now the time has come for you to leave earthly school and transition to a higher evolutionary stage of development. The imperfections with which mankind has burdened itself during its development are not characteristic of this stage. Therefore, only those of you who fully submit their lives to the Divine Law will be able to transition to that stage. When you are studying in earthly school, you are allowed to do different misdeeds for a certain period of time. Yet proper models are pointed out to you. There is a principle in pedagogics that an individual has acquired knowledge only when he or she is able to apply it in practice. Therefore, you are given an opportunity to acquire Divine knowledge and put it into practice.

There are people who are more successful in their acquisition of the Divine science, and there are those who have not been able to understand even its basics yet. Yet, all of you have to complete your earthly school. And each of you needs to demonstrate readiness for further learning.

We speak about proper models, about the models that are characteristic of the world in which you have to transition. You cannot transfer to the next grade until you have learned the lessons of the previous grade. Therefore, you are required to manifest the qualities that are typical of the Divine world. You have to gradually give up the manifestation of any negative qualities that you have acquired throughout your earthly evolution. The substitution of the old and the outdated with the new can only be made by you yourselves, by making choices in your life.

Everything has gotten mixed up in your life — the good and the bad, the Divine and non-divine. Only you yourselves can clean up your world by abandoning non-divine manifestations and aspiring to Divinity. We cannot do it for you. We can give recommendations and provide our Teaching, but you yourselves have to solidify your theoretical knowledge in practice.

Do not think that you have a lot of time. The situation in your world is worsening every day. The vibrations of the physical plane are rising involuntarily, and you get into challenging conditions where you are trying to return to the behavioral stereotypes that you are used to, but everything that had previously brought you pleasure no longer attracts you. You cannot understand why the things that used to be pleasant for you do not bring you the same satisfaction. You continue to follow old behavioral stereotypes in your life, but you understand that they have lost their meaning.

You need to follow the rising vibrations of the physical plane in your behavior; otherwise you will fall out of space and time and will not be able to continue your evolution.

From now on, everything that is capable of elevating your consciousness will bring you satisfaction. Everything that lowers vibrations will cause aversion and rejection.

Of course, not all people are able to realize what is happening. However, for the majority of people it is becoming clear already that neither alcohol, nor music that is destructive to the surrounding environment, nor past hobbies give them satisfaction. The search for something new is becoming wider and wider.

You are given recommendations on how to protect yourselves from the influence of everything that brings low vibrations. When you are able to bring the Divine models into your life, you will be able to feel fulfillment and harmony. Of course, not all people are able to strive for the proper models. That is a natural and legitimate stage at which there will simultaneously be people with such different levels of vibrations, that when they meet each other in the street, they will perceive each other as aliens.

The mix of the good and the bad on Earth has to be sorted gradually. The process of sifting out the ashes from cinders is taking place in the Divine thresher.

And you are living now, during this time. That is why it is very difficult for you. However, this process has a beginning and an end, as does everything in the physical world.

It is a necessary process that at first small areas will form on Earth where people with this new consciousness and new way of thinking will live; and then there will be more and more areas of this kind. Gradually, Earth will become free of the places around the world where low vibrations prevail. With time, water and fire will wipe off all such places on Earth, where the bearers of old thinking and low vibrations are concentrated.

New places on Earth will be available for the representatives of the new race, who are starting to come on the planet already.

Now is a very difficult time when literally every person considerably changes the situation on planet Earth with his or her choices.

We give you our support and our help. There has never been such a close collaboration between your world and the world of the Ascended Masters. We are waiting for the situation on Earth to change to such an extent that we will finally be able to come visit you and give our instruction directly, avoiding intermediaries. You yourselves are creating such conditions for us now by changing your consciousness and trying on new garments, pure garments woven from your perfect thoughts and feelings.

I have come to you as a representative of your elder brothers who have finished earthly school and are waiting for you at the Higher planes of Existence.

I AM your elder brother, Jesus.

A Teaching about the necessity to keep your lower bodies pure

Beloved Kuthumi
July 4, 2007

I AM Kuthumi, who has come again in order to give another Message to the people of Earth. I have come on this day to remind you about your duty. Many of you, before taking on this incarnation, had received special training at our schools and ashrams located on the subtle plane.

You attended our classes and prepared for the mission. Many of you, during your adolescent years, still retained subtle recollections about the need to do something for the world. Your hearts were burning with the flame of Service, but nothing around you reminded you about your duty.

Now I have come to remind you about the purpose of your incarnation. All the fuss of life should become secondary. You need to know how to set priorities in your life. There are primary tasks and there are secondary tasks. There are eternal tasks, there are the tasks of the current incarnation, and there is the daily fuss. When you allow the daily fuss to come over you every day, year after year, your sense organs lose the perception of the subtle plane; you stuff your consciousness with such a great amount of unnecessary information that you are simply unable to seclude yourselves and come into the stillness of our world.

You are very sensitive beings. Your subtle bodies, when attuned to the Higher worlds, are like a Stradivarius violin. However, many of you prefer to drive nails with that violin. Imagine a real Stradivarius violin. Generations of people have been enjoying its charming sounds. You are taught to recognize its value as a true piece of art. Why do you value yourselves less than a violin? You are much better conduits of the energies of the subtle plane. You are capable of transmitting the energies of the Higher worlds into your world. However, you treat the material things of your world with much greater respect than you treat yourselves.

Your unwillingness to listen to yourselves and keep yourselves in purity is related to your psychological problems; and the lack of love for yourselves lies at the root of these problems of yours. You need to love yourselves, not as a physical body but as the manifestation of God on Earth. You are a part of God, and you should take care of all your bodies and maintain them purely as a manifestation of the Divine.

All your bodies need proper care. Your physical body must receive proper nutrition. The higher the vibrations of the food, the less food you need to eat.

Your emotional body needs food in the form of the subtle energies that come from the Higher worlds. Your emotional body constantly needs to feed on the subtle energy. You try to satisfy the hunger of your emotional body by feeding it with surrogates consisting of low-quality music and television programs. You litter your emotional body by constantly putting it in the unfavorable conditions that exist in your world. Try to protect yourselves from the sounds that come from all directions. One hour a day of listening to the radio or watching television is enough to deprive you of communication with the Higher worlds for one month.

Think over what you surround yourselves with in your lives. The vibrations of it all are so distant from those of our world.

One shot of alcohol that you drink or one cigarette that you smoke does not allow you to rise to the Higher etheric octaves for several days. You are forced to constantly reside at the levels of the astral plane because you have tied yourselves to it, like using ropes, by your harmful habits.

Carefully analyze what you load your mental body with. How much time do you spend watching endless soap operas and in conversations with people? Do not be afraid to be left alone with yourself. Learn how to listen to the silence and enjoy the solitude.

Legislative measures must be taken toward those who are trying to upset the world with the sounds of ragged rhythms. Each of those who like to listen to rock music, or to any kind of music with improper rhythms, lowers the vibration of the surrounding space for many miles around. This hooliganism must be stopped.

While the alcohol that you drink and the cigarettes that you smoke lower only your own vibrations and the vibrations of the people who live together with you, the pounding music affects thousands of people. If you knew about the consequences of such hooliganism for your lower bodies, the first thing you would do would be to prohibit your children from to listening to such music forever.

There are very simple measures that allow you to quickly raise the vibrations on the physical plane, and one of these measures is the prohibition of listening to loud music.

You cannot even imagine what influence music has on you. Every night I come to my organ, and inspired by God, I play charming melodies. There are a very small number of people who come to my abode to listen to this music. Even a smaller number of people are capable of reproducing that music in their awakened state of consciousness, writing it down with notes, and presenting it to the world.

Oh, how much I wish for that consonance with the Higher world to be accessible to you through listening to the music that I play on my organ.

If during the day you have been under the influence of your horrible music, even if you heard it only briefly on public transportation or at a store, then that night you will no longer be able to rise to the octaves where my organ is heard.

You must constrain yourselves. You should remember your mission and take all the necessary measures to purify yourselves to such an extent that you are able to fulfill your mission, for the sake of which you have taken on this incarnation. You have forgotten everything, and you yourselves are guilty of this forgetfulness because you do not pay proper attention to taking care of your four lower bodies.

Think about how much simpler it would be for the next generation to fulfill their missions if you had already started to consider the places on Earth now, where the new generation could incarnate and spend their first years of life in stillness and in association with nature. If such places on Earth were created now, the new race of people would be able to come into incarnation. Believe me; many advanced souls are ready to incarnate in order to give their Service to the world. Only the lack of arranged conditions on the physical plane makes them postpone their incarnation for years, and even decades.

Many of the high spirits take on the risk and incarnate in unprepared conditions. What do you think happens? Right after birth, they are compelled to burden themselves with such a large amount of karma, which they take from the people who surround them by absorbing that karma into their auras, that by their fourth year of life, those unique children are no longer capable of unfolding their abilities and serving the world until the end of their incarnation.

It is painful for us to see how the best sons and daughters of mankind perish among you while carrying your burden and dying under its load.

Have you not heard or read everything that I told you today? How many times do you need to hear these simple truths in order to put them into practice?

I am ready to come to you as many times as is needed for you to learn my Teaching. However, your progress will be better if before going to sleep you desire to come to that hall on the etheric plane where I play my organ and if throughout the day you try to protect yourselves from everything that may prevent you from hearing my organ.

I AM Kuthumi, loving you always.

The last warning

Beloved Alpha
July 5, 2007

I AM Alpha, who has come to mankind of Earth on this day. I have come to you and I would like to begin my Message with a joyful event that you, perhaps, have been anticipating in your hearts. This event is related to new opportunities and new Divine Graces for planet Earth.

In conjunction with the Karmic Board, the decision has been made to continue the dispensation associated with the opportunity to work through this Messenger. You know that a very difficult test had to be passed in order to confirm the right to continue the work.[34] That test was taken by our Messenger, and that test was extended to many individuals who are currently incarnated. It was an exam on maturity, on the right to work for God.

Every time when the new Divine opportunity comes down on Earth, it is related to the transmission of new energies, of new, higher vibrations for the planet.

It seems to you that my words do not apply to you, that I am talking about some abstract matters. However, this Message of mine and the opportunity that has come on Earth applies to every resident living on planet Earth.

The vibrations of the physical plane and the planes close to Earth's plane will be further raised. This is connected to the new,

---

[34] Refer to the Dictation "A Teaching on the Initiation of the Crucifixion," Beloved Zarathustra, June 23, 2007, in *Words of Wisdom Volume 2*.

necessary stage of evolutionary development. For you, it is related to the reconstruction of your body and the elevation of vibrations of your physical body and of your more subtle bodies.

The change of vibrations is connected with major changes on the planet. Those who are not able to follow the change in vibrations, the rise of vibrations, will not be able to feel confident in the new conditions. Believe me, goodness and blessings are the only things that we want for you. We know that those of you who are compliant with God's Will and are ready in your hearts to follow God will receive an unprecedented impulse for your development, and the planet will receive the opportunity for prosperity and abundance. However, those who have decided to separate themselves from God, who have become inflated like a soap bubble, will have to reap the consequences of their wrong choices and deeds. This is the Law, the evolutionary Law of this Universe.

That is why the joy that the Ascended Hosts feel, and following them, the best representatives of mankind also feel, will not be shared by many souls who, for their own reasons, have decided to choose a path that is different from the Divine one. You should never forget that you all are inside the abdomen of God, that everything is God. There are cosmic deadlines, about which you are warned. There is time for making the choice. Nobody can say that it has not been said or warned about.

The time for choice is coming to an end. The time frames have run out, and the cosmic harvest season is coming to an end.

The time has come for the good sons and daughters of God to receive the retribution for their kind deeds; and those who have chosen their own path will also receive retribution, but of a different nature.

I am not trying to frighten you. All the terms for warnings have passed. The decision has been made. The decision must be implemented.

There is always the opportunity to choose a different path. Even at the last moment, one scream of repentance is enough to stop the Divine grindstones.

We are waiting and giving you a chance. The wait is coming to an end.

I have come in order to share the joy. However, for many that joy will turn into sorrow. That is because too many efforts and too much energy have been wasted. Everything must be compensated for.

The time to reap is coming. Everyone must receive what he or she has earned over many, many thousands of years wandering in the physical plane of planet Earth.

It will not be a secret if I tell you that the terms about which Beloved Jesus had warned His disciples only now begin to approach and come down to the physical plane.

I am trying to give you understanding and extend the time of your choice. I am trying for you to fully understand the operation of the law and to overcome within yourselves what is repining and is not taking in the Divine Law.

I came on the feeling of tremendous Love for each of you. I came in order to give my Message to the people of Earth. I will feel very sorry if I do not manage to get through to the souls who still can hear me but do not listen, because they prefer to follow the horn that is calling them into nowhere.

I AM Alpha.

A discourse on the aspiration to Victory

Cosmic Being Mighty Victory
July 6, 2007

I AM Cosmic Being Mighty Victory, who has come to you on this day!

I have come from the remote regions of the Universe. It is difficult for you to understand and for me to explain that as soon as your consciousness attains a higher level, you become capable of tearing yourselves away from your home planet and getting drawn to the layers of the etheric octaves of Light which will allow you to acquire the Freedom of travel in the vastness of this Universe. You will gain this state of Freedom and independence from the matter and from the gravitation of any planet or planetary system. However, this will happen to you no earlier than when you are able to overcome the gravity of the matter of your planet in your consciousness.

Your consciousness is currently limited by the time frames and space frames of your planet. You think within the framework of your three-dimensional world. Now the time has come for the stage when you must transform your consciousness and allow it to ascend to the next level of evolutionary development. This process of new consciousness being born inside of you is not always painless. In the same way as a new being is born into your world through pain, you have to be reborn in the throes in order to become capable of carrying the new consciousness. It is truly a burden, the same burden that was carried by all martyr saints of the past. The resistance of the matter is too strong and there are too many forces that counteract the coming of the new consciousness and the new thinking into your world. That is why you are acquiring the new with such difficulty. It is unlikely that the majority of the population of Earth understands what I am talking about.

Many millions of years ago, I was at your stage of evolutionary development. Now I am trying to remember the main difficulty that stood before me as an unsolvable problem. Do you know what it is? It is the gravity of the matter. It is the unwillingness to part with the gross world. It is similar to how the infant must come out of the cradle in order to make his or her first step into the unknown world. You are simply afraid to part with your old and habitual state of attachment to the matter. The matter is your Mother. However, there is also a Father, who is calling you to the ascension to a higher level of consciousness. Otherwise, you are risking staying in your cradle forever.

The new is always frightening. However, it is necessary for you to develop fearlessness and the ability to change your consciousness. You should not be frightened by anything. You should always remember in your consciousness that you are immortal and that God is taking care of you. The transition in your consciousness about which we speak and which you should make will happen inevitably; and that transition will allow you to come to a new turn of your evolutionary development.

Now you are in a flat world. We are calling you to the cosmic expanses; we want you to learn in your consciousness how to leave the realms of the gross world. For that, you need to part with the attachments to the material and soar higher with your consciousness.

There is nothing terrible about changing the form, about aspiring to more subtle experiences. Learn to distinguish the different states of being in which you reside throughout the day. Learn to hold onto the most subtle manifestations of your feelings, which are intangible like a waft of wind on a hot afternoon. Even now you can distinguish the manifestations of the subtle world in your consciousness, and you can manifest the knowledge of these worlds in your world.

It is necessary for you to understand that there is a whole universe beyond the borders of your gross world.

You are like the inhabitants of the forest — the insects, which only see their own world in front of them. Imagine an analogy when a human being comes into your forest. How many millions of years separate your stages of the evolutionary development from each other? Can you imagine giving a message to the insects? However, you and I are separated by the same evolutionary period of time as you and the insects that live in your world. I am trying to give you my Message. It is not so much a message filled with words and inner meaning, but it is primarily a message that contains the aspiration into the future for you, that calls you to your Victory over the mortal consciousness.

I fill you up with the feeling of Love, my Love, and the Love that is characteristic of my level of consciousness. I am trying to give you the impulse of confidence in your power. You will accomplish everything, and your Victory will come to you.

You should simply maintain the aspiration to the Higher worlds in your hearts. You should constantly try to overcome Earth's gravity of the surrounding illusion. Believe me, now there is no task for you more important than the task of elevating your consciousness over all the manifestations of your established, conventional life.

Constant change and constant strenuous efforts are required. In this constant process of overcoming yourselves you are capable of ascending to the next stage of evolutionary development. Nothing can be achieved without effort. Do not flatter yourselves with the thought that the next stage will come to you by itself and you will not have to do anything. No, you will not be able to trick the Divine Law and conquer the next stage on somebody's shoulders and thanks to someone else's efforts.

You will have to put in all the efforts yourselves, rising higher and higher in your consciousness. Besides that, you also need to feel responsible for the people with whom you have a karmic connection. You need to stretch a helping hand to them, just like I am now stretching a helping hand to you by giving this Message.

Everyone who has a higher level of consciousness must help those who are lagging behind or have gotten stuck on the Path. When you were children, you were taught to help the younger ones. Now you need to remember that. There are many people around you who need your help and advice.

Believe me, there is nothing more significant that can help you on your Path of ascension to the Summit of the Divine consciousness than to help the ones close to you. You cannot even follow the Path yourselves but if you help the people around you to follow it, together with them you will overcome all the barriers and obstacles on your Path.

I was happy to give you today's instruction.

**I AM Mighty Victory,
wishing you Victory on your Path!**

A discourse on the change of the physical plane through the change of consciousness

Beloved Surya
July 7, 2007

I AM Surya, who has come to you again through our Messenger.

I have come in order to attest once again to the fact that we have made the decision to continue our work in the physical plane through our Messenger. This work is related not only to the receiving of our Messages. In reality, the transmission of Dictations or Messages of the Masters is only a part of the mission that we are carrying out on Earth. The Dictations give you the opportunity to become familiar with the direction in which you should advance in order not to end up at the road-side of the evolutionary process. However, in the same way as there are theory classes or lectures, there is also practice. You know that theory without practice is dead. When you only study a science or some literature without putting it into practice, you do not advance anywhere. It is similar to running in place.

That is why we come and create conditions for you in the form of our energies. When you receive and absorb the Divine energy, you also receive the Divine opportunity to transform your consciousness and along with it, to transform your physical plane.

Beloved, it is too little in your times to simply read our Messages. You need to adjust everything in your life in accordance with the principles that you receive from us. You need to analyze your entire life and understand how you can change it. It will be difficult for you because the karma that you have created and the karmic circumstances will not allow you to change your life instantly. However, until you gain the correct image inside yourselves to which you should aspire, nothing will change in your life. First, you realize in which direction you should advance, and next you begin to understand what in your lives prevents you from following the set direction. Then you begin to overcome one obstacle after another in your lives.

Believe me, the obstacles outside of you that you face in your lives have been created by your imperfect consciousness. When you remove the imperfect energy from your subconsciousness and consciousness, when you change your inner orientation and direction, and the vector of your aspirations, then all outer circumstances in your lives begin to change.

You do not get the perfect conditions and the opportunity to develop in accordance with the Divine principles right away. No, you overcome the imperfect state of your consciousness, and the outer circumstances of your life also begin to change. The passivity of the matter does not allow quick changes in the outer circumstance of your life. Some time must always pass for the outer circumstances to transform in accordance with the change of your consciousness. However, the principle is always the same: First you change yourselves, and then the outer circumstances change.

It has been said many times, and I will repeat it now: Each of you has karma that is related to the misuse of the Divine energy in the past. This concerns not only this incarnation but also your past incarnations. That is why this karma holds back your development and does not allow you to instantly change all circumstances of your lives. Sometimes you have to make tremendous efforts in one direction in order to overcome just one aspect of your energies that have not been worked off yet. There might be many such aspects.

Each of you performed deeds in the past that are associated with the breach of the Divine Law. Now the time has come to realize that you misused the Divine energy and to take measures so that these wrong deeds of yours do not happen again.

First you remove the wrong quality from your consciousness, and then your life changes in proportion to the efforts that you make in the right direction.

You should act in the same way when performing any activities in the physical plane. If you are striving to do something in the physical plane — even if it is a very virtuous deed, such as a deed directed to the fulfillment of the Masters' plans in the physical plane — but you have a karmic burden in your energy field, then your karma will not allow you to complete the deed that you begin. You first need to part with your imperfections, and then perform the work for God. You will not be able to perform work for God until you become perfect builders.

You will say that there are no perfect builders in your world. That is truly so. That is why you are required to make constant efforts in the right direction. Even when your imperfections do not allow you to complete work for God, you can and should continue to make your efforts in the right direction. After some time, all the energies that had been qualified wrongly by you in the past will burn in the Divine fire of your virtuous aspiration.

That is why we teach you to not stop on your Path. Take action, make mistakes, redo, but continue your efforts. That is because when you begin to do something, we have the ability to help you, to correct your efforts and direct them properly. When you do not do anything, we cannot interfere. The energy must flow, it must change, and then it is easier to control.

This is a constant and interpenetrating process: the change of your consciousness and the actions in the physical plane. When you take action, you have the ability to work off your karma during your actions. The karma is worked off not only by means of prayer and choices that you make. The karma is also worked off by means of proper actions directed at the transformation of your physical world. When you have the right motive and are moving in the right direction, you have the ability to work off your karma very fast. As a comparison, I will tell you that you will need 10,000 hours of uninterrupted prayer in order to work off the same karma that you would work off if you performed work for God, such as some action related to building an Ashram for our Messenger.

I have approached an important topic that concerns the fulfillment of our plans in the physical plane. It is necessary for us to get settled in a pure location where we can begin to perform work on leading the perfect models downwards into your world. We need a place on Earth where we can begin to take action. First, you need to create such a place in your consciousness. Prepare your consciousness in order to live and work in accordance with the Masters' plans, and then the Masters trust you to work for them.

Therefore, you have a lot of work ahead of you on the transformation of your consciousness and on the transformation of the physical plane of planet Earth.

We will be where you allow us to be. We will be where your vibrations allow the elevation of the vibrations in a location to such an extent that we can be among you and talk to you.

I looked into the future. However, you are able to accelerate this future with the acceleration of the change of your consciousness.

I AM Surya,
and I was with you on this day.

A Teaching on the Transition

Lord Shiva
July 8, 2007

I AM Shiva, who has come to you again!

Shiva I AM!

I have come to you on this day! I have come!

I am happy today that I have the opportunity to speak through my Messenger again!

Each time I come in order to support the connection between our worlds and to continue your instruction. You know that now the time is coming when it is necessary to part with the illusions of your consciousness. You know that your victory over death is inevitable, if only you are able to elevate your consciousness to the level of your immortal part.

You are like a matryoshka doll. Every time when you open another matryoshka, you see a new one. The same is the principle of your development. When you part with your physical body, you simply transition in your consciousness to a higher vibrational level. You will continue to come into incarnation and take on physical bodies until you learn how to constantly reside at a higher energy level.

Therefore, our task is to prompt your consciousness to transition to a higher energy level. This gradual process will simply accelerate now. You are slightly behind the cosmic deadlines, and that is why we have to hasten you.

You follow us for as long as you are able to change your consciousness. When you begin to understand many things better than we, as it seems to you, and prefer to explore new-fashioned teachings and practices, we do not interfere. It can be very amusing to observe how you fancy yourselves as very high cosmic beings. You think that you are great cosmic beings. However, before you actually become these great cosmic beings, you have to graduate from earthly school and consecutively pass through all the stages along the Path.

Therefore, when you are being called to the instant elevation of your consciousness and to transition to a different energy level, if I were you I would strongly question how realistic is what is being offered.

For millions of years we have been following the evolutionary development of mankind. In terms of comprehending the Divine Truth, your consciousness has not advanced very far in the past thousands of years. You should not confuse the development of your intellect with the development of the Divine consciousness. It is still very hard for you to comprehend the simple Divine Truths related to reincarnation and the Law of karma. It is a great difficulty for you to overcome a small attachment or an inconspicuous habit. This happens because the greatest difficulty is related to overcoming the attachment to the physical plane.

It seems strange when you are offered to instantly receive big initiations and achieve considerable advancement on the path. If I were you, I would think about at what expense this great advancement will take place. Who will give you the energy to transform your karmic loads? And on what terms do your benefactors engage in your fast advancement? Does it not resemble the sale of your soul, of your life energy, to the devil?

Try to understand how the Cosmic Law operates.

When, due to the Law of free will, you make your choices and lower your vibrations, you come down to the material world, deepening into the matter more and more. After that, you will need a great amount of energy, which must be equal to all the Divine energy that you have once misused. That energy must come to you under certain terms.

Imagine that a miracle has happened and all the energy that you had misused for millions of years has come back to you instantly. Considering the density of your physical body and your vibrations, how will you be able to withstand that energy? For your being, it will be similar to an explosion of a supernova. Your consciousness will not be able to instantly adjust to the new energy level. That is why we teach you a gradual evolutionary path. In the course of an accelerated evolution, almost all humanity would die. We do not have the desire to promote your death. We have the desire for you to continue your evolution at a higher energy level.

Think carefully and compare my words with many of the teachings and theories that you come across and that are related to an instant leap. Who will give the energy for that leap?

I am telling you this as a being that has been granted the power and called to contract the illusion. I am telling you that it is impossible to instantly transition to a level of consciousness of greater quality, unless that transition is accompanied by the death of almost all human individuals inhabiting the planet Earth. We teach the evolutionary path and we give the knowledge, thanks to which you will be able to naturally elevate your consciousness to a higher energy level. In that way, a greater number of beings living on Earth will be able to continue the evolution. Any revolutionary change of vibrations can happen only when the efforts that we make are not successful in the near future.

We believe that the majority of you are ready to continue the evolution and to change the vibrations of your body to such an extent that you will survive in the new conditions. However, you should also make the efforts to extend the evolution and to not end up in unfavorable conditions that exist on the planets that had desired to separate themselves from God.

All that follows the Divine Law existing in this Universe must be provided with everything necessary for its evolutionary development. All that does not wish to follow the Divine Law will face greater and greater hardships until a complete termination of development occurs, and the angels of death will escort the remnants of the soul to repolarization.

You are given exactly as much as is needed to make a conscious choice of the path and to continue your evolution. We have not spoken so clearly and in such detail through any other Messenger of the past or the present.

I AM Shiva! I came today in order to provide your consciousness with important information for thinking over in the stillness of your heart and for making the decision.

I AM Shiva.

A Teaching on Buddha Consciousness

Gautama Buddha
July 9, 2007

I am Gautama Buddha, who has come to you again.

I have come to you on this day in order to tell you about the main aspect of our work that we are conducting on Earth. This main aspect is related to the change of consciousness of the people on Earth. Actually, this principle of our work has not changed for many millions of years.

As soon as a person reaches the level of Buddha in his or her consciousness, everything that surrounds this person in his or her life acquires completely new meanings and significance. That is because for an ordinary person what is only a sequence of events and a change in the state of thoughts and feelings, for Buddha it represents the book of Life, which he is able to read, turning the pages one after another. When you attain the level of consciousness of Buddha, you make the transition in your consciousness to the next level of evolutionary development.

I am not giving my Message only to Buddhists or only to those who believe in me as the Lord of the World, Gautama Buddha. I am giving my Message to all of humanity and to the people who are able to understand it, grasp it, and carry it out into the life. In reality, it is not as important what the next stage of the evolution of your consciousness is called, but it is important that you ascend to that stage of your evolutionary development with fewer losses.

I spoke to you this year[35] during the time when Earth was going through yet another critical moment, another critical point. From time to time, there are situations on Earth that require urgent interference from many legions of Light. I asked you for help during that critical moment because you need to be imbued with the responsibility for everything that happens on planet Earth.

The level of Buddha consciousness allows you to rise in your consciousness to the level where neither national, nor financial, nor political, nor religious differentiation matters to you. That is because you rise above any differences that have been created by human consciousness, and you are able to see only the Oneness behind all the diversity of life.

In your world, the people who have achieved the Buddha consciousness are not able to stay among crowds of people for a long time. That is because the level of Buddha consciousness presupposes rendering help to all human individuals who need help. As soon as a true Buddha enters your cities, he sacrifices his level of consciousness and gives away all of his achievements in order to provide help to those in need. There are so many of those who need our help in your cities. There are so many calamities and miseries in your world. That is why the Buddhas who come into your world perform the act of self-sacrifice by dissolving in you, by dissolving their perfect energies into the ocean of people, and by that, they change the consciousness of mankind and allow people to comprehend the existence of the Higher Law that operates in this Universe.

There are other human individuals who have come into your world in order to provide the connection between the worlds, in order to serve as a source of Light for your world, and as a lighthouse that shows the way among life's miseries and troubles. There are always people who carry the fire in their hearts and are ready to serve humanity. If you look carefully around you, you will

---

[35] Refer to the Dictation «About the current situation on Earth," Gautama Buddha, March 7, 2007, in *Words of Wisdom Volume 2*.

be able to see the level of Buddha consciousness behind ordinary human manifestations.

I have come today in order to help you to understand that your consciousness is very flexible, and many of you are able to rise in your consciousness to the level of Buddha throughout the day. The only point is that you maintain that state as long as possible. In order to do that, you will have to create life conditions that will allow you to return to harmony as soon as possible, even when you lose balance. Many of you experience very elevated states of inner harmony and peace. There are not many Buddhist monasteries where the monks are able to attain such elevated states of consciousness. Now you need to expand this state and make it prevailing in your life. You need to achieve the stage at which nothing that happens in your lives could make you come out of the state of Divine harmony and peace.

You need to continue making such efforts one after another because the extent to which you are really able to maintain the state of peace and harmony within yourselves will determine how many surrounding people you will be able to pass your state of harmony, peace, and happiness. The situation on the entire planet depends on how many people will be able to constantly reside in the harmonious state of consciousness. All hurricanes, cataclysms, and natural disasters are only the manifestation of discordance in the consciousness of mankind as a whole.

You cannot endow everyone with Buddha consciousness, but you can spread your harmonious inner state to the people around you. Your aura is able to expand, and those who come into the field of your aura experience the effects of it. Many people think that others have dropped out of the habitual state of elevated consciousness, and they will try to lower their vibrations using the universal means of lowering vibrations: alcohol, tobacco, and loud music with ragged rhythm. However, the process of the penetration of the high vibrations into your world will increase. The quality of the consciousness of the individuals who will sustain harmony in big cities will increase. The power of your consciousness in the subtle plane will cause the opposition of the entire legions of forces that support Manu, to maintain the illusion. However, always remember that your power is strong when you do not participate in the battle. You force out the negative energies of this world with the strength of Love in your hearts; and with the strength of your Love, you refine the negative energies into the positively-directed vector of harmony, peace, and Love.

You must always be aware of your connection with many, many souls of Light on the planet. Together you form the network of Light that is dispersed around the planet. In every country and in every town, there are people who have volunteered to bear the Light in order to illuminate the Path for those who are still wandering in the darkness.

Achieving the Buddha consciousness is not the ultimate goal of your incarnation. You should not strive for personal achievements. You should aspire to help those who need your help. If a real Buddha faces the question of whether to continue his perfection in God or to sacrifice all his achievements in order for humanity to continue their evolution, a real Buddha will sacrifice all his achievements for the continuation of earthly evolution. The ability to sacrifice oneself for the Common Good is the quality of all Buddhas and Bodhisattvas of the past and the present.

I wish you success in gaining the state of Buddha consciousness.

I AM Gautama Buddha, your brother.

The final Message of the summer cycle of Dictations

Beloved El Morya
July 10, 2007

I AM El Morya, who has come to you on this day.

I have come in order to inform you that the summer cycle of Dictations, which we have been giving through our Messenger, is over. Today I have the honor to give you the final Dictation of this cycle.

As always, we are sad to end our association with you. We become closer to each other during the cycles of our Messages. We see how many people go on the Internet every day with palpitating hearts in order to read our Messages. The wonder of our association continues during all the days allocated for the transmission of our Messages.

Today, in the final Message, I would like to once again note the importance of the event that we have managed to continue the given dispensation. It has been decided at the Great Central Sun that it is necessary to continue our work through this Messenger. I am glad, and the Heavens are glad that this opportunity has been extended.

Now, during our future work, we would like to come even closer to you. When we are far away, your consciousness cannot fully comprehend our existence and our presence. Therefore, our task is to come closer to you, and your task is to become closer to us by raising the level of your consciousness, and then we will be able to perform work on the physical plane together.

One is afraid of the unknown. What is obscure causes fear and anxiety. Our task is to make the communication between the worlds ordinary.

We wish that there were not any shades of religion or dogma in our communication. It is time to put the association with us, the Masters of humankind, on the new foundation of collaboration and mutual help. We do not come to you for you to waste your time on reading our Messages. We come to you in order to inspire you to perform work on the physical plane.

All your ordinary work should be set on the new foundation and done in accordance with the Divine principles.

It is not necessary to do anything extraordinary; you should not fear that you will come under the influence of another cult. The difference between a sect and a true Teaching is that the former creates exclusivity for its followers. There is no exclusivity. Anyone can become a follower of the Ascended Masters Teaching. In order to do that, you only need to carry out in your lives the Divine principles and moral behavioral patterns that we teach you. You need to shift the focus in your daily life and do everything from a new angle — the angle of service to the Common Good, to the work of the Masters, and to the evolution of planet Earth.

There is nothing that we would want to conceal from you. The restriction of the information that you receive is solely related to the limited nature of your consciousness and to the limited nature of the consciousness of our conduit, our Messenger. You set this restriction for yourselves because you are not trying to change yourselves, your consciousness, and after that, change your lives by setting the proper priorities in your life and acting according to the Teaching that we give you.

We come so that you constantly check your vibrations and the compass of your heart against our orienting points that we set for you.

If you read carefully all the Dictations from the very first Message that we gave through our Messenger on March 4, 2005, until today's Dictation; if you read all these Dictations with one purpose — to understand what you should do in your lives now, you will obtain answers to all your questions. Everything that you need is given to you. Now it is your turn. Show us that you have learned our Teaching. Show us what you are able to do on the physical plane guided by our Teaching.

Every deed on the physical plane that you perform successfully based on our principles allows us to expand the effect of this dispensation.

Therefore, think about how you can do our work collaboratively. If you need our help, write letters to us. If you need our advice, appeal to us and you will receive advice in your heart.

We are never slow to render our help. The whole question is whether you can sustain our energies that we give you to fulfill the work on the physical plane.

Every time when one of you is ready to take on the responsibility and perform our work on the physical plane, we give our blessing, our help, and our energy. You begin the work vigorously. However, only several months pass and your determination and willingness to work for God fade away. You find thousands of excuses and thousands of reasons that make you abandon our work and return to completing the projects that, as it seems to you, are more important and more profitable, giving something to you personally.

I am warning you — before you take on the responsibility to perform work for the Masters, please evaluate everything a thousand times. That is because we give you the energy, and if you misuse the energy that we give, if you direct it at completing your own projects, then all the energy that you use inappropriately is qualified as the karma of the unfulfilled duties before God and the Masters, or in other words, the karma of betrayal. You know that this type of karma is the hardest to work off and it is accompanied by great difficulties not only in this life but also in several future lives.

However, if you do our work selflessly, with all your heart, then you earn tremendous good karma, which will allow you to fulfill our tasks with even greater success in the future.

God does not want you to be poor or struggle financially. If you make proper choices and apply your efforts in the right direction, then abundance will come into your life. You need to learn how to properly use and spend the Divine energy; and if you manage to find the balance between the wise fulfillment of your personal projects and performing work for the Masters, then you will never feel the shortage of energy, including the monetary energy in your life.

God requires you whole. All your life must be devoted to the Divine Service. However, there are too few individuals among you who are done with their personal karma and their ancestral karma. Therefore, you still have karmic debts left in the form of taking care of the people close to you: children, parents, and anyone with whom you have a karmic connection. This is where you need to find a wise balance between the energy that you will spend on fulfilling the work of the Masters and the energy that you direct at caring for your family and the people with whom you are connected by karma.

This is not an easy task. However, how successfully you solve it determines your future.

I came today in order to give the final Message of the current summer cycle. There is so much that I want to tell you, but there is no more opportunity for that.

Thanks to all of you who support the fulfilment of our plans on the physical plane and take on the burden to perform our tasks.

I AM El Morya, until the next time!

Appendix to Cycle 6 of the Messages

Appeal from the Masters to the people of Russia

Part of a speech given by Tatyana N. Mickushina in Moscow, March 27, 2007

Yesterday when I was meditating with Lord Maitreya, He said something to me...

Every time when some event of the Masters is over, I call upon my Teacher and He tells me what the next thing is, what is necessary to prepare.

For example, a month ago it was necessary to ask about a seminar in Bulgaria, and I asked this question, and Lord Maitreya answered it in the following way: "After the seminar — The Path of Initiations — everything may change significantly."[36]

I did not understand what it was all about. And then yesterday I was meditating and again asked the same question: "What is going to be done further?"

"Until you reach the corner, you cannot see what is further."

Over the course of an hour I received a flow of thoughts, which were not formed in a Dictation, but these were very serious things and I can only repeat them as I understand them.

In fact, the mantle of the Messenger of the Great White Brotherhood was given to me in March 2004. It has been three

---

[36] The seminar "The Path of Initiations" was held in a suburb of Moscow from March 15-18, 2007.

years since the Messenger of the Great White Brotherhood and the mantle have had the opportunity to be present in Russia. And that is the time limit that has been given to the nation and to the country.

You know the story with Jesus. He entered Jerusalem on a donkey. And before that He had preached for three years among the people of Israel. They had met Him with palm branches and had shouted "Hallelujah," but afterwards, on Friday, they crucified Him.

In this way, the nation, on behalf of the people who caught Jesus, tortured, and killed Him, made their choice.

And the people of Israel have been scattered around the world.

Russia is a very important country. And now it becomes obvious why this is so. For in the course of seventy years, Russia had an opportunity to achieve the level of consciousness, passing through its tests like a nation, (i.e., not only separate people pass through initiations but also whole nations), and Russia had the opportunity to reach the level of consciousness that could allow it to make an important choice for the future.

And you know that Blavatsky and the Roerich's could not live in Russia. They gave their Teachings beyond the borders of Russia. And for the whole 20th century, the Great White Brotherhood has been giving the Teachings on the territory of America. There were many Messengers and movements through which this Teaching has been given. And from the Dictations of the Masters, we know that the focus of the Light was taken from the land of America and carried to Russia.[37] The focus of Light is not something that can be touched. This is something that is inside a human being. This is just an ability of the human being to emit the Divine Light, which is received for the whole nation. In 2004 — three years —

---

[37] Refer to the Dictation "We are establishing our focus of Light in the Land of Russia," Beloved Lanello, April 6, 2005, in *Words of Wisdom Volume I*.

the changes that have taken place after these three years can be seen with the naked eye. The Divine energy on the physical plane is being manifested as a monetary energy, and Russia is meant to be a rich country, provided it passes this Initiation.

When the Teaching was given in the territory of America, America became a rich country. The question was how the nation would use the given Light. And America went along the path of worshiping the golden calf. The Light, which the Masters had been giving in America for the whole 20th century, went for some external things that people chose, such as the wealth of this world and serving that world.

Now there is no time. What took decades in America, now it is given to Russia. Three years. And the country is faced with a choice. And what happened to America is happening in Russia now (it has to make its choice). What will it choose? Will it choose the Spiritual, Divine Path, or will it choose the path of worshiping the golden calf? This is the choice the nation is making.

I asked: "What is going to be done further?" A summer cycle of Dictations was planned in June and July, and there had to be a seminar. However, Maitreya did not allow it. They did not give me the chance to work.

They say that Russia has not given anything to me during that time. I do not even have a place to live. The way that people treat the Messenger tells a lot to the Masters...

And the problem is not in me. In fact, it is very difficult for me to talk about all this. For at a human level, it seems that I want something for myself. In reality, I don't need anything. However, this is really very serious.

And if the Masters take the focus of Light, then Russia will not pass its test.

Usually a nation makes its choice through people, through people like those who were present at the killing of Jesus, and through those people who have an opportunity to be present at this meeting. Therefore, God is talking to you...

God is talking to you...

And it is possible that this meeting is the last one... I don't know...

This is what I understood yesterday from my meditation with Lord Maitreya.

Explanation of the "Appeal from the Masters"

I am not a homeless person. I have a one-room apartment in the center of Omsk, close to the Irtysh embankment. And if such significant changes hadn't happened recently in my life, I would have continued to live quietly.

It all started when I began to receive the Dictations of the Masters. It was the first cycle of the Dictations; one Dictation was given every day from March 4th to June 30th, 2005. By the end of this cycle I was extremely overtired and exhausted. There was no one near me who would explain to me what was going on. I received a Dictation, published it on the website, and sent it out to subscribers. Then, I went to my summer house or to the park, where I sat or lay on the grass and couldn't move for hours. I just looked at the sun.

I asked the Masters, what is going on? They told me that I will not be able to live in the city and I should move to live in nature.

But I didn't have the opportunity neither to buy a house nor to engage in exchanging my apartment for a house because all my time was busy Serving.

The Masters told me that I will not be able to live in a village or in a settlement. "Living in society, you will have to adapt to the society. We wish an Ashram to be built where we would establish our own rules."

In autumn of 2005, the Masters mentioned a new cycle of the Dictations. They also said that they will no longer give the dictations in Omsk. The people found a house for me in Altai, Chemal, where I moved on December 11th, 2005. The Dictations began on the 12th of December. Thus, I managed to receive the Dictations of the winter cycle 2005-2006. The owners of this house were far from the Teaching, so I was not allowed to receive the Dictations in this house.

In the spring of 2006, when it came time to receive the next cycle of the Dictations, I had to find a new place. By some miracle, the place was found — this time in the Moscow region.

As I was receiving more and more Dictations, the flow of energy was being increased. And, despite the fact that the duration of the cycles of the Dictations became less, all the time during the receiving of the Dictations, I felt various strange ailments and aches in different parts of my body and in different organs. The people who were with me in the same house during the receiving of the Dictations felt the same as me. As soon as the Dictations were over, all of the diseases come to an end.

Every act of receiving a Dictation is tremendous work for me, on the verge of physical impossibility. Every time, more and more pure conditions for the receiving of the Messages are needed because more and more energy is transmitted.

Every time, it gets harder and harder time to find a place to receive the Messages. When we were in Bulgaria, we were looking for a place for nine days, spending the night each time in a new place. By some miracle, I managed to find a place and receive the Dictations, although after nine days of wandering across Bulgaria and after several days of moving from Omsk to Bulgaria via Moscow, I felt very bad.

When God wants people to pay attention to the problem, He carries the situation to the point of absurdity. And when this year we were looking for a place to receive the Messages of the winter cycle, we spent a total of one and a half months to find this place.

First, we were looking for a place near St. Petersburg, combining this search with the preparation for the seminar "Inner Path." The St. Petersburg group was relieved when they found out that I got an offer to take the Dictations in Cyprus, and they gladly saw me off on the train.

However, I did not go to Cyprus. I visited Moscow and the Crimea. The Masters were ready to give the Dictations in any place that would be appropriate for it, but such a place was not found.

We arrived in Moscow. During the week, we toured the Moscow region looking for a place and again we miraculously found a place in the Vladimir region. All that transferring around wore me out to such an extent that I was striving with great difficulty to feel normal in the first days of receiving the Dictations. And I just barely made it to the end of the cycle.

All these years, when I have been working in the post of the Messenger of the Great White Brotherhood, my vibrations had risen continuously. And I stopped being able to bear a stay in the city for a long time. I just get sick and unable to work.

However, my presence also affects others around me.

When I was last in Omsk, I had no opportunity to even meditate. My apartment is on the second floor of an old five-story building (its common name is "Khrushchyovka"). As soon as I start meditating, my neighbors immediately play loud music. And it is not Bach, Beethoven, or Mozart as you might guess. And this is understandable. Our auras are constantly in contact because of the closeness. People just want to return to their natural vibrations, and this can be done by using nicotine, alcohol, or listening to contemporary music.

Thus, even when I do not receive the Messages, my vibrations are much different from the vibrations of the surrounding space. My sensitivity has also been increased greatly. I can feel people with low vibrations at long distances, I can feel the vibrations of the place, and I feel the impact of contemporary music at a distance of one kilometer.

I can feel the vibrations of houses. Every house is not good for me. In some houses, I literally make myself go in by force. Every house is impregnated with the energy of the people who lived or stayed in it. And because all people are imperfect, they superimpose their imperfect vibrations on the walls of their houses. I can feel it. Thus, I can only stay in relatively new houses.

It is impossible to stop evolving. You can go either forward or go backward (i.e., degrade).

The main thing is the level of my vibrations. It is exactly what allows the Masters to work through me and give the Teaching on a completely different, new level. The receiving of the Messages is not the primary but the second-order effect, you might say. The main thing is to keep and conduct the Divine vibrations into this physical world.

I must control myself, my inner state, carefully because my state of consciousness affects the receiving of information from the etheric level. And if I allow disharmony or imperfection, it will lead to distortion of the Message, and the karma will lie on me. The same is true of the place that I live in. Any disharmony around me leaves a mark.

I can control everything concerning my lifestyle and meals, but it is impossible to control external circumstances and other people.

I need silence and lack of people, but I think that is the most elusive thing because in order to work at the level of the present day, we need to have everything that will help to avoid wasting time on home maintenance, heating, and taking care of things. I need to work on the Internet. That is why I can't be away from civilization. Above all, people need contact with me. It makes no sense to engage in individual self-perfection. You can blow up like a bubble and burst. I must constantly keep in touch with people who go along the Path and need help and advice.

The Masters want actions to be performed on the physical plane. For this, it is necessary to stay in contact with society. So, the Masters were faced with the situation on the physical plane that must be resolved. I can't resolve this situation, because I don't know how to resolve it. A collective decision, a collective choice of the nation, is required.

I am ready to continue to bear any difficulties and overcome myself, but the Masters say that the time has come for the people of Russia to make choice. Hence, their ultimatum.

And this is not only a test for the country but also for me personally, because it is very difficult for me to explain this and ask for something without knowing what...

I receive offers from other countries. But I was born in Russia. I love Russia. And I will leave here in the extreme case when I cannot work here any longer.

Tatyana Mickushina
Love and Light!

Messages of Ascended Masters

Words of Wisdom

Volume 2

Tatyana N. Mickushina

Buy Books by T. N. Mickushina on Amazon:
amazon.com/author/tatyana_mickushina

Websites:
http://sirius-eng.net/ (English version)
http://sirius-ru.net/ or http://sirius-net.org (Russian version)

Made in the USA
Columbia, SC
11 March 2025